CALL for Mobility

STUDIES IN COMPUTER ASSISTED LANGUAGE LEARNING

Edited by Anna Turula

VOLUME 3

Prior to publication, the quality of the work published in this series is blind reviewed by an external referee appointed by the editorship. The referee is not aware of the author's name when performing the review.

Joanna Pitura / Shannon Sauro (eds.)

CALL for Mobility

PETER LANG

Bibliographic Information published by the Deutsche Nationalbibliothek
The Deutsche Nationalbibliothek lists this publication in the Deutsche Nationalbibliografie; detailed bibliographic data is available in the internet at http://dnb.d-nb.de.

This publication was financially supported by the Pedagogical University of Cracow

ISSN 2364-1339
ISBN 978-3-631-74455-0 (Print)
E-ISBN 978-3-631-74835-0 (E-PDF)
E-ISBN 978-3-631-74836-7 (EPUB)
E-ISBN 978-3-631-74837-4 (MOBI)
DOI 10.3726/b13451

Peter Lang – Berlin · Bern · Bruxelles · New York · Oxford · Warszawa · Wien

This publication has been peer reviewed.

www.peterlang.com

Table of contents

Joanna Pitura
Pedagogical University of Cracow, Cracow, Poland

Shannon Sauro
Malmö University, Malmö, Sweden

Introduction

This volume brings together a collection of ten chapters which explore different facets of CALL for mobility, discussed during the 2016 PL-CALL conference.[1] The theme was conceived in response to the use of tools and devices found in CALL that facilitate the formation of communities and learning environments in which learners and teachers are often not in the same place. This can pose a challenge for educators as this situation generates constrained access to content and can limit participation in language class activities. However, the prevalent ownership of portable devices brings about additional opportunities, resources, and norms that can be taken advantage of for language learning and teaching purposes.

Mobile phones and other portable devices are well suited to learning scenarios which address learner mobility issues, for instance, limited contact time in the classroom faced by weekend students. Such technology also makes new ways of learning possible by affording the activity with regard to the current location and conditions of the learner, disengaging all involved in the educational activity from fixed time and place. More specifically, as Duman, Orhon, and Gedik (2014) explain, "mobile learning (m-learning) refers to teaching and learning with the use of mobile technologies (…), which are potentially available anytime and anywhere" (p. 198). Mobile assisted language learning (MALL) is a branch within m-learning that entails the use of portable devices in language learning that render learning, not possible otherwise (Duman et al. 2014). MALL activities have been delivered via mobile/smart phones, personal digital assistants (PDAs), handheld computers, tablet PCs, MP3/4 players, pocket electronic dictionaries, laptops, notebooks, e-book readers, digital voice recorders, multi-function camcorders, game consoles (Kukulska-Hulme & Shield 2008; Duman et al. 2014). These devices can be effective in delivering rich language learning content, enabling collaboration and interaction, as well as authentic and meaningful use of a foreign/second language

1 PL-CALL is a conference organised annually by researchers and practitioners interested in computer assisted language learning in Poland.

in speech and writing that is not restricted by the classroom walls (Duman et al. 2014).

MALL activities – that can be designed by teachers and accessed by learners "anytime and anywhere" – appear to be well justified in language learning contexts as such activities have the potential to adequately address learner and teacher mobility. Yet, despite the fact that both teachers and students make use of mobile technology for communication and entertainment on an everyday basis, the application and use of mobile technology in instructional settings can present a challenge. It is still not well known how to design language instruction in which learners are to decide – in Kukulska-Hulme and Shield's words – "what, when and where to learn" (2008: 281). Remarkably, action research that could develop, test, and evaluate the pedagogic solutions to address this issue has rarely been used as a form of inquiry in MALL research (Duman et al. 2014). Consequently, learning activities that support learner and teacher mobility require further investigation.

This volume therefore attempts to bridge this gap by providing reports of small-scale classroom-oriented research, allowing for insight into how mobile learning activities can be used in educational settings. The focus of the first part of the volume is on the application of mobile technology for the training of language professionals, i.e. teachers and translators, while the second part of the volume investigates the use of technology fostering mobile language learning.

The volume opens with two chapters that address the issue of telecollaboration, i.e. collaboration between geographically separated classes that make use of digital communication technologies. Barbara Loranc-Paszylk recognises the role that peer assessment plays in developing teacher trainees' professional expertise. Accordingly, she applies peer assessment in a Polish-Spanish telecollaborative learning experience, with the aim of enhancing students' learning outcomes. Anna Turula and Maike Grau, in turn, view telecollaboration as a viable means in supporting virtual mobility. With this goal in mind, they report on an online Polish-German intercultural exchange in language teacher pre-service education.

The next two chapters present teacher trainees as language material developers. Elżbieta Gajek focuses on the creation and use of videos as particularly well suited for language teaching purposes. Gajek's study involves the production of video clips in the course of a teacher training course, seen as developing digital and media competence. Jarosław Krajka considers the issue of developing language teachers' ICT (information and communication technologies) competences so that technology can be applied in the education of Languages for Specific Purposes (LSP), in which the ability to design electronic materials that foster learner and teacher mobility is regarded as an essential skill for a modern language teacher.

The final chapter in this section is written by Małgorzata Kodura who is concerned with translator education and the concept of translation competence. Recognising the requirements of the job market of today, in which translators are expected to be able to work remotely, she investigates the suitability of remote translator training, where the instructor is not physically present to assist the students.

The second part of this volume touches upon the issue of technology for mobile language learning. In a study which explores the use of mobile devices for language learning, Mariusz Kruk argues that mobile devices are now seen as having the potential to facilitate language learner autonomy as learners are given tools that allow them to have more control – and flexibility at the same time – over their learning activity in terms of time and space. Robert Oliwa attempts to establish the usefulness of hand-held devices in providing a mobile language learning environment. In doing so, instructional activities are designed, implemented and evaluated among a group of professionals. The results reveal that the intervention incorporating the language learning component accessed online produced gains in study participants' communicative competence in speech and in writing.

The two ensuing chapters centre on pronunciation and the application of digital solutions that foster its development. Anita Buczek-Zawiła asserts that mobile dictionaries have the potential for developing English pronunciation skills. Her study of two different groups of language learners confirms this claim. In the next chapter, Marek Molenda, Michał Adamczyk, and Paulina Rybińska investigate the feasibility of applying automatic speech recognition (ASR) software to pronunciation training. They argue that Google Cloud Speech API fosters mobility by allowing for flexible access to the application, regardless of space and device.

The volume concludes with a chapter investigating the use of mobile technology for language development, written by Agnieszka Bryła-Cruz. She recognises numerous benefits of podcasts in developing foreign/second language because they can be readily accessed and used by language learners. Bryła-Cruz argues for the pedagogical value of such didactic tools and offers a number of learning activities for the language classroom.

The chapters in this volume reflect research on classroom practice that we hope will help readers gain a better understanding of the function and implementation of mobile technologies in local classroom contexts to support mobility, professional development, and language and culture learning.

References

Duman, G., Orhon, G., & Gedik, N. (2014). Research trends in mobile assisted language learning from 2000 to 2012. *ReCALL, 27*(2), 197–216.

Kukulska-Hulme, A., & Shield, L. (2008). An overview of mobile assisted language learning: From content delivery to supported collaboration and interaction. *ReCALL, 20*(3), 271–289.

Part 1.
Mobile technology for professional training – teacher and translator education

Barbara Loranc-Paszylk
University of Bielsko-Biała, Bielsko-Biała, Poland

Marking the difference – use of peer assessment in a cross-cultural telecollaborative project involving EFL teacher trainees

Abstract: The aim of this chapter is to investigate the impact of peer assessment that was incorporated into a cross-cultural collaborative learning environment in order to maximize the potential benefits of telecollaboration. As demonstrated by a growing body of empirical research, telecollaborative exchanges can be conducive to foreign language and culture learning by affording learners new opportunities for linguistic and cultural experiences. The goal of this particular telecollaborative project was to help the students – EFL (English as a Foreign Language) teacher trainees in Spain and Poland – to enhance their skills in teaching techniques and developing culture-oriented didactic materials.

Peer assessment was hypothesized to help maximize the potential of telecollaboration by increasing students' engagement and encouraging deeper reflection and close collaboration in the set tasks. The self-reported data suggest that in the case of the EFL teacher trainees participating in this project, such increased engagement, reflection, and collaboration developed their professional expertise. Furthermore, a telecollaborative exchange that included peer assessment allowed students opportunities to experience interculturality, both as teacher trainees able to assess work authored by people of other cultural backgrounds, and as students undergoing assessment by peers from another culture.

Keywords: telecollaboration, peer assessment, pre-service teacher training

1. Introduction

The exponential growth of new Internet technologies has revolutionized human communication and made cross-cultural and cross-linguistic contacts unprecedentedly accessible. Within language learning contexts, telecollaboration, also known as online intercultural exchange, is a structured activity organized jointly by educators from partner universities. Its main purpose is to bring together students from different countries to enhance their foreign/second language learning, as well as to help them acquire intercultural competence (Belz 2003). Such telecollaborative exchanges are becoming increasingly popular as a means of providing students with cost-effective access to remotely-located peers who are speakers of another language and representatives of another culture, and therefore help the students become culturally-aware global citizens who are prepared for geographical mobility.

Video-based telecollaboration as an alternative to studying abroad has therefore made it possible to create contact zones (Kern 2014) without sharing the same geographical space. In this research project, peer assessment was hypothesized to help maximize the potential of such telecollaboration.

It is the intercultural element that makes telecollaborative environments unique. O'Dowd (2016: 292) observes that unlike in numerous forms of distance learning that are based on a both synchronous and asynchronous transfer of knowledge via multimodal files, "intercultural dialogue is at the center of learning in telecollaboration, which is based on student-centered, collaborative approaches to learning where knowledge and understanding are constructed through interaction and negotiation".

Many studies on telecollaboration adopt a sociocultural approach and analyse how the context of online intercultural exchange influences student participation (Belz & Müller-Hartmann 2003). The present action research study, which also takes a sociocultural approach, aims at discussing affordances of a telecollaboration project that has been enriched with collaborative peer assessment tasks. It attempts to shed some light on students' perspectives related to their experience of peer assessment in cross-cultural telecollaboration and to provide some indications of the perceived merits of such pedagogical settings.

2. Review of literature

2.1 Advantages of using telecollaboration

In a telecollaboration context the learning experience is substantially enriched, since participants are provided with opportunities for interaction and communication with representatives of other culture(s) who are able to use the same language.

An essential gain resulting from telecollaboration is linked to increased intercultural competence. Byram, Holmes, and Savvides (2013: 251) observe that processes of globalization, the emergence of new technologies and an unprecedented scale of migration have created a new social context in today's world. Therefore, teaching communicative (cultural) competence becomes more and more necessary and it calls upon "consideration of the ways in which people of different languages – including language learners themselves – think and act and how this might impact on successful communication and interaction" (Byram, Holmes, & Savvides 2013: 251).

Byram (1997: 50–53) developed a pedagogical *savoirs* model for intercultural competence and identified five key components: knowledge (of social groups and products and practices), attitudes (of curiosity and openness towards values, beliefs and behaviours of other cultures), skills of discovery and interaction, skills of interpreting and relating (data from one's own and another's culture), and finally, skills of critical cultural awareness (questioning the values, beliefs and behaviours of one's own and other cultures). It is important to emphasize that, in a telecollaborative context, an interculturally competent speaker – apart from being able to demonstrate an appropriate repertoire of knowledge, skills and attitudes to interact with people from a different country or culture – is also required to "display attitudes of curiosity and openness" (Chun 2015: 7).

Several studies which explore affordances of telecollaboration focus on its capacity for creating a virtual community of practice to interact and collaborate, for example in the case of EFL teacher trainees (Dooly & Sadler 2013). Members of communities of practice – as defined by Wenger (1998: 2) – "are informally bound by what they do together [...] and by what they have learned through their mutual engagement in these activities". Dooly and Sadler (2013: 6) found that "knowledge-sharing activities" that included feedback provided by teacher trainers and teacher trainees helped future teachers see how teacher trainers could implement theory into practice in relation to the integration of technology into teaching.

Telecollaborative environments trigger the development of digital skills that encompass not only multimodal modes of communication, but also netiquette and cyberpragmatics. Chun (2015) suggests that in the era of globalization developing e-literacies and digital skills are essential for teachers. This resonates with Royce's (2007: 367) concept of multimodal communicative competence, drawn on the assumption that nowadays interactions in formal and informal language learning occurs increasingly in audio and video modes. Likewise, Orsini-Jones (2015: 45) claims that the role of technology in language learning is "to enhance multilingual and multimodal critical digital literacies, foster meta-reflection and provide unique opportunities for social-collaboration on tasks". In this line of thinking, cyberpragmatics, which is the skill of interpreting others' intended meanings in computer-mediated communication and the ability to apply relevant levels of formality and genre in the process of communication, becomes essential (Yus Ramos 2011: 13).

Therefore, it can be concluded that telecollaborative environments offer affordances to develop skills which are directly linked to working and functioning in the globalized world in the digital age.

2.2 Challenges in telecollaborative projects

According to some studies, online intercultural exchanges, despite their widely-reported positive outcomes, may not always result in successful communication.

O'Dowd and Ritter (2006: 624) point to possible factors that lead to failed communication which they describe as "cases of telecollaborative interaction which end in low levels of participation, indifference, tension between participants, or negative evaluation of the partner group or their culture". The authors (O'Dowd & Ritter 2006: 628) have identified factors that have a disruptive effect on telecollaborative projects and classify them into four categories: individual, classroom, socioinstitutional, and interaction.

Chun (2015: 16), when focusing on the constraints of the learner and the learning contexts in telecollaborative projects, enumerates the following possible challenges: "differences in linguistic proficiencies among the partner classes, willingness of learners to write honestly and openly, cultural differences and conflicts, and the possibility of reinforcing preconceptions and stereotypes of the learners".

Clearly, telecollaboration can facilitate language learning and the development of intercultural communicative competence by affording learners opportunities for authentic linguistic and cultural experiences. Yet it is important to note that mere contact between learners from different geographical locations does not guarantee a successful intercultural exchange, and there are a number of challenges in telecollaborative projects that teachers and learners may face.

2.3 Peer assessment

Peer assessment may be considered the nexus between sociocultural and cognitive perspectives on learning, since in this context, an interplay takes place between collaborative interaction and independent intellectual functioning. As defined by Falchikov (1995: 175), peer assessment refers to "the process whereby groups of individuals rate their peers. This exercise may or may not entail previous discussion or agreement over criteria".

Sociocultural theories stress the collaborative and interactive nature of peer assessment: "It focuses on assessing the process of learning, and putting emphasis on collaborative activity and self-reflection" (Fukai, Nazikian, & Sato 2008: 391). Therefore, this type of assessment affords students the opportunity to not only notice and learn from each other how to construct, and to provide and receive feedback, but it also encourages them to reflect and interpret the experience in order to eventually develop greater learner autonomy.

In the view of cognitive theories, peer assessment means that the cognitive operations needed for successful task completion are first "exercised in collaboration and then presumably internalized for eventual independent problem-solving" (De Guerrero & Villamil 1994: 493). It is also thought to encourage "deep rather than surface learning" (Cassidy 2006: 509).

Various pedagogical advantages of peer assessment are suggested in the literature. Topping (2005: 640) asserts that it "can enhance self-assessment, and [...] yield metacognitive gains". Falchikov (1995: 175) claims that grades assigned as the result of peer assessment are often comparable to those given by teachers, so it has the potential for providing increased feedback without increasing the workload of teachers. Most importantly, he suggests that peer assessment may be even more beneficial to students because it equips them with the following skills: "reflection, analysis and diplomatic criticism". Cassidy (2006: 509) concludes that students usually work harder if they know that they will be assessed by their peers.

From a language learning perspective, peer assessment, when properly introduced, gives students opportunities to develop and practise skills important in language acquisition (Hansen & Liu 2005). Studies in second language writing report that peer assessment is advantageous not only to the students whose work is being peer assessed, but also to the students who perform the assessment task. For example, Lundstrom and Baker (2009) found that the students who peer assessed other students' writing on a regular basis made more significant gains in their own writing skills than those who received peer feedback.

There are nevertheless many concerns related to the validity and reliability of peer assessment. Cassidy (2006: 510) mentions a lack of expertise and formal training as far as evaluative skill is concerned, potential bias, discomfort with the extra responsibility and the perception that it is the responsibility of the tutor to perform the assessment. Furthermore, many of the above-mentioned limitations may negatively influence peer assessment tasks and lead to a central tendency in rating and therefore provide "average" scores for peers, regardless of the actual quality of their performance (Topping 2005).

To conclude, the general view of peer assessment is positive, with studies reporting such advantages as: opportunities to collaborate with others, creation of a space in which peers can support each other, and self-reflection on the learning experience (Fukai et al. 2008), stronger motivation to perform well (Cassidy 2006), and significant gains in content knowledge due to performing the role as assessor or rater (Lundstrom & Baker 2009). Peer assessment as an alternative to traditional teacher-based assessment seems therefore to be a suitable answer to the growing demand for lifelong learners and reflective practitioners.

3. Study: method, data collection

The focus of the current study is twofold. Firstly, it aims at providing insights into the peer assessment process using the students' evaluation sheets and commentaries submitted as feedback to the teaching materials created by the teams from the partner university. Secondly, it attempts to identify the students' self-reported overall views on the most useful and most challenging aspects of this project which involved peer assessment in cross-cultural, telecollaborative settings.

This rationale and the aims of this study were operationalized in the following research questions:

(1) To what extent can peer assessment enhance the goals of the telecollaboration, such as: exchanging teaching techniques and developing culture-oriented ELT (English as a Foreign Language) materials? What kind of benefits can peer assessment provide?
(2) What do the students perceive to be the most useful and the most challenging aspects of achieving the goals of the telecollaboration that included peer assessment?

This study, like other studies based on sociocultural frameworks, tends to prefer the use of qualitative methods (Chun 2015). The telecollaborative project presented in this study was implemented in university settings, and carried out in the classroom in a lab equipped with videoconferencing devices and also via asynchronous communication. The project was undertaken in April and May 2014; it was one of many similar projects organized as a result of collaboration, ongoing since 2011, between two partner universities: the University of Bielsko-Biala (Poland) and the University of León (Spain).

3.1 Participants

The participants were MA students majoring in English Philology and specializing in Teaching English as a Foreign Language (TEFL); they comprised 19 Polish students and 15 Spanish students. Communication between the two cohorts was conducted in English and the average estimated level of the students' competence in this language, as assessed by the tutors, was C1 according to the *Common European Framework of Reference for Languages* (Council of Europe 2001).

3.2 Procedure

The project was organized in three stages. The first stage involved the development of teaching materials. The students in each university cohort were divided into five small teams, each responsible for working on a specific language skill (speaking, listening, reading, writing, and interaction), and were paired up with the respective team from the partner university working on the same language skill. The teams collaborated to create a single teaching unit, which was to undergo assessment later by the peers from the partner university.

The first task for each team was to prepare a lesson plan that would be devoted to developing the assigned language skill in English. Requirements related to the content of the teaching unit were given to all teams: the content of the lesson had to be based on specific, culturally-oriented topics, namely: a famous artist from the partner university country (reading), a tourist destination in the partner university country (speaking), a famous building in the partner university country (writing), a famous sportsman from the partner university country (listening skill), and a famous scientist from the partner university (interaction). The teams also had to find online relevant materials in English and, if necessary, adapt them to the assigned language level (B1). The students were also expected to design activities, develop worksheets and other didactic materials related to their lesson topic.

The sets of lesson plans with the teaching materials developed for this project, i.e. worksheets, recordings, etc., were subsequently exchanged between the respective teams of both cohorts via asynchronous communication. During this stage, peer assessment of the lesson plans and materials sent by the partners was carried out by the teams from each cohort. For example, the Spanish team working on "reading" assessed the lesson plan and related didactic materials on a Spanish famous artist that had been prepared by the respective Polish team, who in return assessed the reading lesson plan and materials on a Polish famous artist prepared by their Spanish colleagues.

The evaluation sheet to help the students assess their peers' work was distributed to all the teams. It consisted of ten questions. The students were requested to provide explanatory answers (as short texts) and, if possible, support them with examples drawn from the work they had assessed. The final question required the assessors to provide a numerical answer – a grade ranging from 1 (the least successful work) to 4 (the most successful work). The following questions were included: Is the structure of the lesson plan correct? To what extent are the activities attractive/diverse? Is the language level appropriate for B1 learners? Is there enough time allowed for the learners to perform the activities? How successfully were the authentic material adapted? Are the activities motivating for the learners? How successfully were the cultural elements incorporated? What are the strengths and weaknesses of the materials?

The evaluation sheets on each teaching unit were completed by the teams from both cohorts, submitted to their teachers and subsequently exchanged between the parties involved so that the students could reflect on the assessment and comments given by their peers from the partner university.

Finally, videoconferencing sessions were held between the respective teams to allow the students from both cohorts the opportunity to discuss their feedback and assessment results. For example, the Polish and Spanish teams, responsible for working on "speaking" presented their feedback to each other.

4. Results

4.1 Evaluation sheets for peer assessment

Three major themes emerged from the analysis of the evaluation reports submitted by the students: firstly, evidence of detailed feedback on teaching materials with respect to content; secondly, evidence of students' reflections on how their own culture was presented in the content embedded in the assessed teaching units; and finally, evidence of collaborative learning provided in appreciative comments about the partner university team's work and inspiration drawn from it.

Many of the reports and commentaries submitted by students support the content evaluation with relevant examples and details. For example, Spanish student [no.2] wrote the following comments: "the timing in your lesson plan is not consistent with the assignment. I think the first task would not require 20 minutes, this is too long and should be shortened. 20 minutes is however enough for the third activity". Two representative comments from Polish students are the following: "In post-listening stage we can find only the task when students check the answers to the activity included in the while listening stage (gap-filling exercise), but your presentation of dialogues as some kind of follow-up activity is definitely a good idea" [no.19], "the self-evaluation checklist may be too difficult for B1 learners, instead you should maybe organize a pair work activity" [no.10].

As regards evidence related to students' reflections on the cultural component embedded in the teaching units, numerous participants' commentaries focused on how their own culture was presented in the lesson unit, expressing both positive and negative perceptions. For example, Polish student [no.18] appreciated the fact that the Spanish team had used an "impressive amount of info about Poland". Student [no.17] wrote: "we appreciate that the you [Spanish students] found comics designed by Dennis Wojda. Some Polish students in our group have never heard about the author, so they could learn something new about our culture". However, some students also expressed disappointment about the choice of cultural content input made by the partner university teams. Spanish participant [no.9] commented: "you [Polish students] use in your reading lesson a lot of stereotypes about Spain, I didn't realize there were so many of them". Polish student [no.1] commented: "I don't understand why have you selected a story about aggressive Polish football fans – we have great sportsmen in Poland".

Finally, we identified evidence of collaborative learning in the appreciative comments about the partner university team's work and inspiration drawn from it in the reports prepared by both teams. A representative quote by Spanish participant [no.3] may serve to illustrate this: "I really like the idea of quiz at the end of the class and giving a prize. I'm going to use it in my teaching practise". Likewise, there is an illustrative comment made by Polish student [no.1]: "The feedback I got from Spanish students during the videoconference was very professional, they didn't want to sound very negative, but gave very useful remarks without hurting our feelings. This a good way to evaluate students".

4.2 Recall surveys at the end of the project

An introspective method based on a recall survey was used to elicit the participants' perspectives. It was conducted one week after the project ended. The anonymous online survey consisted of six items, four of which invited the students to provide their answers to the following open-ended questions: What did you like most/what were the most useful aspects in the telecollaborative project involving peer assessment? What were the most challenging aspects? What changes would you suggest for future editions of the project?

Due to the small sample of respondents, descriptive statistical markers were used to illustrate the results of the questionnaire and to identify the dominating tendencies present in the participants' responses. While analysing the students' responses on self-perceived most useful and most challenging aspects of peer assessment in the cross-cultural telecollaborative project, it became clear that there were certain differences between the two cohorts and thus the major themes identified in the participants' responses will firstly be presented separately.

The Spanish students' perceptions of the most useful aspects predominantly regarded gains in teaching expertise related to materials development. Clearly, the majority of the Spanish participants found this element of the project helpful and practical (53%: 8 out of 15 participants mentioned this gain). An illustrative comment by Spanish participant [no.2] presents this perspective: "It was useful in the sense that it opened many doors and ways for the creation of the final teaching unit. It was also a good practice on what is to plan a lesson and teaching units". Another illustrative comment by Spanish participant [no.7] presents this perspective: "We became aware of how we have to do a lesson plan, also useful because we had to put ourselves in teachers' shoes, so we could see things from another perspective".

Other useful aspects of the project mentioned by the Spanish participants were related to the intercultural dimension of the project and indicated a degree of curiosity and openness towards the partner culture; two Spanish students reported that for them the most useful aspect of the exchange was "to see how lesson plans are developed in different countries" (Spanish students [no.6] and [no.9]).

Likewise, the intercultural dimension of the project was signalled as the most useful aspect in the comments provided by Polish participants: 11 out of 19 Polish participants (58%) considered the exchanging of ideas about teaching and practising teaching skills with peers from another country as the most useful aspect of the project. An illustrative comment representing this tendency was delivered by Polish student [no.13]: "we had an opportunity to exchange teaching ideas and experiences with people from different country, we could also get to know how the Spanish system looks like".

The second most popular theme identified in the answers provided by the Polish participants was related to the enhancing of teaching expertise; 8 out of 19 Polish students (42%) mentioned this aspect and the following quote serves as a good illustration: "It was useful because of self-evaluation of our teaching skills, we could find our good and bad points as far as teaching English is concerned we could practise what we learned in the course" (Polish student [no.15]).

Interestingly, 3 out of 19 Polish students (16%) considered the development of collaborative skills to be the most useful aspect of the project. This is illustrated for example by the following comment by Polish student [no.14]: "it was useful because it improved our group work".

Students from both cohorts also described those aspects of the project involving peer assessment that they considered to be the most challenging. Dominating tendencies identified in the students' responses included willingness to perform well in tasks and be innovative, using digital skills effectively, and coping with stress and fear of public speaking and, again, certain differences were identified among the two groups.

The majority of Spanish participants (11 out of 15) reported experiencing problems during the initial stage of the project, that is finding appropriate culturally-oriented authentic materials online which could be adapted and then included in their lesson activities (5 out of 15 students reported this). One comment by Spanish student [no.14] illustrates this well: "It was quite difficult to take into account our Polish audience, researching Polish customs was time-consuming".

Twenty-six per cent (4 out of 15) of Spanish participants reported that the biggest challenge for them was related to trying to be innovative and perform well in designing a teaching unit because they knew they would be assessed by peers from another country. This is illustrated for example by the following comment by Spanish student [no.9]: "we tried hard to be innovative, we did not want to let down our Polish friends".

Almost half of the Polish participants (9 out of 19) also reported difficulties in finding online appropriate authentic materials in English related thematically to given topics in Spanish culture. A further 9 out of 19 participants considered that the final stages of the project, which involved peer assessment and speaking in front of a new audience during the videoconferencing session, posed the biggest challenge of the project for them.

5. Discussion

In the first instance, the evaluation sheets completed by the students from both cohorts were analysed to answer the first research question: (1) To what extent can peer assessment enhance the goals of the telecollaboration, such as: exchanging teaching techniques and developing culture-oriented ELT materials? What kind of benefits can peer assessment provide?

Firstly, it can be hypothesized that the students were more engaged in the telecollaborative task and wanted to perform better because they knew their peers from the partner university would evaluate their work. This resonates with Cassidy's (2006: 509) claim that students usually work harder if they know that they will be assessed by their peers. Several comments made by students who enumerated "trying to be innovative" as the most challenging aspect may substantiate this conclusion.

Secondly, the opportunity for students to receive feedback on their work from peers at the partner university fostered reflection, which in turn contributed to enhancing their teaching expertise. The student teachers were not only merely presenting their work to each other, the feedback they received from their peers at the partner university on their own work helped them reflect on their teaching expertise. The appreciative comments made about the partner university team's work and the inspiration drawn from it can be interpreted as evidence of the intense reflection and collaborative learning that was taking place.

Furthermore, the peer assessment task required the students to solidify content knowledge on the material being assessed, since peer reviewers had to assess work according to given criteria. The fact that, in many of the commentaries submitted by the students, evaluation of content was supported by relevant examples and details may serve as evidence of this gain. These findings support the observations made by Lundstrom and Baker (2009) as well as those made by Fukai et al. (2008: 391) that peer assessment "may help students to not only observe how others give and receive feedback but also to determine how to take responsibility for their own assessment".

Last, but not least, participation in the cross-cultural peer assessment also triggered the drawing of comparisons, which, as Liddicoat and Scarino (2013: 61) assert, leads to reflection, which is "a core element in developing interculturality". These authors further advocate that telecollaborative exchanges should provide "opportunities for analysis and reflection" (Liddicoat & Scarino 2013: 108) for the learning experience to be effective. Therefore, thanks to the peer assessment task, which led to the processes of analysis and reflection, the students were able to experience interculturality both as teachers, in that they could practise assessment (which is an inherent part of the teaching profession) on work authored by students from another country, and also as students, by being evaluated by teachers from another country.

To sum up, our findings suggest that peer assessment incorporated into the telecollaborative project between EFL teacher trainees helped maximize the goal of telecollaboration by affording teacher trainees opportunities to engage in the task, reflect on their teaching expertise and learn from each other, as well as practise their teaching skills in this novel intercultural environment.

These findings are in line with the results reported by Dooly and Sadler (2013) who found that, through participation in a virtual community of practice created as a result of telecollaboration involving groups of student teachers in Spain and the US, who collaborated online to give peer feedback and evaluation of several teaching activities, teacher trainees were able to assimilate competences needed for their future classroom work and were provided with "opportunities unavailable in more traditional teacher education classrooms" (Dooly & Sadler 2013: 4).

The second research question – What do the students perceive to be the most useful and the most challenging aspects of achieving the goals of the telecollaboration that included peer assessment? – can be answered using the data collected in the recall survey.

The students' perceptions of the most useful aspects overlap with the findings from the evaluation sheets presented above. They can be classified into the following categories: aspects related to gains in teaching expertise, aspects related to the intercultural dimension, and aspects related to collaboration.

A large number of the Polish (42%) and Spanish participants (53%) indicated that they were able to enhance their teaching expertise through the opportunity to practise their skills in developing and evaluating teaching materials, and this was the most useful aspect of the telecollaborative exchange that included peer assessment.

Participants from both cohorts indicated aspects related to intercultural dimensions of the exchange as being the most useful ones. The majority of Polish participants (58%) and 12% of the Spanish students pointed to benefits deriving from practising teaching skills with peers from another country. Thanks to the opportunity, future teachers, members of the same "community of practice" could gain a new intercultural perspective on EFL teaching. It is also worth stressing that the intercultural dimension of this telecollaboration project was not limited to creating a contact zone allowing for interaction between students from two different countries. The students were required to find online authentic texts or visuals that described the partner culture and embed them in the teaching materials. As a result, they could reflect on how their own culture was presented by the students from another country. The commentaries concerning the choice of cultural content made by the students from the partner university suggest that they were sensitive to the depiction of their own culture. They acknowledged informed as well as sophisticated choices of materials. However, they did not appreciate their own culture being presented in a stereotypical way or when it was presented not in a stereotypical, but in a negative way.

Finally, the development of collaborative skills, as a result of achieving the goals of telecollaboration that included peer assessment, was considered to be the most useful aspect of the exchange by only 16% of the Polish students. This finding, i.e. a somewhat limited appreciation of collaborative skills development by Polish students, is in line with the observations made by Kurek and Turula (2013: 254); these authors pointed to the culturally-grounded deficit of collaborative skills observed among Polish students, who tend to understand collaborative tasks as the final compilation of individually completed tasks rather than as a joint collaborative effort. It may be worth noting at this point that in Hofstede's dimensions of cultural differences (Hofstede & Hofstede 2005) Poland is classified as a masculine society. In masculine societies (like the Polish one), the "system rewards students' academic performance, students compete with each other in class [and they] try to make themselves visible". In contrast, in feminine societies (like, for example, the Spanish one), "the system rewards students' social adaptation, [and they] practice mutual solidarity" (Hofstede 1986: 314).

The aspects which the students found most challenging were related firstly to insufficient digital skills to develop the teaching materials (33% of Spanish students and 47% Polish students found these aspects challenging). Such answers could have been caused by the fact that online availability of materials on Polish and even Spanish culture in English may be limited, therefore finding relevant materials on, for example, Polish architecture, sport or art in English required more intensive effort and careful searching.

The second most challenging aspect may be related to the anxiety and pressure resulting from the peer assessment task, and especially from the perspective of the students who realized they would be assessed. Four out of 15 Spanish participants reported that the biggest challenge experienced by them in the telecollaboration that included peer assessment was trying to perform well and be innovative in designing a teaching unit in order to achieve a good result during the assessment. Almost half of the Polish participants (9 out of 19) believed that speaking in front of a new audience during the videoconferencing session when the peer assessment results were discussed posed the biggest challenge for them.

6. Conclusions

Although the challenge of peer assessment, which puts additional pressure on those being assessed, needs to be considered, the overall results of this study suggest that incorporating the peer assessment task in telecollaboration can be considered beneficial. The results of this study suggest that peer assessment stimulates intense reflection and activates deeper involvement and enhances collaborative learning on the part of students in the collaboration. In the case of the EFL teacher trainees participating in this project, such increased engagement and reflection enhanced both professional expertise in developing culture-oriented ELT materials. Furthermore, telecollaborative exchange that included peer assessment allowed students opportunities to experience interculturality, both as teacher trainees who were afforded the chance to practice assessment (which is an inherent part of the teaching profession) on work authored by students from another country, and also as students who underwent evaluation by peers from another country. This type of telecollaborative experience could therefore constitute a valuable means of preparing future teachers for functioning in the globalized world and for future work with culturally diverse students.

References

Belz, J. A. (2003). Linguistic perspective on the development of intercultural communicative competence in telecollaboration. *Language Learning & Technology, 7*, 68–117.

Belz, J. A., & Müller-Hartmann, A. (2003). Teachers negotiating German-American telecollaboration: Between a rock and an institutional hard place. *Modern Language Journal, 87*(1), 71–89.

Borthwick, K., Corradini, E., & Dickens, A. (Eds.). (2015). *10 years of the LLAS elearning symposium: Case studies in good practice*. Dublin: Research-publishing.net.

Byram, M. (1997). *Teaching and Assessing Intercultural Communicative Competence*. Clevedon: Multilingual Matters.

Byram, M., Holmes, P., & Savvides, N. (2013). Intercultural communicative competence in foreign language education: Questions of theory, practice and research. *The Language Learning Journal, 41*(3), 251–253.

Cassidy, S. (2006). Developing employability skills: Peer assessment in higher education. *Education + Training, 48*(7), 508–517.

Chun, D. (2015). Language and culture learning in higher education via telecollaboration. *Pedagogies: An International Journal, 10*(1), 5–21.

Council of Europe (2001). *Common European Framework of Reference for Languages: Learning, Teaching, Assessment*. Modern Languages Division, Strasbourg: Cambridge University Press.

De Guerrero, M. C. M., & Villamil, O. S. (1994). Social-cognitive dimensions of interaction in L2 peer revision. *The Modern Language Journal, 78*(4), 484–496.

Dooly, M., & Sadler, R. (2013). Filling in the gaps: Linking theory and practice through telecollaboration in teacher education. *ReCALL, 25*(1), 4–29.

Falchikov, N. (1995). Peer feedback marking- developing peer assessment. *Innovations in Education and Training International, 32,* 175–187.

Fukai, M., Nazikian, F., & Sato, S. (2008). Incorporating sociocultural approaches into assessment: Web-based peer learning and portfolio projects. *Japanese Language and Literature, 42*(2), 389–411.

Hansen, J., & Liu, J. (2005). Guiding principles for effective peer response. *ELT Journal, 59,* 31–38.

Hofstede, G. (1986). Cultural differences in teaching and learning. *International Journal of Intercultural Relations, 10*(3), 301–320.

Hofstede, G., & Hofstede, G. J. (2005). *Cultures and Organizations: Software of the Mind*. New York: McGraw-Hill.

Kern, R. (2014). Technology as pharmakon: The promise and perils of the Internet for foreign language education. *Modern Language Journal, 98,* 340–357.

Kurek, M., & Turula, A. (2013). Praca zespołowa online: uwarunkowania kulturowe i edukacyjne — próba analizy. In J. Stańczyk, & E. Nowikiewicz (Eds.), *Dydaktyka językowa a kompetencje ogólne* (pp. 247–259). Bydgoszcz: Nauczycielskie Kolegium Języków Obcych w Bydgoszczy.

Liddicoat, A. J., & Scarino, A. (2013). *Intercultural Language Teaching and Learning*. Chichester: Wiley Blackwell.

Lundstrom, K., & Baker, W. (2009). To give is better than to receive: The benefits of peer review to the reviewer's own writing. *Journal of Second Language Writing, 18,* 30–43.

O'Dowd, R. (2016). Emerging trends and new directions in telecollaborative learning. *CALICO Journal, 33*(3), 291–310.

O'Dowd, R., & Ritter, M. (2006). Understanding and working with "failed communication" in telecollaborative exchanges. *CALICO Journal, 23*(3), 623–642.

Orsini-Jones, M. (2015). A reflective e-learning journey from the dawn of CALL to web 2.0 intercultural communicative competence (ICC). In K. Borthwick, E. Corradini, & A. Dickens (Eds.), *10 Years of the LLAS Elearning Symposium: Case Studies in Good Practice* (pp. 43–56). Dublin: Research-publishing.net.

Royce, T. (2007). Multimodal communicative competence in second language contexts. In T. Royce, & W. Bowcher (Eds.), *New Directions in the Analysis of Multimodal Discourse* (pp. 361–403). Mahwah, NJ: Lawrence Erlbaum.

Royce, T., & Bowcher, W. (Eds.). (2007). *New Directions in the Analysis of Multimodal Discourse*. Mahwah, NJ: Lawrence Erlbaum.

Stańczyk, J., & Nowikiewicz, E. (Eds.). (2013). *Dydaktyka językowa a kompetencje ogólne*. Bydgoszcz: Nauczycielskie Kolegium Języków Obcych w Bydgoszczy.

Topping, K. J. (2005). Trends in peer learning. *Education Psychology, 25*(6), 631–645.

Wenger, E. (1998). Communities of practice: Learning as a social system. *Systems Thinker, 9*(5), 2–3.

Yus Ramos, F. (2011). *Cyberpragmatics: Internet-Mediated Communication in Context*. Amsterdam, Philadelphia, PA: John Benjamins.

Anna Turula
Pedagogical University of Cracow, Cracow, Poland

Maike Grau
University of Education, Freiburg, Germany

Distributed teaching presence in a telecollaborative project

Abstract: This chapter presents the results from a study of an online intercultural exchange in language teacher pre-service education, involving two groups of students at a German and a Polish university. The overall aim of the project was promoting virtual mobility, and telecollaboration was seen as a useful tool in this respect.

After being introduced to the project and to each other, the participants of the online intercultural exchange created short video clips. In regular oral debriefings students were asked to evaluate the process, the role of the facilitators, and their own group dynamics. Observation notes taken during these debriefings, as well as an anonymous post-project questionnaire, placed a specific focus on aspects of teaching presence (TP), based upon categories from Anderson et al. (2001), accommodated within the Community of Inquiry Framework proposed by Garrison et al. (2001). Since the focus was upon distributed teaching presence, the respondents were asked to evaluate how the requirements described in different categories of TP were fulfilled by both their teachers and their fellow students. The data show that the distribution of TP inherent in the project design matched the students' perceptions in some parts, but was evaluated as weak in other areas, a factor which will have to be reconsidered in future projects in order to create a learning environment which fully benefits all participants.

Keywords: telecollaboration, online intercultural exchange, distributed teaching presence, action research

1. Introduction

In this chapter, we look at student virtual mobility in telecollaboration described by Guth and Helm (2010: 14) as "Internet-based intercultural exchange between people of different cultural/national backgrounds, set up in an institutional context with the aim of developing both language skills and intercultural communicative competence (as defined by Byram 1997) through structured tasks". The main focus is teaching presence (TP; defined and described in more detail in Section 2), a concept based on Anderson et al. (2001), which is analysed within the Community of

Inquiry Framework proposed by Garrison et al. (2001). The purpose of the action research described in this chapter was twofold: to find out how different aspects of the teacher's involvement were perceived and evaluated by the participants in the project; and to inform our future telecollaborative planning. Meeting the former objective was meant as our contribution to the broad research pertaining to teaching presence; the latter aim was related to our intention to organise similar exchanges in the future, in a better, more effective and motivating way. In order to create these projects as rich learning environments through learner engagement and autonomy, we placed a particular emphasis on distributed TP, i.e. ways of sharing the teacher role between all participants.

First, we introduce the theoretical framework which we used for this study and we establish its relevance for the context and purpose of this study (Section 2), carried out during the Freiburg-Krakow intercultural online exchange in 2015–2016. Then we present the context of the study, paying special attention to local specificity, especially the educational cultures to which the telecollaborating groups belonged. We also describe the two courses, their outlines and objectives (Section 3). Section 4 contains the presentation and discussion of the research data obtained by means of two tools during the online intercultural exchange in question: a questionnaire, implemented at the end of the study, as well as observation notes taken during in-class discussions of the project carried out at both universities.

While presenting the Freiburg-Krakow exchange, its progress and the data gathered alongside the project execution, we are fully aware of one thing emphasised by many telecollaboration practitioners: online intercultural exchanges are complex learning (and teaching) environments. We see this as an asset, yet we are aware that it can also result in tensions and issues. It is our belief that we, as teachers, should help students see this complexity as a learning opportunity, preparing them for and supporting them in resolving communication issues. Hence we hope our future exchanges will benefit from this study, and we hope our readers will as well.

2. Review of literature: teaching presence

Teaching presence has a special place and an exceptional role to play within the framework of Community of Inquiry (CoI), a model of critical thinking and practical inquiry. It was proposed by Garrison et al. (2001) for the purpose of studying teaching and learning in a text-based online environment. Teaching presence is both a part of the network – the other two presences being cognitive and social – and its organizing force; the "binding element in creating a community of inquiry" (Garrison et al. 2001: 96); the source of "online instructional orchestration" (Shea et al. 2010: 17). It is defined as the "design, facilitation, and direction of cognitive and social processes for the purpose of realizing personally meaningful and educationally worthwhile learning outcomes" (Anderson et al. 2001: 5). Design, as clarified by the proponents of the model, is the creation and re-purposing of learning materials as well as establishing the overall plan of the course. Discourse facilitation has the purpose of addressing differences and misunderstanding between the members of the community of inquiry, motivating learners to participate, regularly monitoring the process of inquiry and, if necessary, familiarizing students with the discourse of the community of knowledge to which a given CoI belongs (Benbunan-Fich et al. 2005). Finally, direct instruction is about clear definition of objectives, reinforcement of the understanding of instruction through regular feedback, and guidance offered in response to students' concerns (including technical problems).

Each of the three aspects can further be broken down into a number of descriptors of teaching presence (Table 1).

Table 1: Design, discourse facilitation and direct instruction. Descriptors based on Anderson et al. 2001

DESIGN	DISCOURSE FACILITATION	DIRECT INSTRUCTION
setting curriculum	identifying areas of (dis)agreement	presenting content/ questions
designing methods	seeking to reach consensus	focussing the discussion
establishing time parameters	encouraging/ acknowledging/	confirming understanding
utilising medium effectively	reinforcing students' contributions	diagnosing misconceptions
establishing netiquette	drawing in participant/ prompting discussion	injecting knowledge from different sources
	assessing the efficacy	responding to tech problems

As has been shown by research, teaching presence is an indicator of online instructional quality and is positively correlated with student satisfaction (Picciano 2002; Shea et al. 2003; Bangert 2008; see also Shea et al. 2010 for an overview of relevant research). Shea et al. (2005) report "a significant link between students' sense of learning community and their recognition of effective instructional design and directed facilitation on the part of their course instructors" (59). They also point out that high levels of student-instructor interaction correlate positively with higher levels of learning (cf. also Jiang & Ting 2000; Shea et al. 2003; and Dzuiban et al. 2005). In turn, weak teaching presence results in the impoverishment of student discourse (Meyer 2003; Finegold & Cooke, 2006), negatively affecting cognitive presence in CoI. Some studies also show a positive correlation between teaching presence and social presence (Gilbert & Dabbagh 2005; Shea et al. 2006). As pointed out by Garrison et al. (2010), in their otherwise quite critical summary of studies into the utility of CoI, "the main finding over the last decade with regard to teaching presence is the growing evidence as to the importance of this element. Teaching presence is seen as a significant determinant of student satisfaction, perceived learning, and sense of community" (7).

In light of this, given its conceptual meaning, its three different aspects and its research-proven utility, teaching presence seems to be of paramount importance in online intercultural exchanges. Its influence on the effectiveness of the exchanges as well as students satisfaction is emphasised in Turula and Raith (2015) and Turula (2017). These two insights corroborate telecollaborative research results reported to-date. Even if the publications in question may not explicitly refer to the TP concept, they address the three main aspects of TP: design, discourse facilitation, and direct instruction. For instance, the significance of the design of tasks for online collaboration has been emphasized in a number of publications (e.g. Müller-Hartmann & Schocker-v. Ditfurth 2013; Kurek & Müller-Hartmann 2017). The facilitation of discourse, in the face of physical and – even more importantly – cultural distance, can be a deciding factor as to whether prejudice and stereotypes are successfully dealt with or reinforced (Guth & Helm 2010).

Alongside research into teaching presence per se, there is growing evidence of the importance of *distributed* teaching presence, which is the main focus of our study. Distributed teaching presence, as we use the term, is the responsibility for the design, discourse facilitation and direct instruction shared in a telecollaborative community of inquiry between the cooperating teachers as well as between the teachers and their students and among the students themselves. CoI literature to-date offers some insights into the problem. Shea et al. (2010) note the importance of the *students*' teaching presence, observing that "when the instructor's participation within the threaded discussion drops to zero students attempt to recreate 'instructional equilibrium'" (137). Therefore, they argue that "there may be a need to focus more attention on the distinct roles of learners in online education separate from the role of the instructor" (Shea et al. 2010: 139); a similar position on the necessity for student involvement in the process – or distributed teaching presence – is argued for in Shea and Bidjerano (2010). When it comes to teaching presence in online intercultural exchanges, the recent study by Kurek and Müller-Hartmann (2016) sheds some light onto how design, discourse facilitation and direct instruction responsibilities are shared between the two telecollaborating classrooms. The authors emphasise both the need for inter-class coordination as well as the unique contributions on both sides, resulting from teaching styles and educational cultures represented in the exchange. Sharing responsibilities between classrooms, their teachers and – especially – the students is what contributes to the feeling of independence and a sense of responsibility in the latter. These two are aspects of student autonomy, a capacity developed as a result of telecollaboration, as observed by Hauck et al. (2012).

As our review of literature reveals, in spite of its potential relevance, teaching presence in telecollaboration is not yet broadly researched. This chapter is an attempt to fill in the gap. We look at how the responsibility for design, discourse facilitation and direct instruction is shared between the two teachers and their students in an online intercultural exchange, how it contributes to the virtual mobility of the participants and what can be done to further increase this mobility. At the same time, though, the findings presented here will be subject to analysis whose results cannot, by any means, be treated as generalisable. We carried out the study described as action research, with a purpose typical of such studies: bettering the pedagogical measures to be applied in the future telecollaborative exchanges we are planning.

3. Distributed teaching presence in the Freiburg-Krakow exchange (2015–2016): the project plan and objectives

Before the study into distributed teaching presence is described, it is necessary to introduce the context in which the online intercultural exchange between the University of Education, Freiburg, Germany and Pedagogical University, Krakow, Poland took place. We then outline the exchange itself, specifying its objectives and timeline.

3.1 The Freiburg context

The University of Education Freiburg is a university in southern Germany with a focus on teacher education. The telecollaborative project was embedded in a seminar on film-based language teaching, an elective course offered by the university's TEFL (Teaching English as a Foreign Language) department for students in their final semesters of the primary or secondary education programmes. The courses in this last module can be chosen to cover various key aspects of TEFL and they are assessed through a portfolio, in which students include samples of work from classes, reflections on their professional education as English language teachers, and a classroom research project they carry out on a topic of their choice. The class in question was also open to international exchange students and consisted of 12 German and 7 international students from China, France, Russia, Spain and Switzerland, working at different levels of English language competence, teaching experience and background knowledge in TEFL. Except for one mature student, the participants were in their early to mid-twenties, and there were 16 female and 3 male students in the group.

The first five weeks of the course consisted of a general introduction to approaches and methods for working with films in language teaching, followed by the telecollaborative project as an experience-based introduction to producing films in English language teaching, as well as an opportunity to learn first-hand about telecollaboration in education.

3.2 The Krakow context

Pedagogical University in Krakow (PUK), where the Polish group participating in the exchange was based, is a leading teacher training institution in Poland. Like most Polish universities, it is rather traditional and generally very teacher-centred when it comes to the instruction mode as well as one-size-fits-all in terms of course offerings. Once in a chosen study programme, students are enrolled into a group with a common weekly study schedule. Participation in classes, with the possible exception of lectures, is compulsory, and each student earns a credit based on in-class performance (in which attendance is usually a factor) and some form of a final exam.

The online telecollaborative exchange described in the present chapter was implemented as part of a 2-year CALL teacher training programme offered at the School of Modern Languages and Literatures of PUK, during a 15-hour *Introduction to CALL* course taught in year 1 of the programme. Student participation in the course was compulsory, and carrying out the tasks of the telecollaboration was a course-completion requirement. The Krakow group consisted of 21 students, 14 females and 7 males, 23–25 years old, all Polish.

Prior to the telecollaborative project, the group took part in 6 hrs of class, during which different multi-literacies, as defined by Pegrum (2009), were addressed. The students performed different activities in which they developed their knowledge and skills as regards different digital tools (digital literacy); information search and evaluation (search and information literacies); and online collaboration (participatory literacy). Special emphasis was put on multimedia literacy: the students learned how to make video tutorials, making use of relevant tools and guidelines.

3.3 The Freiburg-Krakow exchange

The collaborative project covered seven weeks of class time, excluding the three-week Christmas break. As an introduction, participants were asked to individually upload a short video clip on the project platform on Wikispaces, in which they could present themselves and a typical day in their lives. During class time at both sites, students watched the clips and wrote comments and questions to their peers. In the same session, the students in Krakow and Freiburg were asked to form pairs or groups of three, which were then randomly assigned a partner pair or group at the other site, resulting in 9 international teams. These teams were then assigned to create what we labelled a "TEFL clip", i.e. a short film which teaches an item of English language or culture. This included deciding on the topic of the film, on the tools to create it, and on the role each team member was to have in the production process. After the deadline, the clips were commented and voted on by all project participants, with a view to finding out whose clip got the most positive comments and was thus the "winner" of the project.

3.4 Distributed teaching presence in the Freiburg-Krakow telecollaboration – the plan

While designing the exchange, we decided that teaching presence in this telecollaboration would/should be distributed between us and our students. This is why we provided the structure, aims and overall task requirements (a TEFL clip) of the project, while leaving task management and completion to our students. A more detailed explanation of how we projected the distribution of responsibilities can be found below, in relation to the three aspects of teaching presence and their descriptors.

As shown in Figure 1, in the area of design, the overall plan was provided by us, the teachers, including general guidelines as regards the methods, media and netiquette, as well as the project milestones and their deadlines. However, it was up to the students to work out the internal plan of the project, including the topic of the clip and the individual steps to be taken for the sake of task completion, together with their time parameters. The choice of tools as well as netiquette for their group interactions were also left entirely to the students themselves. Regarding discourse facilitation, we provided for weekly in-class discussions of the project in progress, during which areas of disagreement were diagnosed and remedial actions were undertaken: ways of reaching consensus were considered; encouragement and prompting were applied in the cases of insufficient contribution; and the overall efficacy of steps taken in the project was gauged. However, the fact that the meetings were held once a week did not allow for any impromptu reactions to achievement and problems in all five areas, so we predicted that most of discourse facilitation in the project groups would happen beyond our control. Finally, when it comes to direct instruction, we predicted that presenting content and diagnosing misconceptions would be mainly our responsibility. Yet, considering the considerable autonomy of our students working on the task, we thought that focusing discussions, confirming understanding and injecting knowledge would be shared equally between us and our students. Responding to technology-related problems, in turn, would almost entirely be in the hands of the students.

Figure 1: The planned distribution of teaching presence in design, discourse facilitation and direct instruction (indicated for teachers in bold; and for students—italicised)

DESIGN	DISCOURSE FACILITATION	DIRECT INSTRUCTION
Setting curriculum	**Identifying** *areas of (dis)agreement*	**Presenting content/** *questions*
Designing *methods*	**Seeking** *to reach consensus*	**Focussing** *the discussion*
Establishing ti*me parameters*	**Encouraging/** *acknowledging/reinforcing students' contributions*	**Confirming** *understanding*
Utilising *medium effectively*	**Drawing in participants/** *prompting discussion*	**Diagnosing misconcepti***ons*
Establishing *netiquette*	**Assess***ing the efficacy*	**Injecting knowledge** *from different sources*
		Respond*ing to tech problems*

4. The study

4.1 Research questions

As outlined in the literature review section, questions relating to distributed teaching presence in online cooperation are still under-researched, so this study is exploratory in that it is aimed at generating questions for further analysis. As an action research project, the knowledge gained from this research is purposeful, aiming at improving future project design and facilitation (e.g. Burns 2011).

This is why our research questions centre on the students' perception of different aspects of the teaching presence in a telecollaborative project (Research Question 1); on how and to what extent these perceptions coincided with the plan of the exchange we delineated in Section 3.4 (Research Question 2); as well as how our project plan should be amended to improve the quality of future exchanges (Research Question 3).

- Q#1: What are the students' perceptions of the different aspects of teaching presence: design, discourse facilitation and direct instruction for their teachers and their partners?
- Q#2: What is the relationship between the perceptions and the distribution of teaching presence planned for the exchange?
- Q#3: What should be changed in the future Freiburg-Krakow exchanges to help better distribute teaching presence?

4.2 Research tools and data sources

The data for the study consist of the content produced by the students and available on Wikispaces, observation notes, which were taken during in-class sessions and exchanged between the facilitators; and a questionnaire, administered electronically and filled in by the students after the project. The first two items on the questionnaire were inspired by a survey found in Garrison (2011). They consisted of 11 statements[1] pertaining to teaching presence which the students were supposed to rank on a 0–3 Likert scale (0=not at all; 3=a lot); the ranking was performed twice: for the teachers (Questionnaire Question 1) and the partners (Questionnaire Question 2). Additionally, the questionnaire contained a number of open-ended questions about the most important thing the students learned, as well as their recommendations regarding the teacher's role in such an exchange. The answers to the first of the open questions were subject to data crunching by Wordle.[2] In the case of the recommendations, student answers were categorised and added up within each category.

4.3 Data presentation. Distributed teaching presence: a comparative perspective

Concerning the task, its completion and students' attitudes towards it, there are a few points to be made based on the content produced by the students and uploaded on the wiki (W) as well as the teachers' observation notes (ON). First of all, it can be noted that all nine teams completed the task and submitted their clips online. Six out of the nine clips had a language focus, two had a culture focus, and one had a language and culture focus (W: access 19 Jan 2016). If we consider this in the context of the observation notes showing that the Freiburg students opted for

1 Examples of these statements are: "The goal of the exchange was evident to me", "I got regular feedback that helped me carry on with the task".

2 This tool has been used for a similar purpose by Williams (2008), a study which inspired ours in the realm of data crunching by Wordle.

culture-focused content of the TEFL clip, while the Krakow students preferred to concentrate on teaching grammar (ON: email exchange 10 Dec 2015), it can be said that some compromises were definitely made on both sides, especially on Freiburg's. Secondly, in relation to student attitudes to the exchange, the observation notes contain a record of student satisfaction with the in-group dynamics and staying on task (ON: email exchange 11 Dec 2015; 18 Dec 2015; 8 Jan 2016) as well as proof of some frustration (ON: email exchange 11 Dec 2015; 8 Dec 2015). The concerns voiced during in-class discussions usually pertain to the lack of – or slow – response from the other side or reluctance to use straightforward online communication tools (the complaint voiced by some Krakow members of the teams; ON: email exchange 18 Dec 2015; 13 Jan 2016); and to grammar-centredness, reluctance to choose interesting topics preferred by the other side, and excessive teacher-reliance of the partners (reported by some Freiburg members of the teams; ON: email exchange 10 Dec 2015). Finally, when it comes to the peer-to-peer aspect of the exchange, both sides admit they stayed on task and did not socialise much (ON: email exchange 8 Jan 2016). As regards learning from each other, Krakow students claim to have taught their partners the use of some digital tools, whereas Freiburg teams admitted having left the technicalities in the hands of the Polish partners, because many of the Freiburg participants felt they did not have the same level of technical know-how and experience (ON: email exchange 5 Feb 2016). As a result, it can be inferred that the group members typically divided up the tasks accordingly, which is illustrated by the "winner clip", an animated tutorial on prepositions, in which the animation was created by the team members in Krakow, whereas the voice-over comment was written and recorded by the students based in Freiburg, after the team had decided on the general topic and the idea for the film (ON: email exchange 21 Jan 2016). Apart from the technology, the clips and the project data show that there were other learning processes going on, e.g. regarding teaching methodology, as can be seen in a group which decided on a grammar-based topic much earlier than the other groups and were the most successful group in terms of enthusiasm and task satisfaction (ON: email exchange 17 Dec 2015). In this group the topic was put forward by the Krakow group members; and the Freiburg students, both enrolled in the primary programme, suggested using storytelling through the medium of a hand puppet as their methodology. They went on to perform and film a scene in Freiburg, which was then framed by the Polish group members' voice-over comment and explanations of the grammar rules (ON: email exchange 21 Jan 2016).

As regards the results of the questionnaire, Figures 2 and 3 (below) show how the students in both groups perceived the teaching presence of their teachers and peers.

Figure 2: Freiburg students' answers concerning perceived teaching presence (N = 15).

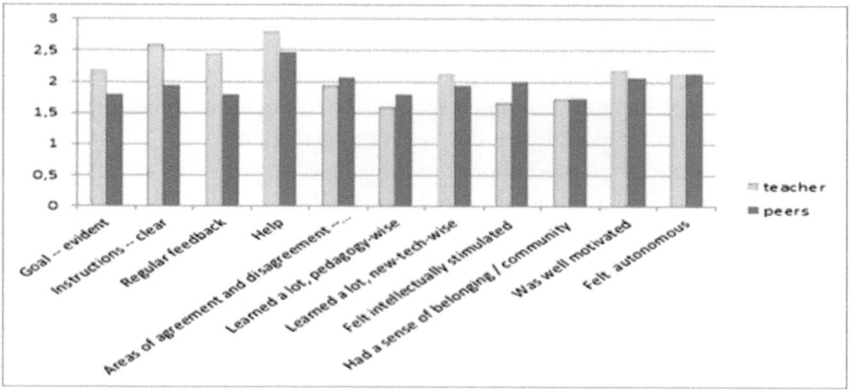

Figure 3: Krakow students' answers concerning perceived teaching presence (N = 21).

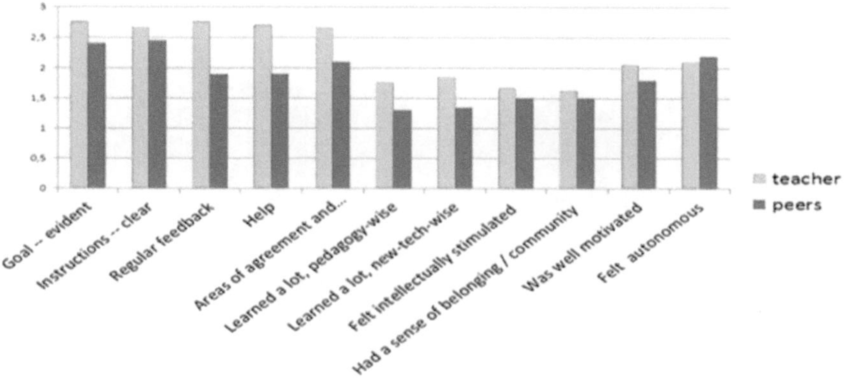

When it comes to the perceptions of the Krakow students, the teachers' TP was felt more strongly than that of the peers in almost all the areas, with particular regard to making the goal of the exchange evident, providing clear instructions, regular feedback and general help. The only descriptor which was ranked higher for the peers than for the teachers was the feeling of autonomy. For students at the Freiburg end of the project, quite similarly to Krakow's, the most important role the instructor(s) played in the project was providing the context, i.e. the goals and instructions for the task, but also giving regular feedback and support. For the Freiburg students the three areas in which the peers' teaching presence was perceived to be more important than the teachers' were mediation and conflict-resolution, intellectual stimulation, and facilitation of learning of pedagogically relevant contents. Finally, in two areas contributions by teachers and peers were perceived to be equally relevant, namely the creation and maintenance of a sense of belonging and the support of student autonomy. While the teachers clearly dominated in the students' perceptions, the role of peers seems to be almost equally important – especially for the Freiburg participants.

When asked about the most important thing they learned in the exchange, both groups emphasise communication-related issues and the ability to compromise. The majority of answers (28 out of 35) given by all participants in the project, regardless of their context, refer to their learning regarding online communication, whereas answers which mention technology-related gains are much fewer (7 out of 35). The importance of compromise and similar aspects of teamwork in item 3 can be seen clearly in the visualization of the words used most frequently in Figure 4 below.

Figure 4: The answers to the question about the most important thing learned in the exchange; crunched by Wordle.

Finally, as regards their recommendations as to the role of the teacher in an exchange of this sort, the students give guidelines pertaining to each of the three aspects of teaching presence: task design and choice (design), socio-affective support (discourse facilitation) as well as instructions and monitoring (direct instruction). The answers are similar in both partnering groups, with "choice" being frequently mentioned by students in Krakow (and not in Freiburg), as illustrated by this comment to question 9 (choice): "Provide students with the internet access and give them a lot of freedom, limited only by some deadline steps so that they could see their progres [sic] as well as so as to motivate them more". Another answer includes aspects of all areas of TP, including the "socio-affective support", which was more frequently mentioned by Freiburg students: "The whole project should be planned with the co-teacher before the projects [sic] starts. Clear instructions and task for the learners and weekly meetings and support". Figure 5 below shows a distribution of the topics mentioned in the students' answers, and a categorization into the three areas of TP.

Figure 5: Students' recommendations as regards the teacher's role in an online intercultural exchange.

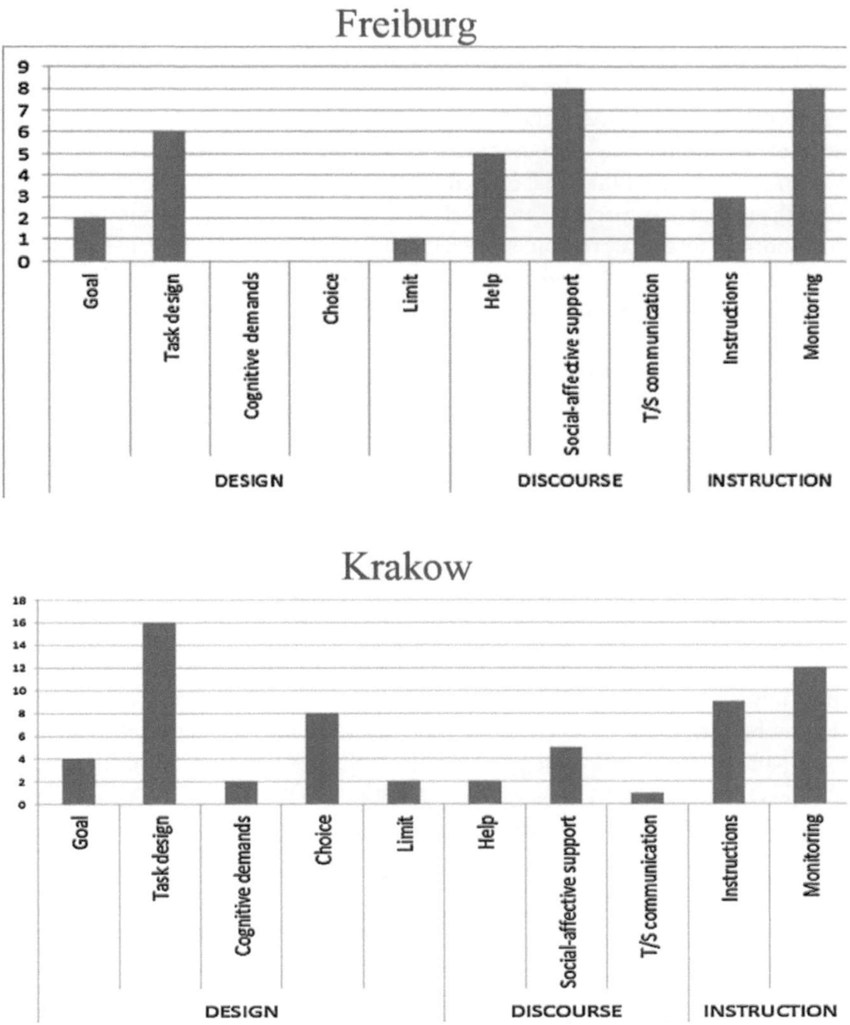

4.4 Discussion

Based on the data presented in Section 4.3 we propose the following answers to our three research questions.

When it comes to research question 1, concerning the nature and quality of the perceived distributed teaching presence in the project, a few observations can be made based on the data coming from both sources, the observation notes and the questionnaire. First of all, the teacher's TP is generally more strongly felt than that of the peers, while, admittedly, the ratings for both are mostly comparable. More specifically (Figures 2 and 3), in the area of direction (goal), task design and general help, both groups feel the teaching presence quite strongly (their teachers' presence rated higher than that of their partners). However, both groups acknowledge the role of their partners and teachers in making them feel autonomous. This corroborates findings presented in telecollaboration literature to date (cf. Hauck et al. 2012, among others) and emphasises the role of virtual mobility in developing and sustaining student autonomy. As our results show, the partners may be more effective in this process than the teachers.

The issue of peer-to-peer learning is an interesting one. As shown in Figures 2 and 3, Freiburg students seem to feel they have learned more from the Krakow students than vice versa in terms of social (dealing with disagreements) and cognitive (pedagogy, intellectual stimulation) aspects. As we are discussing students' perceptions rather than facts here, this may be a question of personal evaluation of the project experience. This is, to a certain extent, confirmed by the compromise made: greater on the Freiburg side, if we compare preferences as to the theme of the clip (focus on form vs. focus on culture; cf. observation notes) and the actual outcome of the telecollaboration, i.e. the clips, which often focused on a grammar topic. In any case, the ability to *compromise* is emphasised by both sides as the most important thing learned (Figure 4). It is interesting to see how communication on both ends depended a lot on *patience*. Most comments relate to the need to be patient, compromise, etc.; group work (organisation, communication); or, a little less frequently, to technology. Data pertaining to the final area of peer-to-peer learning are a basis for another interesting observation: the perceptions of who taught what to whom, technology-wise, seem to diverge on both sides (observation notes): while the Krakow students felt they imparted their new-tech knowledge to their partners, the Freiburg team members thought they abstained from the technology aspect of the clip production rather than learned in the process. At the same time, though, what really happened during and between the telecollaborators in this respect was clearly team-specific, as illustrated above by the set-up of the "winner" clip as opposed the "puppets" clip (observation notes).

As for research question 2, regarding the observed TP distribution vis à vis the plans made for the telecollaborative project (Figure 1), the strong teaching presence in the area of design and direct instruction is concordant with the plan, and is, most probably, the result of task design: a steady framework, clear guidelines as to what was expected and when as well as good in-group management: the international groups were practically on their own during task completion. At the same time, it is both obvious and slightly disappointing that the perceived TP was quite weak in the area of discourse facilitation, shown in the low rating of the social and cognitive quality of the process. This may have resulted from the fact that there was most probably too much room for decision-making as regards the product itself and, consequently, too little time to see to the cognitive and social aspects of the intercultural contact. Some of the teams, even though they were motivated in the beginning, got involved in discussing the theme of the clip, likely losing the discourse focus in the process. This may have resulted in disappointment or even caused a "them" vs. "us" situation rather than a team spirit, as noted for some of the groups during in-class observation (cf. ON, numerous examples containing "They do/don't" complaints). This seems to have been more strongly felt on the Freiburg side, as can be seen in the students' recommendations for the role of the teacher in telecollaboration (Figure 5). On the other hand, however, the fact that all students emphasise working towards compromise may be indication enough that there was a lot of activity which could be labelled discourse facilitation, even if it was not explicitly included in the students' answers.

Finally, regarding research question 3, we have identified the following steps to be taken to ensure the improvement of both the quality of the exchange and the ways in which teaching presence can be distributed in an online intercultural exchange. If we compare these observations with the plan we had devised prior to the exchange (cf. Figure 1), we would like to propose the following improvements (Figure 6): (i) in the area of design – a stronger guidance of the students' technological and methodological choices throughout the whole project. Considering the heterogeneity of the group, we as instructors need to raise awareness of different backgrounds among the students through more emphasis on the preparation and interpretation of the introductory tasks; we also need to set parameters for methods and tools which are available for all participants to take this responsibility off the students' shoulders and give more room for a real intercultural encounters. Additionally, the timeline needs rethinking as the 3-week break in the middle of the project is detrimental to its momentum and coherence; (ii) in the area of discourse facilitation – more affective support should be offered, especially in the area of consensus seeking and diagnosing and resolving misunderstanding as well as acknowledging participation and progress; teacher assessment, alongside student evaluation, is to be given upon task completion to make the whole process more formative and beneficial to the future teachers; and (iii) no substantial changes will be made in the area of direct instruction, which seems to have worked well.

Figure 6: Reworking the original plan of TP distribution in a telecollaborative project (as before: for teachers in bold, for students in italics, underlining for future change in the setting).

DESIGN	DISCOURSE FACILITATION	DIRECT INSTRUCTION
Setting curriculum	**Identifying areas of** *(dis)agreement*	**Presenting content/** *questions*
Designing ***methods***	**Seeking to reach** *consensus*	**Focussing** *the discussion*
Establishing ti*me parameters*	**Encouraging/ acknowledging/***reinforcing students' contributions*	**Confirming** *understanding*
Utilising medium effectively	**Drawing in participants/** *prompting discussion*	**Diagnosing misconcepti***ons*
Establishing *netiquette*	**Assessing** *the efficacy*	**Injecting knowledge** *from different sources*
		Respond*ing to tech problems*

5. Conclusions and teaching implications

At first sight, the project we discussed in this chapter could be called an example of successful online intercultural exchange: all groups were able to complete the task requirement to collaboratively produce and upload a clip in the given time frame. However, a closer look at the task process shows that there are aspects in the design and the facilitation of this cooperative learning environment which can be improved despite the positive overall result.

In light of the importance of the teacher role for successful telecollaboration shown in the research to date – both directly focusing on the concept of TP (Turula & Raith 2015, Turula 2017) as well as addressing its three aspects (Guth & Helm 2010, Müller-Hartmann & Schocker-v. Ditfurth 2013; Kurek & Müller-Hartmann 2017) – the framework of teaching presence, or distributed teaching presence was used to learn more about students' perceptions of their own roles and those of the teachers. The analysis of the data presented above shows that the most important discrepancies between our planned DTP and the one perceived by the participants and diagnosed, based on the research data, seem to lie in the areas of design and discourse facilitation, while the students showed most agreement with the way the direct instruction was delivered throughout the project.

In the first area, task design, the frequency of the word "patience" in the student data for describing their learning processes suggests that the timing of the exchange is a parameter which needs to be considered even more carefully. Avoiding the effects of a long break seems to be imperative for further planning. The data also show that the international teams were struggling with the first part of their assignment, which was to decide on a topic of common interest. Narrowing down the students' options so they would not lose the social and cognitive focus seems to be a direct consequence of these issues. An easier and earlier consensus would also support group-building in the sensitive first few weeks of the project, in which a growing alienation, resulting from a seemingly impossible compromise, can be frustrating for the participants and thus lower their initial enthusiasm.

Managing complex learning environments which are created between different institutional and cultural backgrounds involves decision-making on many different issues. In line with research in similar projects (e.g. Kurek & Müller-Hartmann 2017), the data presented in this chapter suggest that facilitating an easy flow of communication through well-organised task design has to have a high priority in managing such projects. At the same time, making the negotiation processes between the instructors as transparent as possible for the participating students seems to be equally important in order to help them understand the diversity of context factors and thus to support their autonomy and the distribution of teaching presence among all participants. This latter factor – fostering and sustaining student autonomy through telecollaboration – seems to be of utmost importance in virtual autonomy: it is both a factor increasing student motivation to engage in such mobility as well as its much-desired by-product of autonomy (Hauck et al. 2012).

References

Anderson, T., Rourke, L., Garrison, D. R., & Archer, W. (2001). Assessing teaching presence in a computer conferencing context. *Journal of Asynchronous Learning Networks, 5*(2), 1–17.

Bangert, A. (2008). The influence of social presence and teaching presence on the quality of online critical inquiry. *Journal of Computing in Higher Education, 20*(1), 34–61.

Benbunan-Fich, R., Hiltz, S. R., & Harasim, L. (2005). The online interaction learning model: An integrated theoretical framework for learning networks. In S. R. Hiltz & R. Goldman (Eds.), *Learning Together Online: Research on Asynchronous Learning Networks* (pp. 19–37). Mahwah, NJ: Lawrence Erlbaum Associates.

Burns, A. (2011). Action research in the field of second language teaching and learning. In E. Hinkel (Ed.), *Handbook of Research in Second Language Teaching and Learning* (Vol. 2, pp. 237–253). New York: Routledge.

Dzuiban, C., Shea, P. & Arbaugh, J. B. (2005). Faculty roles and satisfaction in ALNs. In S. Hiltz & R. Goldman (Eds.), *Learning Together Online: Research on Asynchronous Learning Networks* (pp. 169–190). Mahwah, NJ: Lawrence Erlbaum Associates.

Finegold, A. R. D., & Cooke, L. (2006). Exploring the attitudes, experiences and dynamics of interaction in online groups. *Internet and Higher Education, 9*, 201–215.

Garrison, D. R. (2011). *E-Learning in the 21st Century: A Framework for Research and Practice* (2nd ed.). London: Routledge/Falmer.

Garrison, D. R., Anderson, T., & Archer, W. (2001). Critical thinking, cognitive presence, and computer conferencing in distance education. *American Journal of Distance Education, 15*(1), 7–23.

Garrison, D. R., Anderson, T., & Archer, W. (2010). The first decade of the community of inquiry framework: A retrospective. *Internet and Higher Education, 13*, 5–9.

Gilbert, P. K., & Dabbagh, N. (2005). How to structure online discussions for meaningful discourse: A case study. *British Journal of Educational Technology, 36*(1), 5–18.

Guth, S., & Helm, F. (2010). *Telecollaboration 2.0: Language, Literacies and Intercultural Learning in the 21st Century.* Bern: Peter Lang.

Hauck, M., Fuchs, C., & Müller-Harmann, A. (2012). Promoting learner autonomy through multiliteracy skills development in cross-institutional exchanges. *Language Learning and Technology, 16*(3), 82–102.

Jiang, M., & Ting, E. (2000). A study of factors influencing students' perceived learning in a web-based course environment. *International Journal of Educational Telecommunications, 6*(4), 317–338.

Kurek, M., & Müller-Hartmann, A. (2016, April). Should I tell my partners or should my teacher do it? – Group formation processes in telecollaborative projects. Paper read at New Directions in Telecollaborative Research and Practice: The Second Conference on Telecollaboration in University Education, Dublin.

Kurek, M., & Müller-Hartmann, A. (2017). Task design for telecollaborative exchanges: In search of new criteria. *System, 64*, 7–20.

Meyer, K. (2003). Face-to-face versus threaded discussions: The role of time and higher-order thinking. *Journal of Asynchronous Learning Networks*, 7(3), 55–65.

Müller-Hartmann, A., & Schocker-v. Ditfurth, M. (2013) Developing teachers' intercultural communicative competences for task-supported language classrooms. *Fremdsprachen Lehren und Lernen, 42*(2), 85–98.

Pegrum, M. (2009). *From Blogs to Bombs: The Future of Digital Technologies in Education.* Crawley: UWA Publishing.

Picciano, A. G. (2002). Beyond student perceptions: Issues of interaction, presence, and performance in an online course. *Journal of Asynchronous Learning Networks, 6*(1), 21–38.

Shea, P., & Bidjerano, T. (2010). Learning presence: Towards a theory of self-efficacy, self-regulation, and the development of a communities of inquiry in online and blended learning.environments. *Computers & Education, 55*(1), 1721–1731.

Shea, P., Li, C. S., Swan, K., & Pickett, A. (2005). Developing learning community in online asynchronous college courses: The role of teaching presence. *Journal of Asynchronous Learning Networks, 9*(4), 59–82.

Shea, P., Pickett, A. M., & Pelz, W. E. (2003). A follow up investigation of teaching presence in the SUNY learning network. *Journal of Asynchronous Learning Networks, 7*(2), 68–80.

Shea, P., Sau Li, C., & Pickett, A. (2006). A study of teaching presence and student sense of learning community in fully online and web-enhanced college courses. *The Internet and Higher Education, 9*(3), 175–190.

Shea, P., Vickers, J., & Hayes, S. (2010). Online instructional effort measured through the lens of teaching presence in the community of inquiry framework: A re-examination of measures and approach. *International Review of Research in Open and Distance Learning, 11*(3), 127–154.

Turula, A. (2017). Teaching presence in telecollaboration: Keeping an open mind. *System, 64*, 21–33.

Turula, A., & Raith, T. (2015). Telecollaboration insights: Learning from exchanges that fail. *The EuroCALL Review 23*(2), 19–37.

Williams, H. (2008). The politics of Obama versus McCain using Wordle. Available at: https://heatherwilliams.wordpress.com/2008/06/20/the-politics-of-obama-versus-mccain-using-wordle/ (date of access: 9 February 2017).

Elżbieta Gajek
University of Warsaw, Warsaw, Poland

Integrating language, intercultural and digital skills in a teacher training programme through home-made videos

Abstract: Adapting and producing teaching materials is part of teaching. Using and creating video for language learning support comprehension and the linguistic performance of students. The idea of home-made one-minute educational video clips oriented on language, culture or communication is well grounded in language learning pedagogy (Willis D. 1983; Lonergan 1984; Coombe & Kinney 1999; Hill 1999). Such videos integrate language skills, intercultural competence, and digital skills. They also make repetitive tasks such as rehearsal or rote learning attractive and motivating. Through situated learning procedures student teachers learn how to create their own learning environment, and how to incorporate their own and their pupils' schemata into language learning. In a study conducted in Poland, home-made video clips were introduced into a teacher training programme to develop digital and media competence in a holistic way. The study analysed the production of over 250 video-clips made by pre-service teachers of languages as part of their teacher training course requirements. The clips were intended for a variety of educational purposes, e.g. introducing new language, illustrating usage, enhancing practice, documenting performance, and assessment, and were produced over a period of six years (2008–2014). They used subtitles, intertitles, and narrative revoicing a story to achieve their educational aim. The ability to produce home-made video-based activities as materials for teaching and learning languages require integration of various skills and competences. The results show that pre-service teachers are able to integrate their professional knowledge with intercultural competence and digital skills to enhance a variety of teaching techniques including the creation of multimodal texts.

Keywords: language teacher training, home-made video, media competence, situated learning

1. Introduction

Making a video for professional purposes can be a challenging yet rewarding task for student teachers as it requires a high level of intellectual agility and mobility as well as the integration of numerous skills and techniques. This chapter traces the process of developing home-made videos by students on a teacher training programme in Poland. It reports on a qualitative study describing the various approaches adopted by the student teachers in producing their videos. It further presents the content analysis that served to identify the various elements which were integrated while making the videos.

Using videos for language learning and teaching has been discussed for over three decades (Willis D. 1983; Willis J. 1983; Lonergan 1984). "Video is a medium which is replacing print. It is changing both the way we learn and the way we interact with each other" (Deubelbeiss 2015: 2 after Anderson 2010). However, the use of video still requires in-depth investigation and discussion in order to identify the areas of potential benefits, the most pedagogically sound techniques, and any added value of teaching the language with the use of video-clips. Given the availability of user-friendly hardware and software, language teacher programmes are under pressure to include as part of their teacher preparation the use of video for both teaching productive and receptive skills. Visual messages convey meaning. They also have their own grammar which is embedded in local and global cultures. The language of visual communication is controlled globally by mass media which unify their content (Kress & van Leeuwen 1996). Understanding the grammar of the picture is essential for its use as language learning material. In this area multimodal linguistics research aims (Kress & van Leeuwen 1996; Bateman 2008) overlap with those of educational research (Kalantzis & Cope 2000; Bateman 2008).

There are various approaches to video use in the classroom. Firstly, teachers and students use ready-made videos available on the Internet, e.g. in knowledge repositories for developing receptive skills such as watching and listening. Secondly, teachers assign tasks in which students manipulate the content of video and audio material by adding captions or revoicing the clip to enhance reading, writing, and/or speaking. Alternatively, students and teachers may produce their own video clips in a class project or as a task in an international cooperation partnership among schools such as eTwinning or Global Gateway which provide natural contexts and needs for video activities. All the approaches above allow for various educational purposes. Video-based activities not only enhance language skills but also contribute to the development of visual literacy, intercultural competence, digital skills, etc. So they can be applied interchangeably depending on the teaching and learning aims, the language level of the students, their computer literacy, and other competences such as media and visual literacy, musical skills, etc.

All the aforementioned activities which involve creating home-made videos for educational purposes require intellectual mobility. CALL tasks aimed at the production of audiovisual materials enhance integration of various competences both professional and personal gained in formal and informal contexts. They draw on intellectual agility that is required to fulfil the task.

Educational theory and research show the benefits of holistic and integrated approaches to learning; Jean Piaget (1970) and cognitive constructivists (Piaget & Inhelder 1966) claim that learning is an active process and should be holistic not fragmented. It should relate directly to the learner's environment. What is more, it is not possible to give knowledge to anybody. It needs to be constructed through experience. CALL tasks aimed at home-made videos create opportunities to integrate classroom activities with the learner's environment within intercultural and digital contexts. Lev Vygotsky (1981) and social constructivists emphasize the role of the zone of proximal development in which learning is possible but with the systematic help and support provided by the teacher or other people. It can be assumed that pre-service teachers are more or less competent users of information and communication technologies (ICT). They also possess some professional teaching skills. They are in their proximal development zone. What they need is help, encouragement and scaffolding to initiate the task of making their own video. This is in tune with Seymour Papert, a constructionist, who adds that a digital learning environment stimulates learner activity (Papert 1980; Papert & Harel 1991). Without easily accessible digital tools the idea of creating home-made videos would remain a potential but not a manageable activity.

Situated learning theory emphasizes "the relationship between learning and the social situation in which it occurs" (Hanks 1991: 14). Lave and Wenger (1991) define situated learning as a way to encourage social participation in co-creation of knowledge in a community of practice. They do not perceive teaching and learning as transmission of decontextualized knowledge from the teacher to the learners but as a process taking place in a particular social and physical environment. Efe et al. (2011) following Anderson et al. (1996) and Wilson (1993) claim that situated learning takes place when "(1) learning is grounded in the actions of everyday situations; (2) knowledge is acquired situationally and transfers only to similar situations; (3) learning is the result of a social process encompassing ways of thinking, perceiving, problem solving, and interacting in addition to declarative and procedural knowledge; and (4) learning is not separated from the world of action but exists in robust, complex, social environments made up of actors, actions, and situations" (Efe et al. 2011: 557). This theory explains the processes that take place in the production of video clips for teaching and learning.

As the location of the video as well as all the props and heroes are clearly set – they are embedded in the learner's social and physical environment the activity aimed at language learning and teaching is no longer decontextualized. Creating video-clips with the use of technology makes it possible for learners to relate to their proximity in learning a foreign language. By recording or encouraging learners to video record activities situated in real-world contexts, teachers provide realistic experiences that are easier to transfer, so enriching instruction (Willis & Cifuentes 2005).

However, there are still voices that claim that technology involved in the process of manipulating and producing video clips distracts learners who are not focused on the linguistic and cultural content but rather play with the technology. Also the issue of the digital divide is worth raising here as in many learning environments the technology needed for media tasks is not available to all students.

Looking at the issue from the teacher training perspective, it is evident that student teachers have to be equipped with the attitudes, approaches and skills which give them grounds for further professional development. As video is indeed the new textbook (Deubelbeiss 2015), pre-service teachers need to learn how to use video with learners and how to adapt it for their learners' needs.

2. Review of literature: video-clips in language learning and teaching

Video projects are used for different purposes, e.g. learning language elements and skills, stimulating discussions, consolidation, strategy and cultural awareness, building intercultural and international communication (MacWilliam 1990; Stempleski & Tomalin 1990; Sherman 2003; Deubelbeiss 2015). They are embedded in clear social contexts usually related to the learners' social environment. What is more, using the video and participation in a video project requires complex processing of language and of the visual content of the message being conveyed.

2.1 Receptive use of video

Video clips are either used in class as teaching materials or watched extensively for entertainment (Stempleski & Tomalin 2001). In subtitling countries, frequent exposure to linguistic input in foreign languages has become anecdotal (Danan 2004). Thus, it is taken for granted. The level of language acquisition in dubbing and subtitling countries has been discussed by Dollerup (1974), d'Ydewalle and Pavakanun (1997), Díaz Cintas (2008), Gottlieb (1998) and Caimi (2008) among others. It has been suggested that the media impacts significantly on average language proficiency, particularly among the youth. In subtitling countries, learning foreign languages is part and parcel of one's social activities as is the use of media. Thus, learning languages is well situated in the learners' environment.

2.2 Manipulating video and audio content

Captioning and revoicing video clips is an example of interpretation of the visual content by adding written (subtitles or intertitles) or spoken text to the video. Subtitles appear at the bottom of the screen, intertitles appear in the midst of filmed action as filmed pieces of printed text – they were characteristic of silent films. Captioning refers mainly to subtitling. Learner autonomous subtitling refers to funsubbing (Díaz Cintas & Muñoz Sánchez 2006), whereby people create their own subtitles and upload them on the internet so that they can be shown together with a particular video clip. Some repositories of knowledge such as Khan Academy and Ted.com also ask users to provide subtitles for clips. Talaván (2010: 289) clarifies that "the goal is not to turn foreign language students into subtitlers, but rather to use these audiovisual translation applications for didactic ends".

Revoicing refers, in general, to adding spoken text to a video. It is an intersemiotic translation which covers dubbing, voice over, audiodescription, narration and commentaries (Pérez-González 2009). Language learners get linguistic input while they watch commented sports events, nature films, instructions on how to cook, play a game, do gym, etc. Repositories of knowledge such as KhanAcademy and Ted.com, among others, provide scientific content revoiced. Audio description is a special type of revoicing addressed to visually impaired viewers to enable them to acquire visual information through a verbal description attached to a clip on a separate soundtrack.

2.3 Home-made video clips

The idea of using video as a productive medium has a long tradition, but the fact that video cameras "have increased in portability and decreased in price … attests their use in language learning" (Broady 1997: 61) which was noticed in the previous century as the prerequisite for educational use of video. Nowadays since a video camera is a standard in an average mobile device, video has become a tool for language learning available for all.

Broady (1997: 61) emphasises the integrative role of video noting that in language learning students and teachers deal "not with video alone, but integrated with other media". Video provides input which "can be manipulated and interacted with by individual and small groups". She claims that "video is no longer just a 'resource', but also a medium of interactive communication" and she recommends using video project work as task based student activity as a means of exploiting video for language learning purposes (Broady 1997: 65).

The theoretical grounds for home-made videos are based on situational learning, action-based teaching procedures, the creation of one's own learning environment, and the incorporation of one's own and one's pupils' schemata into language learning. Learners refer to their environment at each step in the process of video creation. For example, they make their video in other lessons e.g. filming a scientific experiment during a science lesson, or recording instructions of how to perform a traditional dance. Then they revoice such texts according to their interests and needs. If they participate in a school exchange project such as eTwinning, they make a video to introduce themselves, to present their school, town, leisure, hobbies etc. This way they open their learning environment to out-of-class stimuli taking photos or making films outside the classroom with their mobile devices: on the way to school, during a school trip and at home. Then they either caption or revoice the visual materials. The video materials may also be the means of intercultural communication. And creative use of video may be developed in imaginary stories.

Video projects, involving home-made videos, can also contribute to a variety of assessment techniques as they allow for holistic evaluation of skills and competences such as language and communication skills, visual literacy, cultural awareness, as well as intercultural and media competences. They also make students aware of the importance of non-verbal and paralinguistic communication (Gajek 2011).

2.4 Teacher training perspective on video production

Pre-service teachers have to be equipped with state-of-the-art academic knowledge on the use of video in language teaching as well as with the practical skill of how to integrate various video-based learning tasks in practice. Captioning can be the first step in developing creative and critical approaches to the video content. Gajek (2008: 112) emphasizes the need for subtitling activities in teacher training programmes to make student teachers aware of their benefits and to prepare them for effective use of video in their teaching practice. Home-made videos allow purposeful use of technology which becomes a means for cultural expression and intercultural communication as well as linguistic activity in a multisemiotic environment. While creating short home-made videos, students are equipped with various professional skills. Among them, the digital skill which allows them not only to replicate the project with learners but also to adapt fragments of other videos to the needs of learners is of special interest as it also extends the vision of how to manipulate the video material.

It is also worth mentioning that home-made video projects also contribute to the development of six out of eight key competences for lifelong learning i.e. communication in foreign languages, digital competence, learning to learn, social and civic competences, sense of initiative and entrepreneurship, cultural awareness and expression.

2.5 European perspective on video projects in language learning

Video projects for language learning are gaining interest among researchers and teachers of various domains, especially among language educators. Many EU funded projects, such as the ones listed below, promote video as a tool for language learning:

- ICTime – ICT as a Tool for Intercultural and Media Education (Belousa et al. 2009)
- Video for ALL – Digital Video as a basic tool for language learning (http://videoforall.eu/),
- Viducate: Digital video as a support for lifelong learning http://viducate.net/,
- Vidusign: Video Education and Sign Language http://www.vidusign.net/ DIVIS: Digital Video Streaming and Multilingualism,
- DIVIS: Digital Video Streaming and Multilingualism http://www.divisproject.eu/.

Two projects, that is LeVis and ClipFlair, are of special interest for this chapter. LeViS Learning via Subtitles and ClipFlair were similarly focused on language learning. LeViS was realised in 2006–2008 by a consortium of seven European Universities. LeViS developed a range of tasks-based activities for language learning in which multimedia were the central part of the activity not peripheral to the activity. The consortium produced a subtitling simulator LvS, which allows learners to actively participate in real-life communication while creating and adding subtitles to audiovisual material. Evaluation of the project results showed that it was well accepted by learners and teachers. The activities proved to be beneficial for learners at various levels and the subtitling tool was perceived as useful for language learning (Sokoli et al. 2011; Incalcaterra McLoughlin & Lertola 2015).

ClipFlair continued the developments and achievements of Learning via Subtitling (LeViS). Its innovative nature proved to motivate learners in a number of different settings, both formal and informal. ClipFlair not only provides subtitling-based activities, as LeViS did, but it also develops revoicing (i.e. dubbing, voiceover, audio description, karaoke signing, reciting, etc.) as a language learning task. Methodology guidelines emphasize the role of audiovisual skills such as watching and AV-listening, AV-speaking, AV-reading, AV-writing. AV-listening refers to listening to words in combination with non-verbal AV elements such as sound or picture. AV-reading refers to reading words written on screen, such as captions to develop visual-verbal literacy. AV-speaking (i.e. revoicing) refers to verbal literacy enhanced by audiovisual clues. AV-writing (i.e. captioning) refers to verbal literacy enhanced by audiovicual clues (Zabalbeascoa et al. 2012: 36).

For ClipFlair, the Polish team (Gajek & Szarkowska 2012, 2015a, 2015b) prepared activities for learners of Polish and English. The tasks addressed to learners of Polish are based on Polish customs and traditions. Home-made video projects were prepared by the team members and students. Another subgroup encouraged the use of the video-based tasks with small children and beginners based on a video made by a pre-service student teacher. There were tasks with captioning and revoicing. Creating video clips contributed to activating students to manipulate audio-visual texts in order to to enhance the learning of a foreign language (Gajek 2015).

3. The study

The aim of the study was to investigate home-made video project use on a teacher training programme focussing specifically on the integrative role of such tasks. The following research questions were formulated:

- What skills and competences are integrated while students work on home-made videos?
- Are students engaged in the activity? Do they perceive the activity as a valid professional task?
- How is situated learning reflected in the video-clips?
- How does video-making impact intellectual mobility, especially creativity, collaboration, and self-expression?

The video tasks were introduced to meet the pedagogical aims of equipping student teachers with professional teaching competences, preparing them for international cooperation, enhancing their intercultural competence, and encouraging them to produce videos for educational purposes.

While working on their own films the student teachers had to bear in mind the educational value of their videos from the teacher's perspective. Among other things, they needed to think about introducing new language, illustrating usage, enhancing practice, documenting performance, explaining cultural phenomena, and assessment. The main assessment criterion was their ability to present learning tasks in which the video could be used.

3.1 The description of the study

To understand the context of the study it needs to be noted that the Polish educational curriculum does not include explicit media education from either a technical or cultural perspective. Some elements of media education, covering its technical aspects, are included, however, in information technology (IT) classes but IT teachers are more focused on programming and coding from the start rather than on the cultural role of the media and creative production of video materials. Thus, pre-service teachers come to the university without a proper grounding in the domain of creating audiovisual texts. That is why giving them opportunities to integrate various competences with professional skills is especially relevant for them as future teachers.

The study was carried out over a six-year period from 2008 to 2014. Each year student teachers prepared video clips as a project task as part of a compulsory course at the fourth year of study. In the first round of home-making videos compiled in 2008, the students were asked to prepare a video which could be used as material for teaching language or to document learning. Starting from 2009, each year the general theme of the project work was slightly different. In the first instance it was based on teaching the language systems, that is, vocabulary, grammar and pronunciation. In the second year it was on teaching culture (target language culture, own culture or global culture). Then, it focussed on addressing the special educational needs of the learners. For the fourth iteration student teachers were asked to prepare clips for the ClipFlair project in which they were engaged. These videos were based on Polish culture. The fifth round focussed on teaching Polish as a foreign language, while the sixth year saw student teachers preparing materials for content and language integrated learning (CLIL). In the final year student teachers documented learning and teaching activities.

This study was qualitative in nature rather than a systematic quantitative investigation. Final conferences were held at the end of each year during which students presented their videos. These allowed for observations, group interviews, reflections, and discussions.

At the beginning, the students were introduced to the basic methodology of preparing a video clip such as planning, storyboarding, making the scene, recording, editing, and publishing. Special emphasis was put on copyright issues. In their own films students were allowed to use supplementary materials from the public domain or those published under Creative Commons licences. Other issues that were considered related to safety and privacy. Students were made aware that if they filmed other people, they needed to obtain their agreement. The students were evaluated on the basis of the educational value of their clips and overall quality of the video.

The students produced 287 clips. They used various audiovisual techniques such as subtitles, intertitles, and narrative revoicing. They filmed themselves and their peers as protagonists e.g. presenting their hobbies such as Irish dances or football. They designed costumes to prepare micro theatre or media shows. They invited their foreign friends to participate in the project to raise intercultural issues. They invited their students – children or teenagers – to present total physical response (TPR) tasks in practice or the application of sign language. They used realia e.g. for cooking national or international meals and for seasonal festivals. In videos intended for children they used puppets, sock puppets, masks, toys, lego blocks, drawings, cut out figures or photographs. They filmed live birds and animals. They also filmed science experiments preparing materials for CLIL. Students were not allowed to use fragments of commercials or feature films. However, one student got permission to use short fragments of Kieślowski's films.[1]

Students used either a camera borrowed from the department (years 2008–2010) or their own cameras. Movie Maker was recommended as the basic tool, but they were not limited to it. Thus, they used a variety of tools such as Flash, screen video recording software or PowerPoint.

The student teachers worked on the videos collaboratively according to a set framework. The teacher trainer provided support, if necessary, to fulfil the requirements of constructivist learning and teaching. The proximity of locations they selected place their videos within the framework of situated learning.

3.2 Analysis of the results

3.2.1 Integrative role of video projects analysed from various perspectives related to skills and competences[2]

As the main aim of the study was to identify the integrative role of home-made videos, the elements which are integrated are presented in detail. To answer the first research question that is: "What skills and competences are integrated while students work on home-made videos?" the following aspects of integration were observed:

1 Krzysztof Kieślowski (1941–1996) was a Polish art-house film director and screenwriter. He is known internationally for *Dekalog* (1989), *The Double Life of Veronique* (1991), and the *Three Colors Trilogy* (1993–1994).

2 cf. Gajek 2011.

Integration of language skills and competences

Video projects allow for a holistic approach to learning, teaching and assessment. They integrate skills and knowledge gained in formal and informal education that may go far beyond the requirements of the school curriculum.

Learners develop language skills: reading, taking notes, writing, editing, speaking and listening. They learn how to select information. They also practice mediation between languages and genres, translation from the first language and from other languages, mediation between written and spoken genres while integrating linguistic and communication skills.

Students negotiate the project with the teacher and with their peers informally, in and outside class. They share the outcomes of their work with their peers or with the school community in a structured, formal way reflecting on comments and instructions and responding to them.

Integration of intercultural skills and competences

In international projects students experience intercultural communication as they need to negotiate the content of their project with foreign partners. They learn by doing using communication strategies which are indispensable in intercultural dialogue. They also transfer cultural information that appears so obvious that it is usually taken for granted by the author of the video. The content and production of a video which forms the basis of an international collaborative project involves a lot of negotiations and interpretation of messages. Students face an unknown, unpredictable cultural otherness in communication and have to deal with it to reach the shared goal.

Integration of nonverbal and paralinguistic aspects of communication

Projects raise students' awareness of the gestures, facial expressions, ways of looking and breathing, body posture, body distance, dress code, etc. Students are able to notice the emotions of the participants during intercultural dialogue.

Integration of visual literacy in communication

Visual literacy is the ability to understand and interpret information conveyed in an image (Dondis 1972; Messaris 1998; Seppänen 2006). Visual literacy is essential at both reception and production levels:

- reception level
  At the level of reception, this literacy becomes crucial for developing intercultural skills, for a proper understanding of cultural messages and the media at

local and global levels. Watching amateur educational videos allows students to learn how to interpret video texts from different perspectives.

- production level
  At the level of production, visual literacy as a skill helps to create visual messages to convey meaning for cultural, intercultural, educational, and media purposes. Working on a video project and editing films help students to better understand media manipulation, e.g. what is shown and how people and events are portrayed, the role of the position of the camera and of editing the film.

Integration of cultural awareness in language learning activities

Video projects help to sensitize learners to their own culture as they present it to foreign partners in an attractive way. Students look at their culture from somebody else's point of view. They develop intercultural skills and critical thinking, and raise cultural awareness when they analyze visual messages from foreign partners.

Integration of media competence in learning and teaching activities

In language-oriented video projects, media competence develops as a side effect because digital media are used as tools for linguistic and intercultural educational purposes. Learners develop audiovisual receptive skills, audiovisual productive skills, as well as critical thinking.

Integration of formal and informal learning

While working on the video-project students use skills and knowledge gained in formal education, e.g. linguistic skills, in addition to skills acquired in informal contexts such as the use of video cameras, intercultural experiences, etc.

Integration of digital skills

As computer technology becomes a tool for learning and for meaningful communication, technical skills are acquired spontaneously. For its more competent users the use of technology is motivating, yet for the less computer literate students it may prove slightly demotivating. Some of the students in his study who had doubts about the level of their digital skills at the beginning, reported a change in attitude by the end of their project as they found the technical work, that is filming and editing, easier than expected.

Integration of cognitive competences

Cognitive competence integrates the competences presented above with thinking skills such as the selection of relevant information, the differentiation of facts from opinions, the interpretation of data and the coherent presentation of results in a verbal and visual way.

Integration of teacher professional competences

A majority of the students designed language learning tasks using the video they prepared; that is they designed pre, while- and post- watching activities. This extended their professional skills in preparing materials for learners and with learners. Observing the results of their peers' work and sharing their ideas built confidence in a variety of possible approaches to the educational use of home-made videos.

In some cases, they created the video with their pupils. One student reported that she started a short language course with her neighbours' six-seven-year-old children. Having finished the project, she wanted to continue teaching them English but without having to film them at the end of each sequence of lessons. The children, however, requested that films become part of their learning which made her create videos on a regular basis. For them learning a language was associated with video documenting their results.

Some of the students included tasks into the video either in the form of questions which appeared as subtitles on the video material in the background or in the form of intertitles between a sequence of video scenes. The tasks were integrated with the video content. This can be perceived as an indicator of the future tendency in the development of educational videos. This also confirms the way student teachers understand and put into practice the statement that video is indeed the new textbook (Deubelbeiss 2015).

Student teachers extended their learning and teaching strategies beyond the ones they had experienced as learners. As advanced proficient language users, participants in global culture they had already developed learning strategies which included the receptive use of video for language learning. Home-made videos helped them to transfer these receptive strategies into creative teaching strategies and exploit them in their teaching practice while addressing their learners' needs.

Home-made videos allowed for further curriculum integration as the learners could record their experiments in science lessons, document school trips, visits to museums. This enhances cross-curricular projects. Recording narration in the foreign language or editing the materials helped students memorize the content and meaningful language for international cooperation or for further use as educational material.

3.2.2 Students' engagement and reference to professional development

The answer to the second research question "Are students engaged in the activity? Do they perceive the activity as a valid professional task?" is based on the qualitative analysis of the videos' content, observations, students' commentaries and group interviews which constitute the ethnographic part of the study.

Students' engagement – from the view of teacher observation

Students were engaged, motivated, and put a lot of effort in preparing their videos. They were proud of the efforts. They had a positive attitude towards the use of home-made video in teaching and learning. Some reported and evaluated the use of the video with their pupils. Although the students were not professional video producers, the quality of the videos was acceptable. However, in evaluating the videos emphasis was put on message transmission and their values as teaching materials. All students fulfilled the tasks willingly, however, there were three instances of sarcastic or ironic approach to the viewers or addressees of the video, e.g. in the video targeted at professional language of cooks and waiters.

Students' reflections

Each year during the final conferences students reported that it had been challenging for them to design the content, to record, and edit the video material. They claimed that they developed new professional knowledge and skills which might be useful in favourable teaching environments, in particular for collaborative tasks. Some of them engaged their guests, friends, and family members so the video creation became a shared experience in their learning and teaching environment. In projects done with pupils they observed and appreciated the learning effects of video-based tasks. In the first years of the study they invented on their own short clips for teaching pronunciation so that learners could observe the lip movements while the speaker uttered a vowel or a consonant. They found this beneficial for learning and were surprised that commercial producers had not used the idea for professional teaching videos. The idea was later implemented and developed in BBC Pronunciation tips (BBC n/d).

3.2.3 The role of situated learning in the video-clips

The answer to the third research question: "How is situated learning reflected in the video-clips?" is based on the analysis of the location of the clips. While students worked on video projects they applied different elements of situated learning which shifted from decontextualized use of words or phrases to situations grounded in their own contexts rich in cultural information and visual clues. They filmed their rooms, flats, university rooms, and places in the city. They filmed themselves, their colleagues and friends, pupils (with their parents' permission) but also their pets and favourite toys. In this way learning becomes more personalized. This resembles language learning in a natural environment as they record their activities in the places they live or visit, the people they interact with, and also present their hobbies. This opens up an informal learning environment. Situated language learning applied in the video task may encourage students to use the language outside the classroom. Last, but not least, the use of non-verbal elements contributes to the development of various skills in learners.

3.2.4 Reference to intellectual mobility

The answer to the fourth research question: "How does video-making impact on intellectual mobility, especially creativity, collaboration and self-expression?" is based on the content analysis of the clips and students' reflections on the video production processes during evaluation conferences.

Video projects as any project work trigger learner's creativity. They allow for the development of various skills and competences in a holistic way. Being involved in a project empowers learners. It enhances intellectual mobility. Learners negotiate the content, the methods of learning, the outcomes and the way the results will be presented. Making a video enhances creative and collaborative work. This changes education from reproductive – students performing the task in a way (sometimes even in "the" way) the teacher knows and expects, to productive where they learn what the teacher expects, but embrace their own individual style, pace, and engagement. This work opens doors for outcomes which exceed the teacher's expectations. In the process of making home videos the teacher's role is rooted in constructivist approaches. The teacher sets the task, facilitates the learner's work, and helps and guides students to targets (to some extent) unknown to the teacher. The learners need to use various skills and competences such as their first language, foreign languages, innovation and enterprise, social skills, digital skills, and cultural expression.

4. Conclusions and further research

The growth in accessibility of digital tools for recording and editing home-made videos for language learning is facilitating the better preparation of student teachers to face professional challenges. Well-grounded in educational theories, home-made video activities enhance learning, help to personalize learning materials, make them meaningful and accessible for the learner, and trigger creativity and a holistic integrative approach to learning with language and technology as tools for human communication.

Further research may explore the effectiveness of the use of home-made videos in cross-curricular (CLIL) contexts – in terms of both language and content acquisition. It could also reflect on the tendencies in teaching under principles of brain friendly education.

However, the idea of making choices in the plot introduced in the interactive video narrative, well exemplified by *A la rencontre de Phillipe* (Murray et al. 1989; Furstenberg et al. 1993) is still far from being resumed either in commercial or home-made form. At the teacher training level such an approach, on the one hand, requires a lot of organizational work as all students need to be involved in one coherent project. On the other hand, it reduces the personal aspect of the students' creation and their responsibility for the final effect, which may decrease the motivation to participate in it.

References

Anderman, G., & Díaz Cintas, J. (Eds.). (2008). *Audiovisual Translation: Language Transfer on Screen*. London: Palgrave Macmillan.

Anderson, C. (2010). How web video powers global innovation. TED Global. Available at: http://www.ted.com/talks/chris_anderson_how_web_video_powers_global_innovation?language=en (date of access: 12 March 2017).

Anderson, J. R., Reder, L. M., & Simon, H. A. (1996). Situated learning and education. *Educational Researcher, 25*(4), 5–11.

Baker, M. (Ed.). (1998). *Routledge Encyclopedia of Translation Studies*. London, New York: Routledge.

Baker, M., & Saldanha, G. (Eds.). (2009). *The Routledge Encyclopedia of Translation Studies*. London, New York: Routledge.

Bateman, J. A. (2008). *Multimodality and Genre: A Foundation for the Systematic Analysis of Multimodal Documents*. New York: Palgrave Macmillan.

BBC Pronunciation Tips. Available at: http://www.bbc.co.uk/worldservice/learningenglish/grammar/pron/ (date of access: 12 March 2017).

Belousa, I., Ciascai, L., Chechłacz, K., Costa, M., Costa, V., Gajek, E., Marchis, J., Opre, A., Pereira, E., & Stakle, A. (2009). *ICT as a Tool of Intercultural and Media Education*. Seixal: Centro de Formacao Rui Gracio.

Broady, E. (1997). Old technology, New Technology: Video makes a come back. In A. K. Korsvold & B. Rüschoff (Eds.), *New Technologies in Language Learning and Teaching* (No.532) (pp. 53–68). Strasbourg: Council of Europe Publishing.

Caimi, A. (2008). Subtitling: Language learners' needs vs. audiovisual market needs. In G. Anderman & J. Díaz Cintas (Eds.), *Audiovisual Translation: Language Transfer on Screen* (pp. 240–251). London: Palgrave Macmillan.

Coombe, C., & Kinney, J. (1999). Learner-centered listening assessment. *Forum, 37*(2), 21–23.

Danan, M. (2004). Captioning and subtitling: Undervalued language learning strategies. *META, 49*(1), 67–77.

Deubelbeiss, D. (2015). Using video in the classroom: A teacher's guidebook. Available at: https://ddeubel.edublogs.org/files/2015/05/Video-In-The-Classroom-handbook-25np00n.pdf (date of access: 21 September 2016).

Díaz Cintas, J. (2008). *The Didactics of Audiovisual Translation.* Amsterdam, Philadelphia, PA: John Benjamins.

Díaz Cintas, J., Matamala, A., & Neves, J. (Eds.). (2010). *New Insights into Audiovisual Translation and Media Accessibility.* Amsterdam: Rodopi.

Díaz Cintas, J., & Muñoz Sánchez, P. (2006). Fansubs: Audiovisual translation in an amateur environment. *Journal of Specialised Translation, 6,* 37–52. Available at: http://www.jostrans.org/issue06/issue06_toc.php (date of access: 2 September 2016).

Dollerup, C. (1974). On subtitles in television programmes. *Babel International Journal of Translation, 20,* 197–202.

Dondis, D. (1972). *A Primer of Visual Literacy.* Cambridge, MA: MIT Press.

Duszak, A., & Kowalski, G. (Eds.). (2015). *Academic (Inter)genres: Between Texts, Contexts and Identities.* Frankfurt am Main: Peter Lang.

Duszak, A., Jopek-Bosiacka, A., & Kowalski, G. (Eds.). (2015). *Tekst naukowy i jego przekład.* Kraków: Universitas.

d'Ydewalle, G., & Pavakanun, U. (1997). Could enjoying a movie lead to language acquisition? In P. Winterhoff-Spurk & T. H. A. van der Voort (Eds.), *New Horizons in Media Psychology* (pp. 145–155). Opladen: Westdeutscher Verlag.

Efe, H., Demiröz, H., & Akdemir, A. S. (2011). A situated learning practice for language teaching classes: Teaching spoken English with authentic sketches. *Sino - US English Review, 8*(9), 549–555.

Furstenberg, G., Murray, J. H., Malone, S., & Farman-Farmaian, A. (1993). *A la rencontre de Philippe.* New Haven, CT: Yale University Press.

Gajek, E. (2008). Edukacyjne znaczenie napisów w tekście audiowizualnym. *Przekładaniec, 1*(20), 106–114.

Gajek, E. (2011). Learner-oriented teaching and assessment through digital video projects. In H. Komorowska (Ed.), *Issues in Promoting Multilingualism* (pp. 287–306). Warszawa: Fundacja Rozwoju Systemu Edukacji.

Gajek, E. (2015). Aktywizowanie ucznia poprzez dodawanie napisów i głosu do materiałów audiowizualnych w nauczaniu języka polskiego jako obcego. In E. Kubicka & A. Walkiewicz (Eds.), *Nowe perspektywy w nauczaniu języka polskiego jako obcego III* (pp. 257–269). Toruń: Wydawnictwo Naukowe UMK.

Gajek, E., & Szarkowska, A. (2012). Audiodeskrypcja i napisy jako techniki uczenia się języka - projekt ClipFlair. *Języki Obce w Szkole, 2*, 106–110.

Gajek, E., & Szarkowska, A. (2015a). Audiovisual scientific text for self-directed Content and Language Integrated Learning (CLIL). In A. Duszak & G. Kowalski (Eds.), *Academic (Inter)genres: Between Texts, Contexts and Identities* (pp. 216–229). Frankfurt am Main: Peter Lang.

Gajek, E., & Szarkowska, A. (2015b). Przekład audiowizualny w edukacji językowej – na przykładzie materiałów naukowych w projekcie ClipFlair. In A. Duszak, A. Jopek-Bosiacka, & G. Kowalski (Eds.), *Tekst naukowy i jego przekład* (pp. 243–268). Kraków: Universitas.

Gottlieb, H. (1998). Subtitling. In M. Baker (Ed.), *Routledge Encyclopedia of Translation Studies* (pp. 244–248). London, New York: Routledge.

Hanks, W. F. (1991). Foreword. In J. Lave & E. Wenger (Eds.), *Situated Learning. Legitimate Peripheral Participation* (pp. 13–24). Cambridge: Cambridge University Press.

Hill, B. (1999). *Video in Language Learning.* London: CILT.

Incalcaterra McLoughlin, L., Biscio, M., & Ni Mhainnín, M. Á. (Eds.). (2011). *Audiovisual Translation Subtitles and Subtitling Theory and Practice.* Bern: Peter Lang.

Incalcaterra McLoughlin, L., & Lertola, J. (2015). Captioning and revoicing of clips in foreign language learning using clipflair for teaching Italian in online learning environments. In C. Ramsey-Portolano (Ed.), *The Future of Italian Teaching: Media New Technologies and Multi-Disciplinary Perspectives* (pp. 55–69). Newcastle upon Tyne: Cambridge Scholars Publishing.

Kalantzis, M., & Cope, B. (Eds.). (2000). *Multiliteracies: Literacy Learning and the Design of Social Futures.* London: Routledge.

Komorowska, H. (Ed.). (2011). *Issues in Promoting Multilingualism.* Warszawa: Fundacja Rozwoju Systemu Edukacji.

Korsvold, A. K., & Rüschoff, B. (1997). *New Technologies in Language Learning and Teaching* (No.532). Strasbourg: Council of Europe Publishing.

Kress, G., & van Leeuwen, T. (1996). *Second Edition 2006. Reading Images: The Grammar of Visual Literacy.* London, New York: Routledge.

Kubicka, E., & Walkiewicz, A. (Eds.). (2015). *Nowe perspektywy w nauczaniu języka polskiego jako obcego III.* Toruń: Wydawnictwo Naukowe UMK.

Lave, J., & Wenger, E. (1991). *Situated Learning: Legitimate Peripheral Participation*, Cambridge: Cambridge University Press.

Lonergan, J. (1984). *Video in Teaching*. Cambridge: Cambridge University Press.

MacWilliam, I. (1990). Video and language comprehension. In R. Rossner & R. Bolitho (Eds.), *Current Change in English Language Teaching* (pp. 148–156). Oxford: Oxford University Press.

McGovern, J. (Ed.). (1983). *Video Application in English Teaching*. Exeter: Pergamon Press.

Messaris, P. (1998). Visual aspects of media literacy. *Journal of Communication, 48*(1), 70–89.

Murray, J., Morgenstern, D., & Furstenberg G. (1989). The athena language-learning project: Design issues for the next generation of computer-based language-learning tools. In Wm. F. Smith (Ed.), *Modern Technology in Foreign Language Education* (pp. 97–118). Lincolnwood, IL: National Textbook Company.

Mussen, P. (Ed.). (1970). *Handbook of Child Psychology*. New York: Wiley.

Papert, S. (1980). *Mindstorms: Children, Computers and Powerful Ideas*. New York: Basic Books.

Papert, S., & Harel, I. (1991). *Constructionism*. Norwood, NJ: Ablex.

Pérez-González, L. (2009). Audiovisual translation. In M. Baker & G. Saldanha (Eds.), *The Routledge Encyclopedia of Translation Studies* (pp. 13–20). London, New York: Routledge.

Piaget, J. (1970). Piaget's theory. In P. Mussen (Ed.), *Handbook of Child Psychology* (pp. 703–732). New York: Wiley.

Piaget, J., & Inhelder, B. (1966). *The Psychology of the Child*, transl. H. Weaver. New York: Basic Books.

Ramsey-Portolano, C. (2015). (Ed.). *The Future of Italian Teaching: Media New Technologies and Multi-Disciplinary Perspectives*. Newcastle upon Tyne: Cambridge Scholars Publishing.

Rossner, R., & Bolitho, R. (Eds.). (1990). *Current change in English Language Teaching*. Oxford: Oxford University Press.

Seppänen, J. (2006). *The Power of the Gaze: An Introduction to Visual Literacy*. New York: Peter Lang.

Sherman, J. (2003). *Using Authentic in the Language Classroom*. Cambridge: Cambridge University Press.

Smith Wm. F. (Ed.). (1989). *Modern Technology in Foreign Language Education*. Lincolnwood, IL: National Textbook Company.

Sokoli, S., Zabalbescoa, P., & Fountana, M. (2011). Subtitling activities for foreign language learning: What learners and teachers think. In L. Incalcaterra

McLoughlin, M. Biscio, & M. Á. Ní Mhainnín (Eds.), *Audiovisual Translation Subtitles and Subtitling Theory and Practice* (pp. 219–242). Bern: Peter Lang.

Stempleski, S., & Tomalin, B. (1990). *Video in Action*. New York: Prentice-Hall International.

Stempleski, S., & Tomalin, B. (2001). *Film (Resource books for teachers)*. Oxford: Oxford University Press.

Talaván, N. (2010). Subtitling as a task and subtitles as support: Pedagogical applications. In J. Díaz Cintas, A. Matamala, & J. Neves (Eds.), *New Insights into Audiovisual Translation and Media Accessibility* (pp. 285–299). Amsterdam: Rodopi.

Vygotsky, L. (1981). The genesis of higher mental functions. In J. V. Wertsch (Ed.), *The Concept of Activity in Soviet Psychology* (pp. 144–188). Armonk, NY: M.E. Sharpe.

Wertsch, J. V. (Ed.). (1981). *The Concept of Activity in Soviet Psychology*. Armonk, NY: M.E. Sharpe.

Willis, D. (1983). The potential and limitation of video. In J. McGovern (Ed.), *Video Application in English Teaching* (pp. 17–27). Exeter: Pergamon Press.

Willis, J. (1983). The role of the visual element in spoken discourse: Implications for the exploitation of video in the EFL classroom. In J. McGovern (Ed.), *Video Application in English Teaching* (pp. 29–42). Exeter: Pergamon Press.

Willis, J., & Cifuentes, L. (2005). Training teachers to integrate technology into the classroom curriculum: Online versus face-to-face course delivery (comparative analysis of teacher technology training courses). *Journal of Technology and Teacher Education, 3*(1), 43–54.

Wilson, A. (1993). *The Promise of Situated Cognition*. San Francisco, CA: Jossey-Bass.

Winterhoff-Spurk, P., & van der Voort, T. H. A. (Eds.). (1997). *New Horizons in Media Psychology*. Opladen: Westdeutcher Verlag.

Zabalbeascoa, P., Sokoli, S., & Torres, O. (Eds.). (2012). *CLIPFLAIR foreign language learning through interactive revoicing and captioning of clips. lifelong learning programme – key activity 2. language multilateral project. d2.1 conceptual framework and pedagogical methodology.* Available at: http://clipflair.net/wp-content/uploads/2014/06/D2.1ConceptualFramework.pdf (date of access: 21 September 2016).

Jarosław Krajka
Maria Curie-Skłodowska University, Lublin, Poland

Digital materials authoring and English for Specific Purposes – on characteristics of technology adoption in teacher training

Abstract: Much research has been done to date on introducing information and communication technologies (ICT) into the foreign language teacher's skillset. Various technology integration models have been proposed as well to make sure that technology adoption is as high as possible and that graduates of teacher training programmes can actually teach foreign languages with technology.

However, the education of Languages for Specific Purposes (LSP) teachers receives much less attention, even though English for Specific Purposes (ESP) teacher training is becoming a more and more prominent area of modern philological study programs, given an increasing role of in-house language training. Designing electronic materials, both those more traditional and those oriented at mobile-assisted language learning (MALL; e.g., Memrise, Kahoot, Quizlet), as well as integrating these in a single study programme housed in transferable Moodle, are necessary skills for an ESP teacher of today.

The purpose of this chapter is to provide the outline of an ESP teacher training module, aiming at combining LSP education, multimedia authoring development and field work in an attempt to author Moodle-based e-learning courses for different specialisations. The main aims of the study are to diagnose the level of technology adoption of novice LSP teachers and to verify the applicability of the instructional design of the teacher training process. The study shows how, on the one hand, learning mobility is tapped into by exploiting selected MALL applications, on the other hand, transversal competences allow future teachers' greater job mobility.

Keywords: ESP, authoring, teacher training, Moodle

1. Introduction

Training teachers of Languages for Specific Purposes (LSP) has become a highly significant issue in the contemporary world, given much interest in international communication in the corporate sector on the one hand and the revival of job-oriented education at the secondary and tertiary level on the other. Few university curricula include courses in teaching English for Specific Purposes (ESP) to adults. At the same time, quite a lot of interest in computer-assisted language learning (CALL) creates openings for merging technology-based instruction with ESP instruction.

The purpose of the present chapter is to report upon action research based in a graduate teacher development programme, where a selected course was devoted to merging ESP instruction with computer-based teaching. The participants were guided through the process of diagnosing learner needs, designing curricula, authoring digital materials and evaluating online courses. The whole process was framed in a selected specialist area (henceforth referred to as "specialisation") in authentic real-life contexts.

2. Review of literature

2.1 Technology in ESP education

The crux of research into technology implementation in Languages for Specific Purposes has been with Data-Driven Learning (DDL) and corpus-based materials (e.g., Chang & Kuo 2011; Tribble & Wingate 2013) since this area of applied linguistics assists register and genre analysis of ESP and informs LSP course design and materials development. For instance, specialized corpora were used as a source of information on genres and as a tool for LSP materials development (Hüttner et al. 2009) and discourse analysis proved to be an important starting point for materials writing by student teachers (Sullivan & Girginer 2002). This indicates how either teacher- or student-made corpus studies might lead to greater awareness of the characteristics of specialized language in the area of medical English, business English or English for science and technology.

At the same time, since ESP methodology places great emphasis on needs analysis, coursebook evaluation and materials writing, enhancing the process with selected corpus linguistics techniques to facilitate design of teaching aids and classroom resources is of paramount importance. Thus, corpus self-compilation was reported as highly beneficial in increasing learner language awareness (Charles 2014; Lee & Swales 2006). Positive learner evaluations called for the use of multimedia due to its perceived learning effects, as a means of self-study, in general instruction (e.g., Brett 2000) as well as in online ESP learning (Fan & Xunfeng 2002).

2.2 E-learning authoring in teacher training – from e-tools use to e-courses design

As expressed by Chapelle and Hegelheimer (2004), the indispensable skills of technology use and teaching with technology need to be grasped by teachers in order to provide language instruction effectively in the new millennium. The modalities of technology use for teacher instruction were enumerated by Otero et al. (2005) as follows:

- Technology used as a cognitive tool helps students understand concepts and solve problems.
- Technology used as a communication tool fosters discourse and collaboration among educators, students, parents, and the community.
- Technology used as a management tool increases efficiency for teachers and students.
- Technology used as an evaluation tool helps teachers reflect on instruction and provides feedback on student learning.
- Technology used as a motivational tool encourages and engages students in learning (Otero et al. 2005).

Given the above, involving student teachers in creating materials for teaching ESP learners seems to satisfy most of the abovelisted purposes. As is pointed out by Kramsch et al. (2000), engaging students in the process of creating learning materials is beneficial for motivation and attitude toward learning process and subject matter. The same applies to student teachers, who are, on the one hand, learners of English at the advanced level, and, on the other, practising teachers of languages for specific purposes. Nikolova (2002) emphasises the fact that being involved in the selection of content for the revision activities teaches student teachers (STs) the skills of reflecting and prioritising, which leads to improvement in the learning process on the metacognitive level.

Though expressed more than a decade ago, the point made by Amiri (2000) who advocates that teachers at the M.A. level should be trained not merely as consumers but as both consumers and producers of computer-based materials is even more relevant nowadays, given much easier authoring opportunities opened by graphic interfaces of Moodle and other Learning Management Systems. According to Amiri (2000), knowledge of programming is important to get language teachers involved in the design and development of computer-based materials and should be included as a part of the IT training for language teachers. Thus, more specialised M.A. courses for language teaching should concentrate on various aspects of IT, including end-user programming, learning or instructional design (Amiri 2000).

In order to create an online ESP course which would bring desired effects into the students' language progress, the teacher needs to display particular skills. Hampel and Stickler (2005) identify seven key competencies of online tutors which are presented in the pyramid. Technology authoring and authorship in the development of teacher skills are indicated by Hampel and Stickler (2005) as the two highest levels of the teacher skills pyramid:

1. Level 1 – Basic ICT competence
2. Level 2 – Specific technical competence for the software
3. Level 3 – Dealing with constraints and possibilities of the medium
4. Level 4 – Online socialization
5. Level 5 – Facilitating communicative competence
6. Level 6 – Creativity and choice
7. Level 7 – Own style

The three levels at the bottom of the pyramid encompass skills referring to basic competencies in dealing with hardware and software, without which the design of an e-learning tool is barely possible. "Online socialization" means the ability to build social communities necessary to overcome the feeling of isolation which often accompanies e-learning (Hampel & Stickler 2005). The fifth level is closely related to the previous one, as creating a successful virtual environment is dependent on the sense of community which would then facilitate distance communication and eliminate communication barriers (Hampel & Stickler 2005). Creativity and choice mean that the online tutor is supposed to choose high-quality materials which would suit the needs of his/her students out of a variety of available sources (Hampel & Stickler 2005). The last level concerns the development of the tutor's own teaching style in the online environment (Hampel & Stickler 2005). As taking novice LSP instructors through those levels to the top of the pyramid is a challenge for teacher development programmes worldwide, it is the problem that is addressed in the study below.

Taking into account great interest in the field of e-learning and a plethora of research into designing and evaluating e-learning environments for language instruction (e.g., Aldrich 2004; Bates 2005; Gajek 2004; Nichols 2003; Murphy & Rodríguez-Manzanares 2009; O'Lawrence 2007; Plebańska 2011), it is no wonder that research into multimedia authoring in teacher training is flourishing (see, for instance, Maciaszczyk 2015). At the same time, the popularity of Moodle as an e-learning environment for language instruction (as exemplified, for example, by Brandl 2005; Chinnery 2008; Paulsen 2003; Rice 2004; Zsolt & Bessenyei 2008) calls for implementing Moodle authoring in LSP teacher development courses.

3. Study

3.1 The aim of the research

The researcher was interested, most of all, in incorporating selected technology-based instructional habits and procedures into the holistic process of ESP curriculum development. In this approach, technology is subordinated to the overall teaching aims, as technology itself in one form or another is not the driving force for the innovation, but rather appropriate computer-based procedures are selected to fit the research purpose.

Most importantly, it was interesting to see how the areas of needs analysis, curriculum design, multimedia authoring and peer evaluation are interrelated and can be integrated in the teacher training process. At the same time, since there is fairly little research on training teachers for specific purposes, the study was also supposed to investigate possible pathways for LSP teacher development.

In particular, it was interesting to see what attitudes students have towards the integration of ESP curriculum design and multimedia authoring and what technology choices they make (Moodle-based and external tools, familiar or newly-introduced ones). Finally, the process of technology adoption in the case of Moodle authoring is an interesting case to examine.

3.2 Method

In order to investigate the opportunities of developing teaching skills in the area of LSP within the computer-based environment, a small-scale case study was conducted in a post-graduate class in a medium-sized state university in Poland. Throughout the period of one semester, a group of graduate students of applied linguistics (double-language programme) were guided through the process of ESP digital materials development as follows:

1. Choosing a specialisation, finding informants.
2. Conducting a needs analysis, generalising results, presenting findings to the class.
3. Drawing up a needs-based syllabus.
4. Finding coursebooks, evaluating materials in relation to diagnosed needs.
5. Basic training in Moodle authoring:
   - adding resources,
   - creating collaborative activities and quizzes,
   - managing the course, adding students, giving feedback.
6. Advanced training in external CALL applications:
   - quizzing tools: Kahoot, Memrise, LearningApps, Socrative, ESLvideo, Quizlet, BrainPOP, Voki,
   - audio authoring, video authoring, captioning tools.
7. Course authoring, peer evaluation, in-class presentations.

As indicated in the curriculum topics above, the experimental teacher development course was supposed to join three areas of expertise, generally kept separate in teacher development programmes, namely languages for specific purposes, materials evaluation and development, and digital e-learning authoring. Given that students had already had basic training in the second and third areas (had completed their regular teaching specialisation module in the B.A. programme and had completed a few computer-based classes with a differing focus), the researcher rightly assumed that the integration of the three areas could be successfully accomplished over the period of one semester (30 hours).

The study used post-experience survey, mid-experience learning diaries, ongoing informal interviews and final product analysis as data collection instruments. An important part of the process was also test-driving the e-courses by other student groups so that peer feedback could actually be given from the perspective of a target language user.

3.3 Participants

The participants in the study were a group of graduate students in applied linguistics (double-language programme: English+German, English+French and English+Russian) from a medium-sized university in the east of Poland. The participants were all aged between 22 and 25, mostly female (14 females and 1 male), well-skilled in computers, and acquainted with the elements of CALL thanks to previous classes in the teaching module. They were all highly motivated to participate in the project due to the fact that the teaching specialization was their second (additional) study programme and, as such, it was the one to pay for. Moreover, the students were aware of the chance to gain teaching qualifications in two languages upon the completion of the M.A. study cycle, which is an opportunity difficult to arrange out of university.

The students were divided into 2–3 person-groups and were free to choose their own specialisation to research. The eventual choices were as follows:

1. English for nurses
2. English for sailors
3. Russian for plant nursery farmers
4. English for job-hunting purposes
5. English for IT specialists
6. English for railway workers
7. English for receptionists

Most usually, the specialisations were selected based on students' personal or family connections, since an important part of the process was to conduct a needs analysis with selected informants, investigating wants, needs and necessities, as well as gaining access to relevant subject-domain documents to be able to design the e-learning course.

3.4 Data presentation and discussion

3.4.1 Teaching competence as digital materials authors and needs analysts

As was indicated by the post-experience interviews, students generally perceived they had improved their digital competence, mainly in terms of finding and evaluating materials and digitising them as Moodle activities. They felt they would still need much more practice with Moodle authoring, though they were less apprehensive about Moodle as the teaching environment than at the beginning.

At the same time, the participants appreciated being acquainted with different online tools. Quite surprisingly, it was not only relatively new tools such as Kahoot, LearningApps, Memrise or Socrative that sparked interest among students to create ESP materials, but also well-established packages such as HotPotatoes or Moodle in-built quizzes proved to be equally or even more popular. Some students reported trying different tools, including cutting-edge ones, but perceived these as too complicated and reverted back to "safe" technologies such as HotPotatoes or LearningApps. Therefore, as regards the use of online tools, the courses created by students had some common points but also differed a lot. All had the "knowledge base" in the form of documents, text-, audio-, video-based resources, mostly as links to external materials available on the Internet, created with the use of Moodle resource uploading (books, pages, files, links). As for the practice phase, different students utilised diverse tools – many went for HotPotatoes, since they had become familiar with the package during the IT class in the B.A. programme; others experimented with LearningApps and Memrise. In general, external tools were used for multimedia-enhanced practice within the areas of vocabulary and grammar, while Moodle was used for creation of a knowledge base and management of the learning process.

Some participants, clearly regarding themselves as "technopeasants", claimed they were bad at IT but reported they tried hard and managed to overcome the challenge. Eventually, all appreciated the idea of putting together in-built and external resources within Moodle as a useful tool for organising materials and resources.

Unsurprisingly, participants evaluated their competence as needs analysts relatively high. They claimed that preparing tools, finding informants and conducting needs assessment did not cause major problems. One of the reasons behind that was, however, that the needs analyses executed by the students were of relatively narrow scope, usually limited to 2–3 informants at most, and rarely going beyond the most obvious diagnosis of learners' expectations (Hutchinson & Waters' 1987 "wants"). A narrow scope of needs analysis might be justified in the case of a teacher development course; however, student teachers need to become aware of the necessity of executing a multi-faceted evaluation for more valid results.

A greater challenge proved to be interpreting needs analysis results and designing a tailored curriculum. As indicated in the following comments, one of the participants felt that "I think I can conduct needs analysis, but when it comes to syllabus construction I feel I would do it better with someone else rather than individually". At the same time, another trainee "(…) found it difficult to adjust their needs to the form of the course". Yet another student claimed that he/she "received practical information on how to analyse learners' needs and pieces of advice on how to use them in order to prepare a suitable course". However, in total there was a general agreement that much more practice would be needed to familiarise oneself with the selected specialisation, formulate curricular objectives and create relevant materials.

3.4.2 Course effect on personal teaching repertoire

The participants generally indicated that the "Digital materials authoring in ESP teacher development" course had a significant effect on their teaching competence, both in the area of Moodle authoring and teaching LSP to adults. They became more aware of the necessity of individualising instruction to fit diagnosed learners' needs, saw how multi-faceted English language teaching could be, realised significant differences between teaching children/adolescents and adults as well as between teaching general English and English for Specific Purposes. These findings are exemplified in some of the interview quotations below:

- (…) I realised that English language methodology does not confine itself to simple school classes.
- (…) I learned that while teaching English we have to take into consideration needs of our learner(s) and we can either teach general English or English for specific purposes.
- (…) I am more aware of how complex subject the English language methodology is and that is not all about school and teaching children.
- (…) I found out how important the needs analysis is to create a good course. I learnt how to conduct such an analysis and construct a course.

3.4.3 Peer evaluation of digital authored materials

An important part of the study evaluation procedure was assessment of student-made ESP courses within the Moodle environment. The task was supposed to take 4 weeks, groups of 2–3 students were working on a complete course related to a selected specialisation that would respond to the needs of informants as diagnosed at the beginning of the student project. It was assumed that the aspect of digital authoring would be most demanding for the participants; hence, extended support was provided in the form of email assistance, special duty hours, provision of model courses for inspection and an explanation of the evaluation criteria checklist.

The deadline for course completion was established one week before the final face-to-face meeting so that the other participants could have the opportunity to test drive the materials and be ready with suggestions for improvement. Even though the schedule was announced at the beginning of the semester, not all groups managed to complete the courses in time due to some conflict with study duties and other commitments. For many students, course authoring proved to be more time-consuming than they expected, especially since they found it difficult to manage time on their own without strict supervision of the instructor.

As was indicated by self-assessment and peer review, most areas for improvement concerned the imperfect structure of online courses – navigation, internal structure of topics, and consistency across and within topics were the issues most often pinpointed for change. Students also noticed sometimes chaotic progression, weak openings and closings, or inadequate guidance for students as regards task instructions and progression through the materials. An important area where more effort is needed proved to be providing learner support – for instance, missing objectives for particular topics could be supplied or a more prominent help forum/FAQ section could be created. Also, varying quality of materials, differing difficulty level within the same topic or certain methodological faults such as lack of listening task before the recording were observed.

In general, student teachers felt they were not fully competent at evaluating their peers' courses – not because of lack of technical competence, but due to insufficient specialisation familiarity. In the future, practising evaluation of technical and methodological aspects of online language instruction needs to be focused on more extensively, making student teachers aware of their limitations within narrowly-defined specialisations at the same time.

4. Discussion and final conclusions

To conclude, it can be stated that the findings from the present study confirmed differing levels of innovation adoption (both technological and curricular) existing in previous literature (e.g., Pennington 2004; Rogers 2003). Counter to popular belief and widespread expectations of teacher trainers, only a certain proportion of trainees adopt a newly introduced technology, procedure or method, and not necessarily straight away. Hence, great care needs to be taken in order to allow student teachers to find their own way through the newly introduced innovation, rather than expect them to implement it straight away and in the way transmitted by the trainer. This is especially true with student teachers, who should have already developed autonomous attitudes; imposing instructional solutions upon them could have an opposite result.

The use of Moodle as a hub for various interactive activities on the one hand and the authoring environment on the other was made possible thanks to students' familiarity with the system as learners throughout all the previous years at university. Otherwise, most probably, the ESP trainer would have to reflect on which specific authoring tools to be focused on in the teacher development process. Moodle itself is sophisticated enough to demand quite a lot of training in its different aspects, versatile to encompass different kinds of courses, robust in terms of student and resources management. However, it is not as motivating and engaging as other e-Learning 2.0 tools, such as Kahoot, LearningApps or Memrise.

For the digitally-enhanced ESP courses in the future, the selection and use of online tools would very much depend on the pedagogical purposes of the instructor. If the course is to be taken exclusively online, without the face-to-face component, a complete learning environment would have to be created inside Moodle. On the other hand, if the online component is to supplement face-to-face instruction, one can envisage the use of specific tools for particular teaching purposes – e.g., Memrise for regular vocabulary practice, LearningApps for pronunciation and vocabulary work, Kahoot for in-class warm-up and round-up, as independent study modules with no need for a Learning Management System to bind all that together.

Contrary to what student teachers expected, it was not technical authoring but ESP curriculum design that caused them the most problems. Many trainees focused too much on technical mastery, thinking that acquiring and displaying greater technical skill would guarantee success of technology-enhanced teaching. The somewhat surprising finding of the study was that it was the ESP curriculum design that proved to be the most troublesome area, mostly due to trainees' little experience with selected specialisations.

The dual focus of the class (ESP materials design and e-learning authoring) together with teamwork enabled the trainer to encompass different adopter categories. Needs analysis and materials authoring skills were perceived by student teachers as increasing their employability prospects on the job market.

However, even though student teachers were skilled and trained at various cutting-edge technologies (as well as mobile ones), they tended to rely on "safe-and-familiar" technologies, even though they may be less innovative, in view of upcoming assessment.

To conclude, digital materials authoring and ESP course development are two interesting options for language teacher training at the post-graduate level, once basic ICT competence has been built and general language teaching methodology skills have been developed. Due to the application of the framework of training-through-fieldwork, necessary links between theory and practice, university and the job market, education and employment, are created for the benefit of student teachers' future employability. Obviously, further studies with larger samples are needed to see the possible direction of computer-based authoring in training teachers of languages for specific purposes.

Funding

Maria Curie-Skłodowska University's research funds.

References

Aldrich, C. (2004). *Simulations and the Future of Learning: An Innovative (and Perhaps Revolutionary) Approach to E-learning.* San Francisco, CA: Pfeiffer.

Amiri, F. (2000). IT-literacy for language teachers: Should it include computer programming? *System, 28*(1), 77–84.

Bates, T. (2005). *Technology, E-learning and Distance Education.* London: Routledge.

Brandl, K. (2005). Are you ready to "Moodle"? *Language Learning and Technology, 9*(2), 16–23.

Brett, P. (2000). Integrating multimedia into the Business English curriculum: A case study. *English for Specific Purposes, 19,* 269–290.

Chang, C. F., & Kuo, C. H. (2011). A corpus-based approach to online materials development for writing research articles. *English for Specific Purposes, 30,* 222–234.

Chapelle, C., & Hegelheimer, V. (2004). The English language teacher in the 21st century. In S. Fotos & C. Browne (Eds.), *New Perspectives in CALL for Second Language Classrooms* (pp. 299–316). Mahwah, NJ: Lawrence Erlbaum.

Charles, M. (2014). Getting the corpus habit: EAP students' long-term use of personal corpora. *English for Specific Purposes, 35,* 30–40.

Chinnery, G. M. (2008). Biting the hand that feeds me: The case for e-language learning and teaching. *CALICO Journal, 25*(3), 471–481.

Fan, M., & Xunfeng, X. (2002). An evaluation of an online bilingual corpus for the self-learning of legal English. *System, 30,* 47–63.

Fotos, S., & Browne, C. (Eds.). (2004). *New Perspectives in CALL for Second Language Classrooms.* Mahwah, NJ: Lawrence Erlbaum.

Gajek, E. (2004). Nauczanie języków online. *E-mentor, 2*(4). Available at: http://www.e-mentor.edu.pl/artykul/index/numer/4/id/45 (date of access: 15 November 2016).

Hampel, R., & Stickler, U. (2005). New skills for new classrooms: Training tutors to teach languages online. *Computer-Assisted Language Learning Journal, 18*(4), 311–326.

Hutchinson, T., & Waters, A. (1987). *English for Specific Purposes: A Learning-Centred Approach.* Cambridge: Cambridge University Press.

Hüttner, J., Smit, U., & Mehlmauer-Larcher, B. (2009). ESP teacher education at the interface of theory and practice: Introducing a model of mediated corpus-based genre analysis. *System, 37,* 99–109.

Kramsch, C., A'Ness, F., & Lam, W. S. E. (2000). Authenticity and authorship in the computer-mediated acquisition of L2 literacy. *Language Learning and Technology, 4*(2), 78–104.

Lee, D., & Swales, J. (2006). A corpus-based EAP course for NNS doctoral students: Moving from available specialized corpora to self-compiled corpora. *English for Specific Purposes, 25,* 56–75.

Maciaszczyk, S. (2015). *New technologies in tertiary language education.* (Unpublished doctoral dissertation). University of Warsaw, Warsaw.

Murphy, E., & Rodríguez-Manzanares, M. A. (2009). Teachers' perspectives on motivation in high school distance education. *Journal of Distance Education, 23*(3), 1–24.

Nichols, M. (2003). A theory for eLearning. *Educational Technology and Society, 23*(3), 305–336.

Nikolova, O. R. (2002). Effects of students' participation in authoring of multimedia materials on student acquisition of vocabulary. *Language Learning & Technology, 6*(1), 100–122.

O'Lawrence, H. (2007). An overview of the influences of distance learning on adult learners. *Journal of Education and Human Development, 1*(1). Available at: http://www.scientificjournals.org/journals2007/articles/1041.htm (date of access: 15 November 2016).

Otero, V., Peressini, D., Meymaris, K. A., Ford, P., Gavin, T., Harlow, D., Reidel, M., Waite, B., & Mears, C. (2005). Integrating technology into teacher education: A critical framework for implementing reform. *Journal of Teacher Education, 56*(1), 8–23.

Paulsen, M. F. (2003). Experiences with Learning Management Systems in 113 European institutions. *Educational Technology and Society, 6*(4), 134–148.

Pennington, M. C. (2004). Cycles of innovation in the adoption of Information Technology: A view for language teaching. *Computer Assisted Language Learning, 17*(1), 7–33.

Plebańska, M. (2011). *E-learning: Tajniki edukacji na odległość.* Warszawa: C. H. Beck.

Rice, W. (2004). *Moodle E-learning Course Development.* Birmingham: Packt Publishing.

Rogers, E. (2003). *Diffusion of Innovation* (5th ed). New York: Free Press.

Sullivan, P., & Girginer, H. (2002). The use of discourse analysis to enhance ESP teacher knowledge: An example using aviation English. *English for Specific Purposes, 21,* 397–404.

Tribble, C., & Wingate, U. (2013). From text to corpus – A genre-based approach to academic literacy instruction. *System, 41,* 307–321.

Zsolt, T., & Bessenyei, I. (2008). *Moodle and Social Constructivism.* Sopron: Network for Teaching Information Society.

Małgorzata Kodura
Pedagogical University of Cracow, Cracow, Poland

E-learning in translator education

Abstract: The aim of the chapter is to explore whether remote learning courses, without the physical presence of the instructor in the classroom, can replace regular translator training classes at the university level. The starting point for the discussion is the concept of translation competence and its development through students' participation in the classroom or through independent learning.

Theoretical reflections and observations are supported by results of a survey conducted among students of the Pedagogical University of Cracow on their expectations concerning practical translation classes and their form. The survey revealed that students highly value the e-learning mode for receiving and submitting their translation assignments. On the other hand, students expect and appreciate the active presence of a teacher to provide practical advice as regards the choice of the appropriate translation strategy. Although e-learning activities provide a very useful and practical dimension in a translator education curriculum, they should be supplemented by activities conducted in the classroom setting, both as regards instruction and feedback.

Keywords: translator education, e-learning, blended learning

1. Introduction

The translator in modern times is expected to operate in digital space, via the teleworking and telecollaboration channels, which are imposed by the requirements of the contemporary translation and localisation market. This call for mobility, which means a possibility to work from any place in the world, is welcomed both by clients and by the language service providers. It is also reflected in the structure of academic courses intended for translator trainers, such as specialization modules, where one third of the total hours allocated for the entire course are to be conducted via e-learning, understood as off-campus teaching and learning. This provides a perfect opportunity to introduce educational technology and to develop collaborative skills in students, but requires a revision of approaches to translation competence development. When designing the e-learning part of the course, the teacher should take into consideration not only the content to be taught, but also the expectations and abilities of the students, having in mind the entire spectrum of translator's skills to be acquired. This study attempts to explore the attitude towards online translation courses demonstrated by translator trainees, with a particular focus on the development of translation skills outside the classroom setting.

2. Review of literature

Translator training has been very concisely defined as "creation of skills needed in the labour market of translators" (Pym 2001: 1). What should be especially emphasized at this point is the use of the term "training" instead of "teaching", with the focus on the student as the translator-to-be, placing the learner as the focal point (Samson 2005: 109). Translator trainers are also referred to as "facilitators" (Kelly 2008: 99), which pertinently describes their role in helping students acquire translation competence, i.e. "[t]he knowledge and skills the translator must possess in order to carry out the translation" (Bell 1991: 43).

As regards a precise definition of translation competence to be acquired by future translators, various models have been suggested by researchers, of which three have gained particular recognition, i.e. the PACTE model (PACTE Group 2003), described in details below, the model proposed by Kiraly (2006) and the EMT model (EMT Expert Group 2009). In Kiraly's (2006) componential model, the so-called translator super-competence comprises three groups of sub-competences: social competences, which includes such aspects as etiquette, negotiation and income; personal competences, composed of autonomy, preparedness for lifelong learning, quality control and professional responsibility; and translation competence per se, incorporating such features as linguistic competence, cultural competence, text typology, norms and conventions, terminology, world knowledge, strategies, technology and research. The model proposed by the EMT (European Master's in Translation) Expert Group (2009), working on the European Master Program in Translation, was developed with the aim of ensuring convergence in translator training in European higher education institutions and to optimise the curriculum. The model includes six categories: language competence, intercultural competence, info mining competence, technological competence, thematic competence and translation service provision competence.

The study described in this chapter is based on the model developed by the PACTE research group (2003). It consists of five sub-competences: bilingual, extra-linguistic, knowledge about translation, instrumental, and finally strategic sub-competence, being the fundamental one. Two of the sub-competencies identified above refer directly to declarative knowledge, i.e. extra-linguistic sub-competence, which is knowledge about the world, including bicultural encyclopaedic and subject specific knowledge, and the knowledge about translation sub-competence, which covers theoretical aspects of translation, such as strategies and techniques or types of problems related to the translator's work. The remaining three involve predominantly procedural knowledge: bilingual sub-competence, which is understood as knowledge required to communicate in two languages, including the interference control feature; instrumental sub-competence, standing for the ability to use various types of sources and technologies applied to translation; and strategic sub-competence, which ensures efficiency of the translation and problem-solving process. These essential elements are supplemented by psycho-physiological features, such as cognitive components, motivation or creativity. Acquisition of some of those sub-competences does not actually seem to require the physical presence of students in the classroom as they represent skills that can be mastered by students on their own; for instance, knowledge about translation sub-competence can be developed by extensive studying, or extra-linguistic sub-competence usually requires independent research by students. Bilingual sub-competence is generally not the focus of translation classes, as it is assumed that students' knowledge of both languages, the source and the target one, is already at the level ensuring proper completion of translation tasks. Although some language learning in fact takes place in translation courses, it is regarded as an extra benefit and not the aim of the class. Nevertheless, certain language exercises that might be of particular interest to future translators, for example involving collocations or idioms, can be practiced using an e-learning platform.

As regards instrumental sub-competence, its development highly depends on the level of computer skills already possessed by the students. For some of them even the use of the e-learning platform presents a challenge, especially when they are not familiar with online tools. And finally, development of strategic sub-competence, understood as the ability to identify translation problems together with available solutions and subsequently choose the most appropriate of all possible options, is the stage where students need the most guidance. Since the work of translators actually consists of decision making, students tend to look for approval for the translation path they take, which is the point at which they look for more face-to-face communication, as revealed in the survey described in this chapter.

In translator education, the issue of e-learning, defined as the pedagogical use of electronic means of communication (Pym et al. 2003), is often brought up with reference to two basic aspects: gaining instrumental competence (Rodríguez 2003: 72; Massey 2005: 630; Bogucki 2009: 93–94) or providing learning environments to enhance process orientation and collaboration (Kiraly 2000: 123–139; Kelly 2005: 88; Marczak 2016: 1–2). At this point, it is worth emphasizing the main feature of e-learning understood as education technology, the overall aim of which should be not only to provide online access to information, e.g. by posting a text on the web platform, but most importantly to enhance learning by engaging students in learning activities, assessing their work, providing distance teaching or managing the learning process (Kelly 2005: 86; Biggs & Tang 2007: 127).

As has been emphasized in the literature (Pym 2001: 2; Kiraly 2005: 27), the use of information and communication technology in translator training can significantly increase employability of translation students. Some academic institutions (e.g. University of Vienna) already use the concept of e-portfolio to provide their graduates with a summary of translation projects to prove their professional experience, so often demanded from prospective employers (Rotheneder 2007: 9).

There is a common agreement among researchers that e-learning in translator training can help develop students' communication skills, especially in the context of virtual communication. As observed by Massey, "e-learning can and does offer workable collaborative, authentically situated solutions for teaching instrumental-professional competence" (2005: 630), since in their future job, novice translators probably will not communicate face-to-face with their project managers or clients, but will instead use other, virtual means of communication. Additionally, educational technology facilitates tandem and group work in both local and international contexts (Kelly 2005: 88; Fernández-Quesada 2015: 35–36; Al-Jarf 2017). Like in other fields of education, e-learning opens new markets for translator training, enabling access to this type of course for those learners who could not afford to participate in traditional university courses because of distance, lack of financial resources, or disability (Pym 2001; Kelly 2005: 88; Arkorful & Abaidoo 2014: 401).

And finally, e-learning enhances and supports the skill of independent learning and life-long education (Sandrelli 2015: 116–117). Students who learn how to search for information or how to use online resources are more likely to acquire the habit of continuous learning, so important in the translator's practice (Pym 2001).

3. Study

Having in mind all benefits of e-learning in translator education, as well as various translator sub-competences that it can improve, it is interesting to examine students' approach to online classes. It is assumed that without the active involvement and positive attitude of course participants, this guided independent translation training may not result in the expected skill development. The main purpose of the study was therefore to investigate possible challenges faced by the students confronted at the same time with two new aspects: the content of the course – translation of written texts, and its form – online activities. Such investigation would lead to the identification of problem areas to be addressed when designing a translation course, to incorporate as many remote activities as is advisable from the perspective of translation didactics, and to balance the requirements of the contemporary job market and students' educational needs.

3.1 Method

The study was carried out in the form of a survey, preceded by a process-oriented observation and followed by a class discussion. The pre-survey direct observation of students working on their translation assignments in the class setting, as well as in their relations between themselves and towards the teacher, led to the identification of five main areas of interest: general preferences of the course mode, feedback method, individual vs. shared work, privacy, ability to focus in the classroom on translation tasks, and reluctance to show draft translations. Although not all questions in the survey directly mentioned the idea of e-learning, their overall goal was to discover what particular translation sub-competences can be successfully developed through online activities, and for which class tuition would provide a more beneficial solution. Since the ultimate aim of the researcher was to design the online part of the translation course, students' preference concerning the feedback system or publication of final projects on the e-learning platform could be of significant value.

The questionnaire was followed by a group interview, where students were presented with the results of the survey and given an opportunity to explain and clarify their opinions. The two additional research methods, observation and discussion in a focus group, were used to strengthen the design of the survey and clarify the results obtained as quantitative data. They also served the purpose of verifying the information provided by students in their answers and giving insight into the research findings for the particular group under analysis.

A survey was chosen as a research method to capture the students' views and their personal approach to the course. To ensure the reliability of results and to prevent students from randomly providing answers, the questions related to the same issue were paired, e.g. "I prefer to read comments about my translation assignments than to listen to my teacher commenting on my work" vs. "I prefer to talk to the teacher in person about my translation assignments than just to read her/his comments". The survey questionnaire, the full form of which is presented in the Appendix, contained ten statements related to students' preferences and attitudes towards translation classes and feedback type. The questionnaire was completed by thirty-six students in the first and the second year of master's degree studies, who were asked to specify to what extent they agreed with the statements provided by choosing one of five responses: I strongly disagree, I disagree, I neither disagree nor agree, I agree and I strongly agree (i.e. using a Likert scale).

3.2 Results

The results of the survey expressed in percentage are presented in Table 1.

Table 1: Results of the survey

SURVEY STATEMENT	strongly disagree	disagree	neither agree nor disagree	agree	strongly agree
I would prefer to have a translation course only as a class activity	3%	58%	28%	11%	0%
I would prefer to have a translation course only as e-learning activities	28%	31%	22%	14%	5%
I believe that a mixed mode is the best option	0%	0%	14%	50%	36%
I prefer to read comments than to listen to the teacher	5%	28%	28%	28%	11%
I prefer to talk to the teacher than to read comments	0%	22%	20%	47%	11%
While doing a translation assignment in class, I like the opportunity to compare	0%	3%	22%	56%	19%
Translation is an intimate activity which requires time and appropriate conditions	5%	14%	14%	42%	25%
I am able to focus on my translation tasks in the classroom setting	0%	19%	25%	50%	6%
I feel uncomfortable when the teacher reads my unfinished assignment	11%	50%	17%	17%	5%
I don't mind it when the teacher reads my translation assignment over my shoulder	8%	53%	19%	17%	3%

It can be seen that most students would not like to have their translation course 100% in either a face-to-face form (as the idea of having a translation course only as a class activity is opposed by 61% of all students, while only 11% would like to have it only as face-to-face meetings) or as e-learning activities (with 59% of all students disapproving of the idea of having the course only as online classes), with the general approval for the mixed type of classes (86% agreeing or strongly agreeing with the statement, and 14% with no specified opinion). This actually follows the idea of conducting translation training programmes in the form of blended learning, combining face-to-face and online learning activities, as proposed for example by Xu (2007), Secară et al. (2009), Janecka and Szarkowska (2009) or Galán-Mañas and Albir (2010).

An interesting point in students' responses is their preference concerning the feedback. 39% of the students declared that they preferred reading the teacher's comments than talking to the teacher, while 58% preferred face-to-face interaction with the teacher. As the students explained in the follow-up discussion, it was easier for them to defend their choices and the strategy applied in direct interaction, which suggests that the development of strategic sub-competence in translation requires closer trainer-trainee cooperation.

What was certainly perceived by students as an advantage of face-to-face classes was an opportunity to compare their work. A great majority of students (75%) strongly agreed or agreed with this statement. Comparisons of different solutions is considered to be a highly thought-provoking activity, inspiring students to search for new paths or strategies, and thus providing another opportunity to develop strategic-sub-competence. At the same time, comparison of individual versions of translated texts encourages students to share their work with others. It is all the more important considering the view that translation is often perceived as a private activity and students are unwilling to show their draft versions or work in progress, as indicated in the results of the survey. 67% of respondents agreed or strongly agreed with the statement that translation is an intimate activity requiring time and appropriate conditions, which can be best achieved in a private setting and not in the classroom. Additionally, only 20% don't mind it when the teacher reads their unfinished translations over their shoulders. On the other hand, it is not the classroom setting that prevents the students from producing a good translation, as 56% of them claim they can focus on a translation task in a classroom. Although students rarely want to share their unfinished projects, they must be prepared that in future work they might be asked to provide incomplete versions or share their suggestions within teams of translators working on the same text. While the online mode offers such a possibility, it brings better results for small teams working on a specific project, and not for classroom assignments. The teacher should encourage the students to engage in online activities as a team of independent translators, first in the classroom environment, to introduce them to the professional mode of working, and then try to transfer this community spirit and collaboration to the virtual world, as it actually takes place in modern translation practice (Massey 2005: 629–631; Cronin 2013: 53).

3.3 Discussion

The results of the study correspond to the findings of other research concerning the drawbacks of e-learning in translator education (Pym 2001; Xu 2007; Ibrahim-González 2011; Arkorful & Abaidoo 2014), such as the absence of human factor or the need to consult the teacher. The researchers examining the issue of students' attitudes towards e-learning often mention lack of physical contact or individualized feedback, which is generally limited. This may lead to distress among students, making them feel isolated and left on their own. The results correlate with the findings by Ibrahim-González who claims that e-learning provides students with more privacy as they can choose to work at their own pace and can use more preparation time (2011: 234). Consequently, online activities allow students to manage their own working time and to become more independent in the acquisition of knowledge. This follows the general shift in the approach to translator education towards empowerment of students, who "have to construct their own knowledge of the profession and their own understandings of their responsibilities and rights as professionals through experience, by collaboratively participating in the authentic activities of professional translators" (Kiraly 2003: 29).

The problem of a loss of motivation and student distress, mentioned by, for example, Pym (2001: 3), can be resolved by designing a blended course, where all students' concerns can be discussed and solved in the class, giving precise instructions concerning their individual online work (Xu 2007: 20–21). Blended learning would provide the essential methodological framework to effectively combine face-to-face classes, online instruction, and the whole range of content objects and assets (Wagner 2006: 44). By combining both modes of learning, students can develop a certain level of responsibility towards their assignments and translation training in general, with the teacher acting more as a guide, helping the students to achieve a higher level of professional competence, rather than as an absolute source of wisdom (Kiraly 2003: 28–29).

4. Conclusions

As follows from the research conducted, despite numerous advantages connected with e-learning activities, it is not advisable for translation courses to be conducted only as online courses. Translator training curriculum should be based on well-balanced blended learning to encourage group work, promote student autonomy and responsibility, ensuring timetable flexibility and the freedom to organize the workload.

To take full advantage of opportunities offered by both modes of learning, the teacher should carefully plan the division of course activities into e-learning and face-to-face classes. Class activities should focus mainly on strategic (decision-making) competence, where the teacher's guidance is most needed, while other sub-competences (linguistic, extra-linguistic or instrumental) can be practiced via e-learning.

As regards feedback, the focus should be placed on individualization. It should include an interactive component, giving students an opportunity to defend their translation strategy choices.

It is important to develop a virtual learning community among students to encourage them to cooperate in online activities. Such a virtual learning community, i.e. a community within online environment, sharing wisdom and recognizing the contributions of other members (Oliver & Herrington 2011: 72), could also be useful as a forum for exchanging and comparing individual solutions, as is the case with virtual communities of professional translators. This would provide another element preparing students to work in professional environments.

References

Al-Jarf, R. S. (2017). Exploring online collaborative translator training in an online discussion forum. *Journal of Applied Linguistics and Language Research, 4*(4), 147–160.

Alves, F. (Ed.). (2003). *Triangulating Translation: Perspectives in Process Oriented Research*. Amsterdam: John Benjamins.

Arkorful, V., & Abaidoo, N. (2014). The role of e-learning, the advantages and disadvantages of its adoption in higher education. *International Journal of Education and Research, 2*(12), 397–410.

Bell, R. (1991). *Translation and Translating: Theory and Practice*. London, New York: Longman.

Biggs, J., & Tang, C. (2007). *Teaching for Quality Learning at University*. Berkshire: McGraw-Hill Education.

Bogucki, Ł. (2009). *Tłumaczenie wspomagane komputerowo*. Warszawa: Wydawnictwo Naukowe PWN.

Bonk, C. J., & Graham, C. R. (Eds.). (2006). *The Handbook of Blended Learning: Global Perspectives, Local Designs*. San Francisco: Pfeiffer.

Cronin, M. (2013). *Translation in the Digital Age*. London, New York: Routledge.

EMT Expert Group. (2009). *Competences for professional translators, experts in multilingual and multimedia communication*. Available at: http://ec.europa.eu/dgs/

translation/programmes/emt/key_documents/emt_competences_translators_en.pdf (date of access: 5 November 2015).

Fernández-Quesada, N. (2015). Just the two of us? The '¿Qué tal?' e-tandem project for translation students. *Procedia – Social and Behavioral Sciences, 173*, 31–36.

Galán-Mañas, A., & Albir, A. H. (2010). Blended learning in translator training. *The Interpreter and Translator Trainer, 4*(2), 197–231.

Ibrahim-González, N. (2011). E-learning in interpreting didactics: Students' attitudes and learning patterns, and instructor's challenges. *The Journal of Specialised Translation, 16*, 224–241.

Janecka, J., & Szarkowska, A. (2009, April). *Designing a blended e-learning translation course*. Paper presented at the Teaching Translation and Interpreting 2 Conference, Łódź.

Kelly, D. (2005). *A Handbook for Translator Trainers: A Guide to Reflective Practice*. Manchester: St. Jerome.

Kelly, D. (2008). Training the trainers: Towards a description of translator trainer competence and training needs analysis. *TTR: Traduction, Terminologie, Rédaction, 21*(1), 99–125.

Kiraly, D. (2000). *A Social-Constructivist Approach to Translator Education*. Manchester: St. Jerome.

Kiraly, D. (2003). Control, chaos or collaboration? In A. Pym, C. Fallada, J. R. Biau, & J. Orenstein (Eds.), *Innovation and E-learning in Translator Training* (pp. 27–31). Tarragona: Servei de Publicacions.

Kiraly, D. (2005). Project-based learning: A case for situated translation. *Meta: Translators' Journal, 50*(4), 1098–1111.

Kiraly, D. (2006). Beyond social constructivism: Complexity theory and translator education. *Translation and Interpreting Studies, 6*(1), 68–86.

Marczak, M. (2016). Developing selected aspects of translation competence through telecollaboration. *English for Specific Purposes World, 16*(48), 1–12.

Massey, G. (2005). Process-oriented translator training and the challenge for e-learning. *Meta: Translators' Journal, 50*(2), 626–633.

Oliver, R., & Herrington, J. (2011). *Teaching and Learning Online. A Beginner's Guide to E-learning and E-teaching in Higher Education*. Perth: Edith Cowan University, Centre for Research in Information Technology and Communications.

PACTE Group. (2003). Building a translation competence model. In F. Alves (Ed.), *Triangulating Translation: Perspectives in Process Oriented Research* (pp. 43–66). Amsterdam: John Benjamins.

Pym, A. (2001). *E-learning and translator training.* Available at: http://usuaris.tinet.cat/apym/on-line/training/2001_elearning.pdf (date of access: 4 April 2016).

Pym, A., Fallada, C., Biau, R. J., & Orenstein, J. (Eds.). (2003). *Innovation and E-learning in Translator Training.* Tarragona: Servei de Publicacions.

Rodríguez, M. (2003). Notes on translator training. In A. Pym, C. Fallada, J. R. Biau, & J. Orenstein (Eds.) *Innovation and E-learning in Translator Training* (pp. 72–73). Tarragona: Servei de Publicacions.

Rotheneder, N. (2007). E-learning and employability in translator training: Introducing e-portfolio and personal development planning at the University of Vienna. *Translating and the Computer, 29,* Available at: http://www.mt-archive.info/Aslib-2007-Rotheneder.pdf (date of access: 4 April 2016).

Samson, R. (2005). Computer-assisted translation. In M. Tennent (Ed.), *Training for the New Millennium: Pedagogies for Translation and Interpreting* (pp. 101–126). Amsterdam and Philadelphia: John Benjamins.

Sandrelli, A. (2015). Becoming an interpreter: The role of computer technology. *Monografías de Traducción e Interpretación, 2,* 111–138.

Secară, A., Merten, P., & Ramirez, Y. (2009). What's in your blend? Creating blended resources for translator training. *The Interpreter and Translator Trainer, 3*(2), 275–294.

Tennent, M. (Ed.). (2005). *Training for the New Millennium: Pedagogies for Translation and Interpreting.* Amsterdam and Philadelphia: John Benjamins.

Wagner, E. D. (2006). On designing interaction experiences for the next generation of blended learning. In C. J. Bonk & C. R. Graham (Eds.), *The Handbook of Blended Learning: Global Perspectives, Local Designs* (pp. 41–54). San Francisco: Pfeiffer.

Xu, S. (2007). Innovation and e-learning in translator education: A Singapore experience. *Translating and the Computer, 29.* Available at: http://www.mt-archive.info/05/Aslib-2007-Xu.pdf (date of access: 4 April 2016).

Appendix

Study questionnaire

Please evaluate the statements below using the following scale:

1. *I strongly disagree*
2. *I disagree*
3. *I neither agree nor disagree*
4. *I agree*
5. *I strongly agree*

a)	I would prefer to have a translation course only as a class activity.	
b)	I would prefer to have a translation course only as e-learning activities.	
c)	I believe that a mixed mode (e-learning + classroom) is the best option.	
d)	Translation is an intimate activity which requires time and appropriate conditions, and which can be best achieved in personal setting, and not in the classroom.	
e)	I feel uncomfortable when the teacher reads my translation assignment while I am still working (in the classroom).	
f)	I don't mind it when the teacher reads my translation assignment over my shoulder.	
g)	I am able to focus on my translation tasks even in the classroom setting.	
h)	While doing a translation assignment in class, I like the opportunity to compare my work with other students' translations.	
i)	I prefer to read comments about my translation assignments than to listen to my teacher commenting on my work.	
j)	I prefer to talk to the teacher about my translation assignments than just to read her/his comments.	
k)	I don't mind it when the teacher reads my translation assignment over my shoulder.	
l)	I prefer to work on my own and hand in only my finished assignment.	

Part 2.
Technology for mobile language learning

Mariusz Kruk
University of Zielona Góra, Zielona Góra, Poland

Autonomy held in the hand or the use of mobile devices by advanced learners of English

Abstract: The main aim of this small-scale study was to investigate the use of mobile devices for learning English by advanced learners of English representing different levels of autonomy. The sample consisted of 149 Polish students majoring in English in years 1–3 of the B.A. program. The data were gathered by means of a questionnaire and analysed quantitatively and qualitatively. The results showed that, among other things, the study participants typically practiced vocabulary and reading in English and they displayed their awareness of benefits and drawbacks of the use of mobile devices for learning this language. In addition, the findings demonstrated that more autonomous students used their smartphones and tablet computers for learning English as well as practicing various language skills and subsystems more frequently than less autonomous learners. More autonomous students were also more cognizant of the opportunities offered by mobile devices when it came to language study.

Keywords: MALL, mobile devices, learner autonomy, language learning

1. Introduction

Mobile-Assisted Language Learning (MALL) provides language learners with opportunities to experience new learning modes that exceed the typical language classroom environment. MALL offers language learners more flexibility and learning choices in terms of language content, means of delivery, learning space, and time. Through mobile devices (MDs) such as smartphones or tablet computers, students have quick access to the Internet, language learning materials, language applications, and they are able to communicate with their peers and teachers anywhere and at any time. The study reported here is a small-scale study carried out in the Polish context. It attempted to investigate the use of MDs by advanced learners of English displaying different levels of autonomy in learning the language. First, an overview of the literature will be offered. It will briefly discuss learner autonomy, the role of technology, the definition of mobile learning (ML) and MDs as well as the applications of MALL. Next, the description of the research project will be provided (including its participants, procedures, data collection tools and analysis). This will be followed by the presentation of the results. The chapter will close with a short discussion and conclusion.

2. Review of literature

For Benson (2011a) computer technology has the potential to foster autonomous behaviour in language learners because it facilitates self-access in learning and provides students with various valuable occasions to take control of their own learning and to self-direct it. What is more, modern technology offers access to a lot of resources for language study and creates opportunities for autonomous learning (Reinders & White 2011). It has to be noted, however, that the relationship between technology-based instruction and the development of autonomy may not be obvious since "unrestricted access to information, without proper guidance and feedback, can in fact inhibit learners from taking more responsibility" (Reinders & White 2011: 1). Nevertheless, as indicated by Benson (2011b: 17), "new technologies are providing opportunities for language learners who lack immediate access to the target language to bypass classrooms and go directly to target language texts and users through the Internet and social media". This claim is of particular relevance to the Polish educational context in view of the fact that usually it is the language classroom where most language practice takes place.

As far as the use of MDs for language learning is concerned, they can support language learners in their learning efforts by offering access to various resources wherever such learners happen to be (Jones 2015). This is because such language involvement might encompass, for example, the use of chunks of free time for language practice, the search for vocabulary in appropriate contexts, or communication on social media (Jones 2015). In addition, by possessing a mobile device, language learners have the opportunity to take the lead, direct their own learning and engage in language activities motivated by their individual needs and situations (Kukulska-Hulme et al. 2007; Pettit & Kukulska-Hulme 2007). Equally important for independent study is the use of software, since, as observed by Godwin-Jones (2011: 8), it is the user who "determines which apps to acquire and how to use them".

In this study, autonomy is understood as "the capacity to take control of one's own learning" (Benson 2001: 47). In view of the fact that the use of MDs for autonomous language learning is important, mobile learning (ML) and MDs must first be defined. As regards ML, no single agreed-upon definition of the concept exists in the literature (Oz 2015: 23). For example, some researchers define ML as an extension of e-learning built upon MDs whereas others view it as learning that occurs anywhere and anytime (cf. Oz 2015: 23). When it comes to MDs, one of the most recent and straightforward definitions of MDs is offered by Kukulska-Hulme et al. (2015). They define MDs as "hand held electronic devices that can be comfortably carried around in a pocket or bag, including MP3 players, digital recorders, e-readers, tablets, and smartphones" (Kukulska-Hulme et al. 2015: 39).

There are a large number of research projects concerned with the use of mobile technology and MDs in language learning. The results of these studies focused on, for example, learners' perceptions and attitudes towards the use of a specific technology (e.g. Cakir 2015; Oz 2015), profiling mobile language learners (e.g. Byrne & Diem 2014), the impact on learning a foreign/second language (e.g. Nah et al. 2008; Cavus & Ibrahim 2009; Zhang et al. 2011), distance language learning (e.g. Demouy et al. 2016) or informal language learning practices (Jones 2015). In addition, a few studies have dealt with the use of mobile technology and autonomy in language learning (e.g. Díaz-Vera 2012; Djoub 2015). It should also be noted that, among other things, researchers have investigated various applications of ML and identified both advantages and disadvantages derived from using mobile technologies (e.g. Miangah & Nezarat 2012), explored the use of MDs for supporting social contacts and collaborative learning (e.g. Kukulska-Hulme & Shield 2008) and offered directions in how to implement ML into language instruction (e.g. Kukulska-Hulme et al. 2015). Finally, the application of MALL for teaching specific language skills and subskills has also been examined (e.g. Saran et al. 2009; Wang & Smith 2013; Wu 2015; Han & Keskin 2016; Khodabandeh et al. 2017).

The study which is reported in this chapter contributes to empirical investigations into to the use of mobile technology and mobile devices in learning a foreign language. As indicated earlier, only a few studies focused on the use of mobile technology/devices and autonomy in language learning. In addition, the shortage of such studies is, in particular, evident in the Polish educational context. The present study's main objective was therefore to delve into the participants' behaviours related to their own learning of the English language by means of mobile devices. More specifically, the study was guided by the following research questions:

1) What levels of autonomy are reported by the study participants?
2) What mobile devices are used by the study participants for studying English?
3) What is the frequency of the use of mobile devices for studying English by the subjects?
4) What are the most and the least practiced language components by the study participants?
5) What apps and resources are used by the study participants and how do they use them?
6) What are the participants' opinions about the use of mobile devices for language learning?

3. Method

3.1 Participants

The participants of the study were 149 Polish adult learners of English as a foreign language. They were majoring in English in years 1–3 of the B.A. program at University of Zielona Góra in Poland. The sample comprised 118 females and 31 males. As found from the demographic part of the questionnaire used for the aim of data collection, the median age of the sample was 21 (min. 19, max. 46), and the median experience in learning the English language of the group was presumably ten years (min. 1, max. 21). The proficiency level represented by the study participants could be described as somewhere between B2 and C1, as specified in the levels laid out in the *Common European Framework of Reference for Languages (CEFR)* (Council of Europe 2001). The sample was obtained by convenience sampling (Friedman 2012: 186). The data were collected by means of physical copy handed out in class by the present researcher. It should also be noted that this sample represents ca. 37% of advanced students of English at the university.

3.2 Data collection and analysis

The data were gathered by means of a questionnaire. It was completed anonymously by the study participants in their regular classes. The tool consisted of four parts:

- the aim of the first part was to collect demographic information concerning the study participants;
- the second part included 20 Likert-scale items representing autonomy-related issues in which the subjects had to mark the extent to which a particular statement was true about them on a 5-point scale, where 5 perfectly described their actions and 1 meant that it did not reflect them at all (e.g. "I have well defined objectives in learning English", "I know my strong and weak points in learning English"). These 20 items came from surveys used in the literature (e.g. Pawlak 2008; Wach 2012) and concerned participants' planning abilities, their self-evaluation abilities, their learning strategy use, their ability to select and implement relevant resources and collaboration. Cronbach's alpha for the Likert-scale items equalled .735, showing an acceptable degree of internal reliability (Larson-Hall 2010: 171);
- the third part of the instrument included two open-ended questions related to the study participants' MDs use habits ("What mobile device(s) do you have and what mobile device(s) do you use for learning English?" and "If you have

a mobile device (e.g. a smartphone, a tablet, PDA, etc.), how often do you use it to practice English?") and 7 closed-ended Likert-type items (a scale of 1–5) focusing specifically on deliberate practice of language skills and subsystems; Cronbach's alpha for the Likert-scale items amounted to .67;
- finally, the last part of the instrument consisted of three open-ended questions which elicited answers concerning the subjects' opinions about the use of MDs for language learning ("Do you find the use of mobile devices useful for practicing English?" and "In your opinion, what are the main disadvantages of using mobile devices for the purpose of learning English?") and their recent activities during which they used MDs in order to practice English.

The collected data were analysed quantitatively and qualitatively. The quantitative analysis encompassed computing the means, standard deviations and percentages for the items requiring numerical responses. Since the data obtained were not normally distributed, the levels of statistical significance were established by the use of the Mann-Whitney U Test. This test is a non-parametric alternative to the independent-samples *t*-test (Larson-Hall 2010: 376). In cases where there was a need to establish association between variables, the Chi-Square test was run. In addition, the open-ended questions connected with the participants' opinions and recent language activities were complemented by qualitative procedures. The students' responses were repeatedly read in order to look for recurrent items or themes and coded.

3.3 Results

RQ1: What levels of autonomy are reported by the study participants?
As mentioned above, the participants of the study were asked to rate the level of their independence in learning English on a scale from 1 ("strongly disagree") to 5 ("strongly agree") in a range of statements linked to autonomous behaviour. The means of the responses were calculated and then interpreted according to the scale presented in Table 1.[1] Using the scale in Table 1, the participants of the study were divided into two groups: Group 1 (G1) – the students who declared an above average level of autonomy ($M = 3.80$, $SD = 0.19$) and Group 2 (G2) – the students who reported an average level of autonomy ($M = 3.12$, $SD = 0.25$). G1 comprised 95 (63.76%) students and G2 consisted of 54 (36.24%) students. The Mann-Whitney U Test showed a statistically significant difference between the groups ($U = 0$, $p = 0.000$).

---

1 The interpretation is based on Wattana (2013: 209).

Table 1: The interpretation scale of mean scores for autonomy-related items of the second part of the questionnaire

Interpretation	Range of mean scores	Distribution of students
High autonomy	4.50–5.00	0
Above average	3.50–4.49	95 (63.76%)
Average autonomy	2.50–3.49	53 (35.57%)
Below average	1.50–2.49	1 (0.67%)
Low autonomy	1.00–1.49	0

RQ2: What mobile devices are used by the study participants for studying English? The data included in Table 2 show that, overall, smartphones and tablets were the most frequently used MDs for studying the target language by the study participants (80.54% and 32.89%, respectively). Some students also used their MP3/4 players (20.13%) and mobile/cell phones (17.45%). E-readers and PDAs were only mentioned by a few respondents (4.70% and 2.68%, respectively). It should also be noted that a number of subjects indicated the use of more than one device.

Table 2: The use of mobile devices by the participants in the study

MDs	Group 1 (n=95)	Group 2 (n=54)	All students (n=149)
smartphone	78	42	120
mobile/cell phone	15	11	26
tablet	33	16	49
MP3/4	24	6	30
PDA/palmtop	4	---	4
e-reader	6	1	7

When it comes to the students manifesting different levels of autonomy, the analysis of the data showed that MDs were used by a greater number of students who declared an above average level of autonomy. For example, 82.11% of the subjects in G1 and 77.78% of the students in G2 used their smartphones presumably for purposes of studying English. The use of tablets was reported by 34.74% and 29.63% of the subjects in G1 and G2, respectively (see Table 2). It should be noted, however, that Chi-Square tests found no significant relationship between the two groups in the use of either of these devices.

RQ3: What is the frequency of the use of mobile devices for studying English by the subjects?

A majority of the respondents (i.e. 66.67%) used their MDs for learning the target language daily and 25.50% used them several times per week (see Table 3). As regards the subjects in G1, 70.53% of them reported the using their MDs for learning English every day and 23.16% several times a week. As for the subjects in G2, 57.41% and 29.63% of its members declared the use of their MDs every day and 2–3 times per week, respectively. Chi-Square analysis revealed that there was no significant relationship between the groups in the frequency of the use of MDs.

Table 3: The frequency of the use of mobile devices by the subjects

	Group 1 (n=95)	**Group 2 (n=54)**	**All students (n=149)**
Every day	67	31	98
2–3 times a week	22	16	38
Once a week	1	1	2
Less than once a week	---	4	4
Other	5	2	7

RQ4: What are the most and the least practiced language components by the study participants?

As can be seen in Table 4, the most frequently practiced target language components in both groups were English vocabulary and reading in English. It should be noted, however, that the students in G1 used their MDs more often in these respects than the students in G2 (the difference in the mean equalled 0.27 and 0.38, respectively). The data included in Table 4 also show that the least practiced language components by members of both groups concerned speaking and grammar. It has to be noted, however, that the students in G1 practiced these language elements more often than their counterparts (the difference in the mean between the two groups amounted to 0.46 and 0.24, respectively). The Mann-Whitney U Test found some statistically significant differences between the two groups in the areas of listening ($U = 1555.5$, $p = 0.000$), speaking ($U = 2070.5$, $p = 0.045$) and reading ($U = 1947$, $p = 0.007$).

Table 4: Language components practiced by the learners in G1 and G2

	Group 1 *M* (*SD*)	**Group 2** *M* (*SD*)
Vocabulary	4.73 (0.51)	4.46 (0.95)
Listening	4.00 (1.06)	3.19 (1.18)
Grammar	3.31 (1.23)	3.07 (1.13)
Speaking	3.18 (1.25)	2.72 (1.38)
Reading	4.42 (0.82)	4.04 (0.99)
Pronunciation	3.72 (1.18)	3.37 (1.20)
Writing	3.71 (1.12)	3.48 (1.18)

RQ5: What apps and resources are used by the study participants and how do they use them?

Qualitative analysis of the data demonstrated that both groups used similar apps and resources in order to practice English. They mostly utilized reference material such as dictionaries and translation tools (e.g. diki, Google Translate). The students also accessed various websites in English and English language learning websites as well as authentic audio-visual resources. It should be noted, however, that instant messaging, videoconferencing and/or social networking services were mentioned only occasionally and mostly by students who declared more autonomous behaviour. In addition, the analysis of the students' responses to the open-ended questions revealed that they used their MDs on their own both during English language classes (e.g. during reading or phonetics classes) and outside the university (e.g. on their way to the university, on the bus or train). It is also interesting to note that some of the subjects combined the use of their MDs for practicing English with fun and pleasure as well as for some private issues. The following excerpts illustrate some of these points:

> I used my smartphone to talk to my friends who are native speakers. I usually focus more on improving my writing skills, as I'm a bit insecure when it comes to spelling but I'm trying to change that lately. To communicate with them I usually choose apps like Skype or any other similar apps.
>
> (G1)

> (…) I used a smartphone. I didn't use any special apps just a music player to listen to audiobooks. I practiced listening skills. I practiced it because I wanted to get used to British accent. I was very helpful. I enjoyed it very much.
>
> (G1)

> I often use mobile devices, such as my smartphone or tablet when I read something in English and I don't know a word. I check it to make sure that I understand a sentence correctly. I check it on my smartphone in a dictionary or on my tablet. I also send a lot of mails in English to get to know what is going on with my English-speaking friends.
>
> (G2)

RQ6: What are the participants' opinions about the use of mobile devices for language learning?

Insights into the participants' opinions about the use of MDs for learning English were yielded by the qualitative analysis of the data collected by the open-ended questions included in the fourth part of the questionnaire. The main finding was that the majority of the students in both groups seem to be aware of the benefits and drawbacks of using MDs. According to the students, MDs are very easy to use, they can be accessed almost everywhere and virtually at any time, they provide a quick access to information, and offer a variety of apps suitable for language learning. It should be noted, however, that some differences between the two groups were also observed. It is interesting to note that the members of G2 focused more on technical and practical descriptions of their MDs. This is not to say of course that the students in G1 did not point out such issues but, at the same time, they consistently seemed to view their MDs as tools which provided them with new ways and/or additional opportunities to access the English language environment and to practice the target language there as well as organize their own learning. Also, the students in G1 frequently claimed that the use of their smartphones and/or tablets had a positive impact on their progress in learning English. The following examples illustrate some of these points:

> I think that using mobile devices is useful and faster than searching something what we need in books. Of course if I have time I am using (a traditional) dictionary and grammar books but if I don't have time I prefer mobile devices, because this is a faster way to get information (…)
>
> (G2)

> It gives me a new idea how to spend my time better to improve my English. (G1)

> In my opinion mobile devices might be helpful during practicing foreign languages. We can find the best form of learning for us and use it, organize our independent way of collecting information.
>
> (G1)

> Yes because it's another way to practice your language (…)
>
> (G1)

> Yes, I do find the use of mobile devices useful. Using them improves pronunciation, listening skills and allows you to contact and speak to people around the world, including native speakers – we can get rid of so-called "language barrier".
>
> (G1)

As mentioned above, both groups listed some disadvantages of using MDs for studying English. First of all, the majority of the respondents claimed that the use of MDs made them stop giving their attention to learning English and made them do something else (e.g. answer incoming phone calls, read/write text messages, use other apps installed on their devices, play games, surf the Internet in order to entertain themselves). Second, a lot of students pointed to the fact that some web pages may contain false or incorrect information and thus there is a need to be able to look for reliable and verified language material. Third, a great number of subjects considered the use of MDs to be quite addictive. Finally, both groups quite frequently drew attention to some technical issues such as the size of the screen or a good connection with the Internet. The following excerpts illustrate some of these issues:

> For example while using your mobile phone you can easily get distracted by other apps or people calling/texting you. So that's the main disadvantage of using mobile devices.
>
> (G2)

> In my opinion, when people use their mobile devices for the purpose of learning English, they find it difficult because the Internet is also a source of entertainment so it disturbs people.
>
> (G1)

> The internet contains a lot of false information and mistakes, so do apps. We have to choose verified sources to learn languages.
>
> (G1)

> (...) Also you can easily become addicted to your smartphone which is dangerous like any other form of addiction.
>
> (G2)

> The main disadvantage is in my opinion the size of the screen. The smaller it is the harder it is to do exercises or read comfortably.
>
> (G2)

The analysis of the data revealed some differences in the students' opinions related to the drawbacks of using MDs for language study. As for the subjects in G1, some of them considered the use of MDs as a source of demotivation, impracticality and something not related to learning a foreign language at all. Such negative opinions can be seen from the following extracts:

> I think that the only disadvantage is the fact that mobile devices make students less interesting in studying and make them less able to remember things. This results in making students less willing to improve their language knowledge.

> If we learn only with using mobile devices for the purpose of learning English we are focused only on the things that are there, not the ones in real life. We can be good at doing exercises per the Internet (for example), but be not able to use these skills for real because of some barriers and being concentrated only on one source.

> They are distractive. They are "all around", so one cannot focus totally on studying, but just on many things and it's not quite like learning but just "checking".

As regards the drawbacks of using MDs indicated by the students in G2, some of them associated the use of MDs with learning the target language in solitude or openly opted for the teacher. Some of them preferred books and they were of the opinion that learning the target language should require more effort. The ease of use of MDs made some of the respondents claim that smartphones or tablets may prevent them from thinking or developing social skills. Some students also indicated that MDs do not provide opportunities to practice verbal communication and that they cannot be used for practicing all language skills. Finally, they also said that the use of MDs can be harmful for health (e.g. they can be bad for eyesight and they can cause headaches). The following extracts from the data illustrate some of these points:

> I think teachers can better teach us than mobile devices.

> In mobile devices we can find everything we need, we don't have to think too much at all.

> We are more lazy because everything is available that easy, so we don't have to take any effort.

> The main disadvantage is the lack of verbal communication which is very important especially nowadays.

> The light from the device and small letters could destroy your eyesight. Spending a lot of time on the device could give you a headache.

4. Discussion and conclusions

The language learners surveyed in this study comprised two groups of students representing different levels of autonomy in learning English. The analysis of the data showed that smartphones and tablet computers were the most frequently used MDs for studying English by all subjects. What is more, most of the study participants used their MDs in order to learn English every day. It has to be noted, however, that the greater use of smartphones and tables as well as the higher frequency of usage of MDs were reported by the group of students who declared an above average level of autonomy. Such findings may indicate a link between the level of autonomy in language learning and the frequency of use of MDs for learning a foreign language (i.e. the higher the level of autonomy the more frequent use of MDs). It should be noted, however, that in the absence of any statistical relationship between the groups in the use and the frequency of the usage of MDs such an assumption should be treated with great caution.

The study also revealed that vocabulary and reading in the target language were the most practiced language components by means of MDs in both groups. Conversely, the least practiced language areas by the members of the two groups included speaking and grammar. It should be noted, however, that despite the fact that both groups reported access to a range of mobile apps and resources, the students who manifested the higher level of autonomy practiced the language skills and subsystems more frequently than their less autonomous colleagues. At the same time, however, it is still somewhat surprising that the more independent students did not spend more time on practicing the productive language skills or grammatical items. While a range of plausible explanations for this finding can be offered, it stands to reason that these students probably have not developed yet a greater awareness of how MDs can be utilized for practicing these language areas. Such a supposition finds support in the fact that the study participants, including the more independent learners, for the most part reported the use of reference materials (e.g. dictionaries and translation devices) but tools, such as instant messaging, were pointed out sporadically.

The results of the study also demonstrated that all the students were aware of the benefits and drawbacks of the use of MDs for learning English. It should be noted, however, that the students who declared more autonomous behaviour were more cognizant of the opportunities offered by MDs (e.g. they organized their learning, they linked learning the target language by means of MDs with progress in learning it). What is more, contrary to the opinions expressed by the students who reported the average level of autonomy, the more independent students, among other things, did not associate the use of MDs with learning in isolation or they did not appeal for a teacher's assistance in learning English. Therefore, it could be argued that the use of MDs somehow assisted these students in the development of the skill of self-directed learning, in which, according to Benson (2001: 8), "the objectives, progress and evaluation of learning are determined by learners themselves". It should be noted, however, that the converse could be equally true; i.e., it was the autonomy of the students that prompted their use of MDs.

The study suffers from a number of weaknesses. Despite the fact that it included a relatively large sample size, the generalizability of the findings is limited for the reason that the group was largely homogenous – the subjects studied at the same university and came from the same cultural background. In addition, the results could have been affected by a number of factors connected with the weaknesses of the data collection tool, related among other things to the selection of statements and open-ended questions, wording of the statements and questions, or the quality of the subjects' accounts of how they really used their MDs for studying English. For these reasons, involving other students from various tertiary institutions and representing diverse cultural backgrounds as well as incorporating multiple data collection tools (e.g. interviews, mobile session samples, narratives) would have presented a much broader picture of the issue in question.

References

Benson, P. (2001). *Teaching and Researching Autonomy in Language Learning.* Harlow: Pearson Education.

Benson, P. (2011a). *Teaching and Researching Autonomy in Language Learning.* London: Pearson Education.

Benson, P. (2011b). What's new in autonomy? *The Language Teacher, 35,* 15–18.

Byrne, J., & Diem, R. (2014). Profiling mobile English language learners. *The JALT CALL Journal, 10*(1), 3–19.

Cakir, I. (2015). Opinions and attitudes of prospective teachers for the use of mobile phones in foreign language learning. *Contemporary Educational Technology, 6*(3), 239–255.

Cavus, N., & Ibrahim, D. (2009). m-Learning: An experiment in using SMS to support learning new English language words. *British Journal of Educational Technology, 40*(1), 78–91.

Council of Europe. (2001). *Common European Framework of Reference for Languages: Learning, Teaching, Assessment.* Cambridge: Cambridge University Press.

Demouy, V., Jones, A., Kan, Q., Kukulska-Hulme, A., & Eardley, A. (2016). Why and how do distance learners use mobile devices for language learning? *The EuroCALL Review, 24*(1), 10–24.

Díaz-Vera, J. (Ed.). (2012). *Left to My Own Devices: Learner Autonomy and Mobile-assisted Language Learning.* Bingley: Emerald Group.

Djoub, Z. (2015). Mobile technology and learner autonomy in language learning. In J. Keengwe (Ed.), *Promoting Active Learning Through the Integration of Mobile and Ubiquitous Technologies* (pp. 194–212). Hershey: IGI Global.

Friedman, A. D. (2012). How to collect and analyze qualitative data. In A. Mackey & S. M. Gass (Eds.), *Research Methods in Second Language Acquisition* (pp. 180–200). Malden, MA: Wiley-Blackwell.

Godwin-Jones, R. (2011). Emerging technologies: Mobile apps for language learning. *Language Learning & Technology, 15*(2), 2–11.

Han, T., & Keskin, F. (2016). Using a mobile application (WhatsApp) to reduce EFL speaking anxiety. *Gist Education and Learning Research Journal, 12*, 29–50.

Jones, A. (2015). Mobile informal language learning: Exploring Welsh learners' practice. *eLearning Papers*, 45, 4–14.

Keengwe, J. (Ed.). (2015). *Promoting Active Learning Through the Integration of Mobile and Ubiquitous Technologies.* Hershey: IGI Global.

Khodabandeh, F., Alian, J., & Soleimani, H. (2017). The effect of mall-based tasks on EFL learners' grammar learning. *Teaching English with Technology, 17*(2), 29–41.

Kukulska-Hulme, A., Norris, L., & Donohue, J. (2015). *Mobile Pedagogy for English Language Teaching: A Guide for Teachers.* London: British Council.

Kukulska-Hulme, A., & Shield, L. (2008). An overview of mobile assisted language learning: From content delivery to supported collaboration and interaction. *ReCALL, 20*(3), 271–289.

Kukulska-Hulme, A., Traxler, J., & Pettit, J. (2007). Designed and user-generated activity in the mobile age. *Journal of Learning Design, 2*(1), 52–65.

Larson-Hall, J. (2010). *A Guide to Doing Statistics in Second Language Research using SPSS.* New York: Routledge.

Mackey, A., & Gass, S. M. (Eds.). (2012). *Research Methods in Second Language Acquisition.* Malden, MA: Wiley-Blackwell.

Miangah, T. M., & Nezarat, A. (2012). Mobile-assisted language learning. *International Journal of Distributed and Parallel Systems, 3*(1), 309–319.

Nah, K. C., White, P., & Sussex, R. (2008). The potential of using a mobile phone to access the internet for learning EFL listening skills within a Korean context. *ReCALL, 20*(3), 331–347.

Oz, H. (2015). An investigation of preservice English teachers' perceptions of mobile assisted language learning. *English Language Teaching, 8*(2), 22–34.

Pawlak, M. (2008). Autonomia w nauce języka angielskiego w liceum: Diagnoza, analiza, wnioski. In M. Pawlak (Ed.), *Autonomia w nauce języka obcego: Co osiągnęliśmy i dokąd zmierzamy?* (pp. 137–157). Poznań, Kalisz, Konin: Wydawnictwo UAM and PWSZ.

Pawlak, M. (Ed.). (2008). *Autonomia w nauce języka obcego: Co osiągnęliśmy i dokąd zmierzamy?* Poznań, Kalisz, Konin: Wydawnictwo UAM and PWSZ.

Pettit, J., & Kukulska-Hulme, A. (2007). Going with the grain: Mobile devices in practice. *Australasian Journal of Educational Technology, 23*(1), 17–33.

Reinders, H., & White, C. (2011). Beyond the language classroom, Language. *Learning & Technology, 15*(3), 1–3.

Saran, M., Seferoglu, G., & Cagiltay, K. (2009). Mobile assisted language learning: English pronunciation at learners' fingertips. *Eurasian Journal of Educational Research, 34*(1), 97–114.

Wach, A. (2012). Computer-mediated communication as an autonomy-enhancement tool for advanced learners of English. *Studies in Second Language Learning and Teaching, 2*(3), 367–389.

Wang, S., & Smith, S. (2013) Reading and grammar learning through mobile phones. *Language Learning & Technology, 17*(3), 117–134.

Wattana, S. (2013). *Talking while playing: The effects of computer games on interaction and willingness to communicate in English* (Unpublished doctoral dissertation). University of Canterbury, Canterbury.

Wu, Q. (2015). Designing a smartphone app to teach English (L2) vocabulary. *Computers & Education, 85,* 170–179.

Zhang, H., Song, W., & Burston, J. (2011). Reexamining the effectiveness of vocabulary learning via mobile phones. *The Turkish Online Journal of Educational Technology, 10*(3), 203–214.

Robert Oliwa
Bronisław Markiewicz State School of Technology and Economics, Jarosław, Poland

Beyond the classroom – hand-held language instruction for business learners

Abstract: The aim of this chapter is to determine if the implementation of a hand-held (mobile) language learning environment as an augmentation of regular English classes would lead to enhanced writing and speaking competence among customer care consultants. Moreover, the study attempts to determine if an instructional model may support such an implementation. The study group included full-time customer care consultants with national and foreign retail sale experience, whose efficacy of dealing with customers in English has an impact on the company's performance and expansion. The study used mixed method design and incorporated an instructional model which was composed of seven different stages. The implementation and delivery of the instructional content occurred in an online learning environment, Canvas which allows its users to access online content on hand-held devices. Results of the study indicate that after a period of working with online content, the learners had developed their English language writing and speaking competence related to the work of the customer care department as well as their general command of English. The conclusions drawn from the study suggest that augmenting a traditional foreign language learning environment with online materials, which learners can access remotely outside a classroom, may help them improve their English and, therefore, benefit the environment they are engaged in.

Keywords: hand-held, learning, languages, model, business

1. Introduction

The quotation from Ulam (1958:30) that "It would appear that we have reached the limits of what is possible to achieve with computer technology, although I should be careful with such statements, as they tend to sound pretty silly in 5 years", highlights how little has changed in terms of technological progress and how dynamic and unpredictable an area it is. Computers are gone from our lives, or nearly gone, PCs to be precise. Nonetheless, what remains is the idea or medium they have embodied. Computers have been methodically replaced with computerish hand-held devices such as tablets or smartphones which often exceed the processing capacities of once-popular desktops. The reasons for such omnipresence of mobile technologies are numerous; however, the most central ones include versatility, mobility, sociability, interactivity and accessibility (Dickey 2005; Minocha & Roberts 2008). Often all these aspects happen concurrently.

Education, consequently, has quickly adapted the new medium because the most central element to any instructional process, the learner, has long taken to computers and the Internet in the process of learning. The very computer assisted learning and its most recent variety, namely mobile learning (m-Learning) aka hand-held learning[1] is defined as "[…] PDAs, smart phones connected to wireless networks enable mobility and facilitate mobile learning" (Jacob & Issac 2008: 19) or "[…] the provision of education and training on mobile devices: personal digital assistants (PDAs), smartphones and mobile phones" (Keegan 2005: 5). The computer- or Internet-assisted learning has drawn the attention of psychology, pedagogy, foreign language methodology,[2] instructional theory and design.[3] However, the impact which it has on students' school attainment requires study and research to identify its worth and define certain guidelines to be followed.

One of the key factors contributing to the success of computer assisted learning, whether it is delivered on a PC, laptop or a hand-held device, is the instructional design or model used to implement it. Skowron (2006: 56) describes instructional design as "[…] the process of planning instruction, delivering instruction, and assessing student learning". Ryder (2005) believes that:

> Models, like myths and metaphors, help us to make sense of our world. Whether derived from whim or from serious research, a model offers its user a means of comprehending an otherwise incomprehensible problem. An instructional design model gives structure and meaning to an I.D. [instructional design] problem, enabling the would-be designer to negotiate her design task with a semblance of conscious understanding. Models help us to visualize the problem, to break it down into discrete, manageable units.
>
> (Ryder 2001: 18)

1 The typology of computer- or Internet-assisted learning has undergone many modifications and includes such acronyms as information and communication technologies (ICT), technology assisted learning (TAL), computer assisted learning (CAL) or web assisted learning (WAL). The two recent contributions include mobile learning (m-Learning) and hand-held learning which both refer to the idea of education or training delivered with the help of portable devices such as smartphones or tablets. Finally, virtual learning which implies that the learning process can be accessed distantly by means of a computer device, over the Internet and it resembles the traditional learning.

2 Polish researchers use the term glottodidactics as a discipline which covers the field of second or foreign language methodology referring to processes of language acquisition and learning.

3 Other terms include instructional system design, instructional system development, and instructional technology.

Models provide both environments and tools which support interaction, collaboration, connectedness, research, and enquiry as well as autonomy and immediate feedback, which consequently assists a pedagogy-founded implementation of computer-mediated instruction.

2. Review of literature: Instructional models within virtual environments

Instructional models, founded on psychological and learning theories (see Figure 1) derive from such authors like Nunan (1988), Block (1991), Bell, and Gower (1998), Tomlinson (1998, 2011), Richards and Rodgers (2001), Crawford (2002), Tomlinson and Masuhara (2010), Littlejohn (2011), McGrath (2013). However, the overall development of the area has produced changes not in the way design processes are managed but in the methods by which content is delivered.

Figure 1: Development of psychological and learning theories.

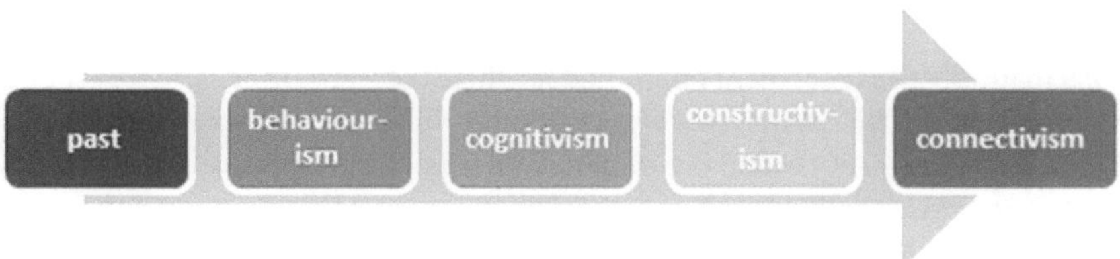

Accordingly, instructional models have gone through a number of modifications over the years and have been under the influence of sundry theories and approaches including Edgar Dale's Cone of Learning (Dale 1969), Skinner's programmed instruction educational model (Skinner 1954), Bloom's taxonomy (Bloom et al. 1956), or Gagné's Nine Events of Instruction (Gagné 1985). The most widely used models, because of their innovativeness and possible application in virtual language instruction, include ADDIE model (Analysis, Design, Development, Implementation and Evaluation[4]) considered the foundation of contemporary instructional design (Reiser & Dempsey 2007), R2D2 model founded on constructivist roots and ASSURE based on learner centeredness (Gustafson & Branch 1997).

Computer and information technologies, including first and foremost the Internet, have been widely recognised, studied and researched in relation to virtual learning, its design, and models (Warschauer & Meskill 2000; Crystal 2001; Lam

4 ADDIE is considered a proto-model which has generated over 100 variations.

and Lawrence 2002; Kim et al. 2012; Koller 2012; Deming et al. 2015). On this basis, two major directions where the development of hand-held learning is going may be discerned. The first is providing access to educational resources of various formats and arrangements. The other direction relates to the buildout and improvement of the instructional environments. As a result, the educational market puts forward various solutions for starting, managing and customising learning environments e.g. learning management system (LMS) or virtual learning environment (VLE), to name just two, all of which regularly complement one another in their functionalities. The offered solutions constitute a range of available possibilities and accurately reveal different features, functionalities but also developments and teaching trends. The emergence of such an abundance of systems representing various classifications and formats[5] adds to the available choice[6] but also to vague differences between their possibilities (Hyla 2005; Stecyk 2008). The market offers free/open source solutions such as Canvas (free version), Edmodo and CourseSites or commercial/paid products such as Blackboard, Schoology or Canvas (commercial version). Setting-up a VLE, which according to Weller (2005) is "[…] a software system that combines a number of different tools that are used to systematically deliver content online and facilitate the learning experience around that content" (2005: 5), involves organizational, didactic and human dimensions (Marczak & Krajka 2014) and can be perceived from the perspective of instruction, customization, data management, assessment, reporting and mobile pedagogy.[7] On top of the above aspects of technology-driven learning, there is the issue of foreign language learning which has become computer-, or more and more frequently, Internet-assisted. The existing research has not established conclusively either the positive or negative effect computers have on students' foreign language learning (Hołowiecki 2014; Kruk & Pawlak 2014; Szerszeń 2014; Turula 2014). Up to now, internet-based foreign language teaching and learning does not seem to have been extensively researched. Nor has a design for Internet-based foreign language instruction been unambiguously provided. Existing doubts may not be left unsettled as they may result in either misinterpretation of certain phenomena,

5 The formats include a learning content management systems (LCMS), content management system (CMS), learning content system (LCS) and massive open online course (MOOC).

6 For a comparison of content management systems visit http://www.cmsmatrix.org/

7 Mobile pedagogy is a derivative of traditional pedagogy and is founded on principles such as accessibility (anytime/anywhere) collaboration, interaction, connectedness, immediate feedback. The term mobile may also refer to mobile devices such as mobile phones or tablets.

distortion of available data or choosing a wrong course of action. As a result, there is a need to study and research if moving foreign language learning online and making it available on computer and hand-held devices will have an impact on students' performance, including the students who study foreign languages for professional reasons. Likewise, it should be studied if such an implementation should adhere to an existing model or provide a model of its own. Outcomes received from such a study may be significant for creators and recipients of the educational process including employers, teachers, material designers, computer programmers, parents, and finally students.

3. The study

3.1 Aim

This study aims to present an account of the implementation of a hand-held language learning environment into regular English classes and its evaluation as far as the improvement of writing and speaking competence was concerned.

3.2 Research questions

The study addressed the following research questions:

Can hand-held language instruction enhance the English writing and speaking competence of customer care consultants?

Can an instructional model support the implementation of hand-held language learning?

The data were assembled in the study with the aim of determining if implementation of a hand-held (mobile) language learning environment for a period of two months (May – June 2016) as an augmentation of regular English classes would lead to enhancing the writing and speaking competence of customer care consultants. The mixed method design included such methods as background questionnaires, interviews, pre- and post-tasks and an evaluation questionnaire. The language resources were delivered via CANVAS virtual environment and followed a model designed by the author. Finally, an analysis and evaluation of the outcomes were carried in the view of the virtual learning environment and instruction model. The researcher had been working with the target population prior to the study as he had been employed by the company to run all the in-house English language courses.

3.3 Participants

The group of employees who took part in the study consisted of 16 full-time adult employees, 15 women and 1 man, working for a customer care department of a Polish retail company with a 600-person workforce. The group chosen for the study was the whole customer care staff who the company employed and who had been taking part in regular in-house English courses. Their participation in such courses was decided by the company board and the customer care manager in particular. The study group had national and foreign trade experience and their good command of English had an impact on the company's expansion and ability to enter markets in other countries. Their key role in the company's expansion which depended, to a large extend, on their good English language skills made them an interesting target of the study. The average age of the learners was 33 (the youngest participant was 26 and the oldest one was 45 years old), 33.87% had a university degree and 13% were secondary school graduates. On average, they had worked in the company for 5 years. Their existent English language competence resulted from the English course they did at secondary or primary schools, university, language school, private classes at home, or on e-learning platforms. Some acquired English while staying in an English-speaking country. As far as the resources the group used for studying English outside regular classes were concerned, they ranged from songs, the most popular source, through films, newspapers and magazines, topic websites, books, and educational software. None of the learners admitted to using computer games to study English.

3.4 Procedure

The instructional model used in the study was designed and developed by the author himself as a result of the absence of an appropriate model available on the market which the company could implement to meet its educational needs. It took into consideration pedagogy, methodology of ELT, instructional design, computer technology, and virtual learning management. The model per se had not been put to the test earlier; however, it was the author's ambition to design, test, and evaluate such a model so as to use it in the future.

The proposed virtual instructional model was composed of the seven stages depicted in Figure 2.

Figure 2: The seven-stage virtual instructional model created for this study.

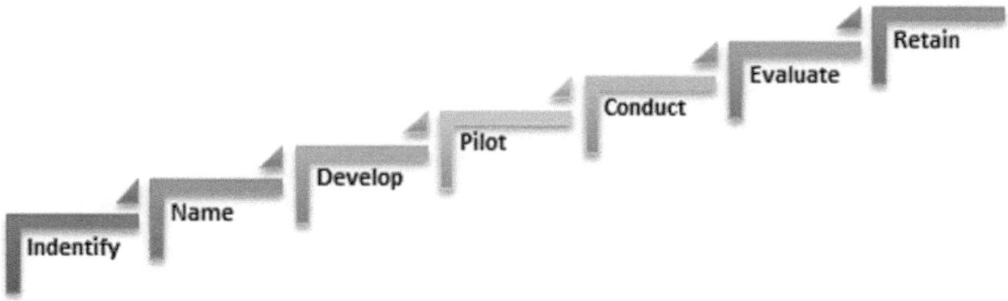

The model was based upon the Canvas learning environment which was used as a platform for material distribution, interaction among learners, feedback, and the evaluation process. The environment includes tools such announcements, assignments, discussions, grades, people, pages, files, syllabus, quizzes, conferences, collaborations. It supports local or outside media formats including text or.pdf documents, graphics, multimedia MP3/MP4 files, PowerPoint and Flash-based applications. It also allows users to embed links to parts of the same course and other websites. The Canvas platform reports on students' attainment with the use of different media such as digital annotations, video/audio comments, rubric assessment, and automatic comments. However, the most central feature of Canvas is its availability on hand-held devices like tablets and mobile phones through special mobile applications for Android and iOS.

It was established during the needs interviews carried out during the *identify* stage (see Figure 2) that the most critical area that needed immediate improvement was providing efficient customer care in English both in speech and writing. The *name* stage defined the syllabus and objectives of the hand-held instruction, technologies, digital tools and pre- and post- tasks. The *develop* stage focused on either designing appropriate customer care resources or finding them on the Internet. The syllabus contained the following areas: claims, returns, refunds, responding to inquiries, ordering, payment, delivery, product description and availability. The resources included local or external text or.pdf documents, graphics, multimedia MP3/MP4 files, PowerPoint, Flash-based applications, tests and quizzes. During the *pilot* stage an induction programme was run with the aim of introducing the Canvas platform to the students[8] and testing the environment in an authentic learning setting to collect the students' feedback on the experience.

8 The idea to run the induction programme stemmed from the conjecture that the study participants may not have been competent virtual environment users and required

Having completed the *pilot* stage, the teacher's and students' comments were collected so as to tailor the online component for all the parties' needs. Following this was the *conduct* stage, the actual instructional stage which implemented all the customer care-related content by means of Canvas tools. The implementation of the content was carried out as an augmentation of the regular in-house English course the Customer Care staff participated in. The resources were published on the Canvas virtual platform which the students could retrieve outside classes on any device, PC, laptop or hand-held, with Internet access in preparation for their classes. These focused on providing regular customer care both in writing and on the phone which involved dealing with claims, returns, refunds, responding to inquiries, ordering as well as payment, delivery, product information and availability. Following the *conduct* stage there was the *evaluate* stage whose aim was to gather information on the students' progress and attainment in the area of writing and speaking competence in response to the online content and instructional model. In addition, this stage intended to yield insight into the students' experience with the model. The final stage of the implemented model, *retain*, aimed at sustaining the material published and proving follow-up resources and tasks to accompany regular English classes. The *retain* stage is still in progress as it is meant for a self-study online environment which is free to access by the participants.

3.5 Techniques and analysis of collected data

The study used mixed method research to measure if augmenting an English course for the customer care consultants with hand-held language instruction could contribute to the improvement of the writing and speaking competence and, therefore, the quality of customer care provided in English. Data collection techniques included a background questionnaire, needs interviews, pre- and post-tasks, and an evaluation questionnaire.

The background questionnaire was administered two weeks prior to the launch of the study with the aim of examining the learners' employment length in the company to see if this had an impact on the results. It also asked about the length of studying English to see if this variable would influence the final outcomes. Finally, the questionnaire inquired about the learners' familiarity with online learning as they would be using a hand-held language learning environment and the relationship between the two might be relevant. The questionnaire was drawn up in Polish in order to avoid any possible misunderstandings and incorporated a Likert-type

---

some practice to understand how it worked. This was confirmed in the computer literacy questionnaire.

scale (i.e., poor, fair, good, very good, excellent). The next step encompassed semi-structured interviews conducted with a mixed amount of open and closed questions firstly among the company's management and then among the customer care consultants to discover the most important needs in terms of providing customer care in English. The following leg of data collection comprised the pre- and post-tasks which involved dealing with customer cases both in writing and on the phone. Both tasks took place on a specified day in the company's head office. Each participant was given a different task printed on a handout which included a detailed background to the subject of the claim and the customers' requirements. The tasks came from an authentic database of claim cases. The students were given enough time to prepare a procedure of dealing with their cases, write an email to a customer explaining required steps, and phone a customer and inform about the company's position on each claim. To show how much the participants improved their linguistic competence, each student dealt with the same task twice. The pre-task took place a week prior to the commencement of the study to evaluate how efficaciously the staff could solve a customer case without the forthcoming intervention. The post-task took place soon after the termination of the intervention to establish if and how much the learners progressed in terms of their writing and speaking competence from the pre-test. Both tasks concerned customer claims regarding faulty products they ordered. While dealing with the claims the students had to follow fixed company policy and guidelines both in writing and on the phone which required appreciating, inquiring and advising customers. In order to document their progress, the students dealt with exactly the same customer claims in the pre- and post-tasks. The criteria used in the assessment included the following:

Writing
- efficiency of dealing with a customer
- following company's policy
- composition
- vocabulary range
- spelling
- grammatical correctness

Speaking
- efficiency of dealing with a customer
- following company's policy
- pronunciation
- interaction
- vocabulary range
- grammatical correctness

Finally, the customer care staff were asked to evaluate the two-month online experience in a questionnaire which was administered a week after the end of the study. Similar to the background questionnaire, it was drawn up in Polish so as to avoid any possible misunderstandings. It used the same Likert-type scale mentioned previously, one multi-select question, and one open-ended question. The evaluation questionnaire asked the learners to assess the following aspects of hand-held instruction: the online component overall, the quality of the resources, the application of the developed skills, and areas where the component could be improved.

3.6 Data analysis

3.6.1 Identify stage

The questionnaire conducted during the *identify* stage revealed that the average employment length of the studied group was 5 years. The longest period of employment was 10 years and the shortest only 3 months. The company's current policy was to provide in-house free English language courses which took place once a week for 90 minutes. However, as the questionnaire showed, all the learners had already undergone some English instruction (see Figure 3). Half of the Customer Care consultants had studied English for more than 10 years, 12.5% for 9–10 years, another 12.5% for 7–8 years and 19% for 5–6 years. The remaining 6% had 1–2 years English studying experience.

Figure 3: Participants' years of English study.

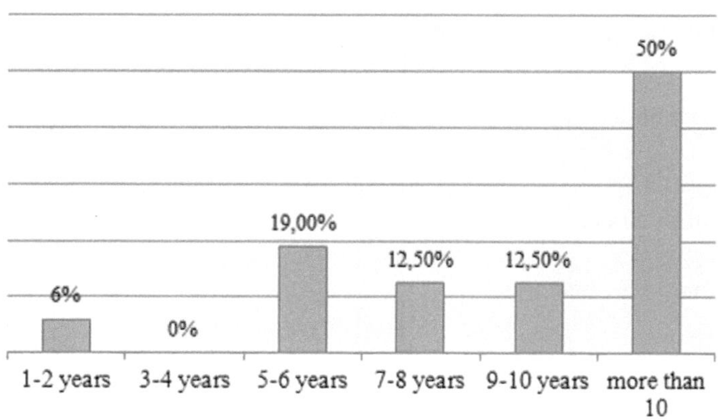

The following part of the questionnaire dealt with the learners' computer literacy. The learners were asked to assess their computer literacy from 1 = poor to 5 = excellent. Nine of the questioned believed it was good (56%), six said it was very good (37.5%), one evaluated it as fair (6%). None of the learners admitted to having either poor or excellent computer skills.

The needs interviews, which were a part of the *identify* stage of the instructional model (see Figure 2), conducted among the company management and the customer care consultants showed that providing effective customer care in English both in writing and speaking was the most critical area which required immediate attention. The areas which were recommended by the company's customer care manager included efficiency in dealing with a customer case, interaction with a customer, and following the company's customer care policy and guidelines. Other recommended assessment criteria included the vocabulary range and grammar correctness for the written part and pronunciation, vocabulary range, and grammar correctness for the oral part. Furthermore, it was articulated by both the manager and the customer care staff that additional resources should be made available on mobile devices such as mobile phones so that the learners could have them at their disposal outside classes or the company's office.

3.6.2 Evaluate stage

In the pre- and post-tasks, five learners were chosen randomly to display their progress in their writing competence (see Figure 4) and speaking competence (see Figure 5) after two-months of access to the resources available on the Canvas virtual platform.

Figure 4: Participants' writing progress.

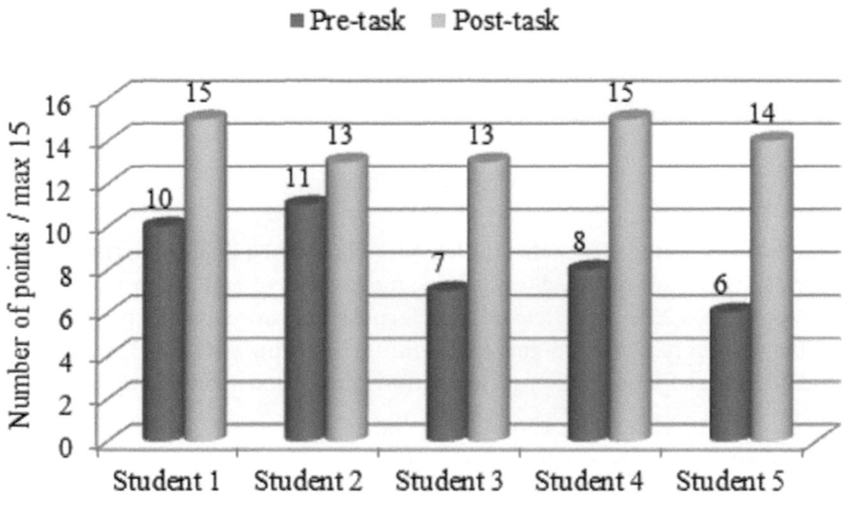

Figure 5: Participants' speaking progress.

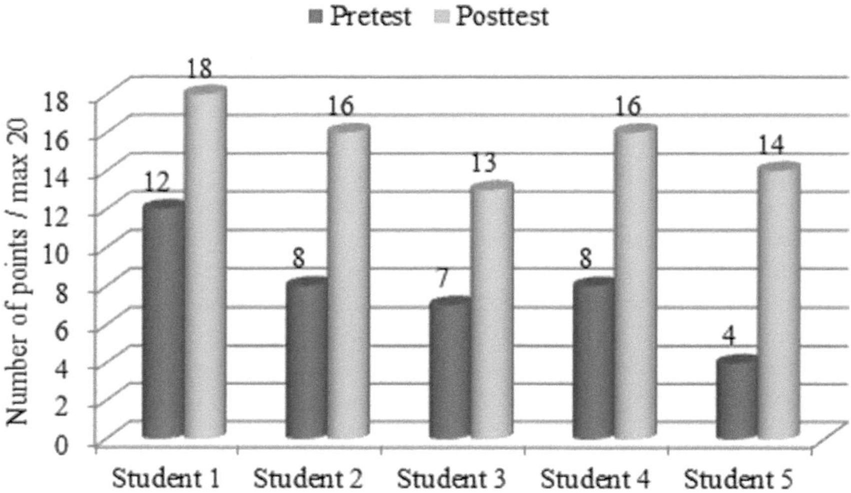

The mean improvement for all the 16 learners who participated in the study was 5.5 points (34%) for writing and 6 points (30%) for speaking (Figure 6). The highest improvement for a single participant on the written part was 8 points (50%) and 10 points (50%) for a single participant for the speaking part.[9]

Figure 6: Improvement between pre-task and post-task.

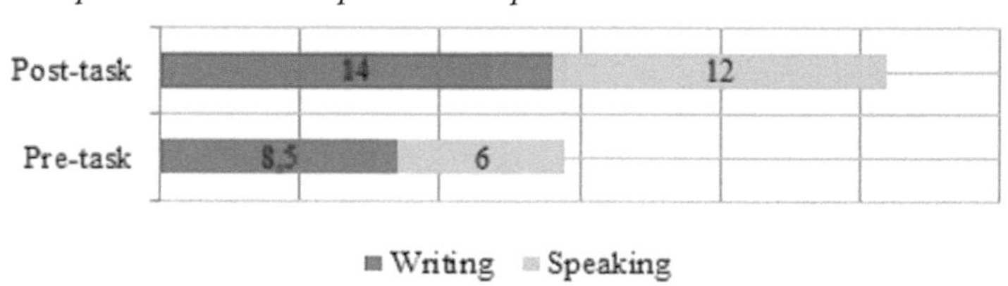

The study uncovered, firstly, that the learners who studied English for the shortest period of time (this included two groups: those with 1–2 and 5–6 years of study) and constituted 25% of participants, made mean improvement of 7 points (44%) for the written part and 8 points (40%) for the speaking part. The learners who studied English for the longest period of time (this included one group with more

9 The difference in the number of points comes from the fact that the two parts used different scoring systems.

than 10 years of study) and constituted 50% of the participants, made mean improvement of 3 points (19%) for the written part and 4 points (20%) for the speaking part. Secondly, it was found that 8 out of the 16 learners (50%) were familiar with online learning platforms. They had some experience working with them, specifically Joomla (19%), Canvas (19%) and Edmodo (6%) learning platforms. One learner admitted to being acquainted with the concept but could not provide any examples.[10] The learners who had prior experience working with online learning environments achieved better results in the post-task. The difference between the pre-task and the-post task for the group with prior virtual platform experience was 4 points (25%) for the written part and 5 points (25%) for the speaking part. The group who had no prior virtual platform experience improved 2 points (12.5%) on the written part and 3 points (15%) on the speaking part.

The questionnaire asked the learners to evaluate the two-month online component As far as the overall opinion about the online component was concerned 81% said that it was good, 12.5% answered it was very good and 6% thought it was excellent. All the learners said that the quality of the resources was very good. As regards the application of the developed skills, 100% of the learners admitted that the online component helped them to provide better customer care. 75% thought that the online component developed their writing and speaking competence to interact with diverse groups of customers. 50% felt confident with their communication/interaction competence in English. Vis-à-vis the learners' suggestions for improvement, 62.5% (10 learners) took their time to offer their ideas. Their suggestions included extending the period of the hand-held instruction, providing more instruction how to use the Canvas platform, constructing content around case studies, and using more translation techniques.

4. Discussion and conclusions

The study asked if implementing a virtual learning environment as part of a regular English course would lead to enhancing the writing and speaking competence of customer care consultants. Moreover, the study addressed the problem of supporting the implementation of hand-held language learning with an instructional model. The collected results may indicate that after the period of the intervention, all the learners improved their language writing and speaking competence as regards customer care. However, their improvement varied depending on two variables,

10 Surprisingly, no student knew the Moodle learning platform which is considered one of the earliest learning initiatives (Arora et al. 2013) whose performance and usability are commonly used for comparison.

namely the length of studying English prior to the intervention and familiarity with online learning platforms. The results demonstrate that the most noticeable progress was made by the learners who had the shortest experience of studying English. On the other hand, the students whose initial English learning experience was the longest demonstrated the least progress in the two areas. In addition, more noticeable progress was achieved by the students who had some prior experience working with virtual environments. Those who had no such experience obtained worse results. The outcomes may therefore suggest that the length of prior English instruction is not an indicator of a possible improvement in linguistic competence. Once students are provided an appropriate online setting, as well as type, amount and quality of input, they may experience enhanced required language competences regardless of previous linguistic experience. This may be due to prior involvement and participation in online learning. As the evaluation showed, the learners held positive opinions about the online component. All the learners said that the quality of the resources was great, and they could provide better customer care owing to the online component. As suggested by some learners, modifications might include providing more technical instruction about tools and applications, focusing on specific case studies, or applying other teaching methods. As the log-on records on Canvas show, the students accessed the hand-held language instruction at different times and places. This may suggest that they enjoyed autonomy, being a part of an augmented classroom on Canvas, interacting with other learners online, viewing what others had done, and receiving feedback on their performance. This will have an impact on both the performance of the company and its individual employees.

Further to the above-mentioned conclusions, the proposed instructional model was found to be valuable in augmenting a regular English course with related online resources. It allowed the author to plan the whole teaching process. Moreover, it helped to identify the learning needs, name the objectives and resources, develop appropriate content, introduce and try out the virtual learning environment, and conduct classes. Eventually, it reminded the author to evaluate the whole intervention and provide follow-up resources for the learners to access after the study.

It is the author's belief that the foremost assets of the study are related to the indications that blending traditional classroom instruction with hand-held learning resources implemented in accordance with an instructional model can be an interesting augmentation to the known methods and techniques which might be beneficial for both learners and their environment. The limitations of the study might relate to a limited sample of participants, length of the study or the instructional model per se. Therefore, a further study is recommended which would include a larger sample of learners, examine their improvement over a longer period of time, use quantitative and qualitative research methods, or employ a different instructional model. As the retention stage is still in progress it is impossible to evaluate if it has served its purpose. Hence, another study of the very retention stage is suggested.

References

Arora, D., Lihitkar, S., & Roy, P. (2013). Virtual learning environment with open source software: MOODLE. *International Journal of Information Dissemination and Technology*, *3*(4), 254–259.

Bell, J., & Gower, R. (1998). Writing course materials for the world: A great compromise. In B. Tomlinson (Ed.), *Materials Development in Language Teaching* (pp. 135–150). Cambridge: Cambridge University Press.

Block, D. (1991). Some thoughts on DIY materials design. *ELT Journal, 45*(3), 211–217.

Bloom, B. S., Engelhart, M. D., Furst, E. J., Hill, W. H., & Krathwohl, D. R. (1956). *Taxonomy of educational objectives, handbook I: The cognitive domain.* New York: David McKay Co Inc.

Crawford, J. (2002). The role of materials in the language classroom: Finding a balance. In J. C. Richards & W. A. Renandya (Eds.), *Methodology in Language Teaching: An Anthology of Current Practice* (pp. 80–92). Melbourne, VIC: Cambridge University Press.

Crystal, D. (2001). *Language and the Internet.* Cambridge: Cambridge University Press.

Dale, E. (1969). *Audio-Visual Methods in Teaching* (3rd ed.). New York: Holt, Rinehart, and Winston.

Deming, D., Goldin, C., Katz, L., & Yuchtman, N. (2015). Can online learning bend the higher education cost curve? *American Economic Review: Papers & Proceedings, 105*(5), 496–501.

Dickey, M. (2005). Three-dimensional virtual worlds and distance learning: Two case studies of Active Worlds as a medium for distance education. *British Journal of Educational Technology, 36*(3), 439–451.

Gagné, R. (1985). *The Conditions of Learning and the Theory of Instruction* (4th ed.). New York: Holt, Rinehart, and Winston.

Gustafson, K., & Branch, R. (1997). Revisioning models of instructional development. *Education Technology Research and Development, 45*(3), 73–89.

Hołowiecki, M. (2014). Wykorzystanie e-learningu, jako formy kształcenia zdalnego na publicznych uczelniach wyższych w Polsce. *Lingua ac Communitas, 24*, 185–206.

Hyla, M. (2005). *Przewodnik po e-learningu*. Warszawa: Wolters Kluwer SA.

Jacob, S. M., & Issac, B. (2008). The mobile devices and its mobile learning usage analysis. *Proceedings of the International MultiConference of Engineers and Computer Scientists*. Hong Kong: IMECS.

Keegan, D. (2005). Mobile learning: A practical guide. Leonardo da Vinci programme of the European Commission. Available at https://www.ericsson.com/res/thecompany/docs/programs/incorporating_mobile_learning_into_mainstream_education/book.pdf (date of access: 2 September 2015).

Kim, S. H., Lee, L. J., & Thomas, M. K. (2012). Between purpose and method: A review of educational research on 3D virtual worlds. *Journal of Virtual Worlds Research, 5*(1), 1–18. Available at https://journals.tdl.org/jvwr/index.php/jvwr/article/view/2151/5973 (date of access: 5 June 2016).

Koller, D. (2012). Daphne Koller: What we're learning from online education. Available at https://www.ted.com/talks/daphne_koller_what_we_re_learning_from_online_education (date of access: 12 May 2016).

Kruk, M., & Pawlak, M. (2014). The use of Internet resources in developing autonomy in learning English pronunciation: A qualitative study. In M. Pawlak, J. Bielak, & A. Mystkowska-Wiertelak (Eds.), *Classroom-Oriented Research: Achievements and Challenges* (pp. 169–184). Heidelberg: Springer International Publishing.

Lam, Y., & Lawrence, G. (2002). Teacher-student role redefinition during a computer-based second language project: Are computers catalysts for empowering change? *Computer Assisted Language Learning, 15*(3), 295–315.

Littlejohn, A. (2011). The analysis of language teaching materials: Inside the Trojan Horse. In B. Tomlinson (Ed.), *Materials Development in Language Teaching* (pp. 179–211). Cambridge: Cambridge University Press.

Marczak, M., & Krajka, J. (2014). Electronic assessment tools in Learning Management Systems – Perceptions of student teachers of foreign languages. In E. Smyrnova-Trybulska (Ed.), *E-learning and Intercultural Competence Development in Different Countries* (pp. 265–278). Katowice, Cieszyn: Uniwersytet Śląski, UMCS.

McGrath, I. (2013). *Teaching Materials and the Roles of EFL/ESL Teachers: Practice and Theory*. London: Bloomsbury.

Minocha, S., & Roberts, D. (2008). Laying the groundwork for socialisation and knowledge construction within 3D virtual worlds. *ALT-J, Research in Learning Technology, 16*(3), 181–196.

Nunan, N. (1988). *Syllabus Design*. Oxford: Oxford University Press.

Reiser, R., & Dempsey, J. V. (2007). *Trends and Issues in Instructional Design and Technology*. Upper Saddle River, NJ: Pearson/Merrill Prentice Hall.

Richards, J., & Rodgers, T. (2001). *Approaches and Methods in Language Teaching* (2nd ed.). Cambridge: Cambridge University Press.

Rosenthal, J. (Ed.) (2000). *Handbook of Undergraduate Second Language Education*. Mahwah, NJ: Lawrence Erlbaum.

Ryder, M. (2005). *Theoretical Sources*. Available at http://carbon.cudenver.edu/~mryder/itc_data/theory.html (date of access: 5 May 2016).

Skinner, B. F. (1954). The science of learning and the art of teaching. *Harvard Educational Review, 24*, 86–97.

Skowron, J. (2006). *Powerful Lesson Planning: Every Teacher's Guide to Effective Instruction*. Thousand Oaks, CA: Corwin Press.

Smyrnova-Trybulska, E. (Ed.). (2014). *E-learning and Intercultural Competence Development in Different Countries*. Katowice, Cieszyn: Uniwersytet Śląski, UMCS.

Stecyk, A. (2008). *Abc eLearningu: System LAMS (Learning Activity Management System)*. Warszawa: Centrum Doradztwa i Informacji Difin.

Szerszeń, P. (2014). *Platformy (glotto)dydaktyczne: Ich implementacja w uczeniu specjalistycznych języków obcych*. Warszawa: Uniwersytet Warszawski.

Tomlinson, B. (1998). *Materials Development in Language Teaching*. Cambridge: Cambridge University Press.

Tomlinson, B. (2011). *Introduction: Principles and Procedures of Paterials Development*. Cambridge: Cambridge University Press.

Tomlinson, B., & Masuhara, H. (2010). Published research on materials development in language teaching. In B. Tomlinson & H. Masuhara (Eds.), *Research for Materials Development in Language Learning: Evidence for Best Practice* (pp. 1–21). London: Continuum.

Turula, A. (2014). Kiedy dydaktyka akademicka jest nowoczesna: o potrzebie dywersyfikacji kształcenia na odległość. *Kultura i Polityka, 16*, 45–63.

Ulam, S. (1958). John von Neumann, 1903–1957. *Bulletin of the American Mathematical Society, 64*, 1–49.

Warschauer, M., & Meskill, C. (2000). Technology and second language teaching and learning. In J. Rosenthal (Ed.), *Handbook of Undergraduate Second Language Education* (pp. 303–318). Mahwah, NJ: Lawrence Erlbaum.

Weller, M. (2005). *Virtual Learning Environments: Using, Choosing and Developing Your VLE*. London: Routledge.

Anita Buczek-Zawiła
Pedagogical University of Cracow, Cracow, Poland

Verifying the usefulness of mobile dictionaries for developing English pronunciation skills – users' reports and achievements

Abstract: Many online dictionaries incorporate information on the pronunciation of items in the form of IPA transcriptions and recordings. These hints, while generally useful, do not assist in developing fluent pronunciation and effortless comprehension of longer stretches of spoken text. A working knowledge of the reduced variants (weak forms) of a number of grammatical words is needed.

The *Oxford Advanced Learners Dictionary*[1] introduces users to this aspect of speech by listing the reduced variant before the strong pronunciation in the form of recording and transcription. This way, users immediately see the specificity of such items and recognize their contribution to communication.

An attempt to verify the usefulness and efficiency of such dictionary use for developing students' English pronunciation skills is reported on in this chapter. Two groups of advanced EFL learners received instruction in pronunciation, one in class, the other no class training, involving transcribing sentences and, as a result, being able to pronounce them accordingly. The second group was advised to seek dictionary assistance. The results achieved in the transcription tasks as well as in the oral production tasks indicate that a good mobile dictionary may be an asset when trying to develop one's oral skills holistically and satisfactorily.

Keywords: online dictionary, pronunciation training, strong and weak forms, connected speech, transcription

1. Introduction

> Perhaps the most obvious use of dictionaries in foreign language learning is as a way of accessing meanings of words, in the form of translations or definitions. But dictionaries have many other uses. Among other things, they are a valuable source of information about the pronunciation of words.
>
> (Bowen & Marks 1992: 14)

Online dictionaries, or, more precisely, any mobile dictionaries of foreign languages, most notably those of English, have steadily gained in popularity among

---

1 http://www.oxfordlearnersdictionaries.com/

users (Niewiadomski 2010; Levy & Steel 2015; Buczek-Zawiła 2016). Whenever students of a foreign language experience problems in their knowledge because of lexical gaps, it is only natural that they solve them by turning to reference works, especially dictionaries. These resources are usually able to resolve many of the questions students have, particularly those which pertain to lexical choices (Mueller & Jacobsen 2016). Among the plethora of these resources available, some have come to be used not only to provide lexicographic insights, but also to inform users of the spoken form of words. This is done chiefly in the form of recordings made available for users to listen to and emulate. Additionally, the IPA[2] transcription is made available in the majority of them. The exact conventions vary from dictionary to dictionary, but the divergences are easy to grasp and follow.

While both types of hints are undoubtedly useful for learning the spoken form of individual words, they do not assist in developing fluent pronunciation nor effortless comprehension of longer stretches of spoken text, commonly referred to as connected speech (Levis 2006; Barańska & Zając 2014). To achieve an easy understanding of connected speech, it is necessary to have both a working knowledge of a number of grammatical words along with considerable practice in their reduced variants. These simplifications, characteristically known as weak forms, are, arguably, one of the most important elements in the English spoken discourse. There are dictionaries, the *Oxford Advanced Learners Dictionary*[3] (henceforth OALD for convenience) among them, which actually introduces users to this aspect of speech. OALD not only lists the reduced variant alongside the regular, strong pronunciation in the form of a recording and transcription, but classifies the weak form as the major variant in the first place. This way, users immediately see the specificity of such items and recognize their contribution to communication. More so, they learn empirically that words may have alternate spoken forms, which are most probably dependent upon the phonetic environment they find themselves in within an utterance. For instance, the OALD entry for the modal verb *must* shows the desirable pronunciation of the item in IPA characters, supplementing the information with recordings. In the examples section it specifically highlights (in bold type print) the use of the item that would require the strong pronunciation.

Bowen and Marks (1992) argue for dictionary presence in pronunciation practice in the following manner:

---

2 Or some other written approximation of actual pronunciation – compare the simulated spelling in, among others, dictionary.reference.com

3 http://www.oxfordlearnersdictionaries.com/

> You can encourage learners to check pronunciation in the classroom by using their dictionaries. When the habit is established and the learners are familiar with the conventions used, they will be able to make use of this resource whenever they need it, in or out of the classroom. [...] Learners can be encouraged first to predict the pronunciation of problematic words, and then to use the dictionary as a checking device. The combination of these two approaches is a valuable contribution towards making learners independent in their dealings with English pronunciation.
>
> (Bowen & Marks 1992: 14)

An attempt to verify the usefulness and efficiency of such dictionary use for developing students' passive and active English pronunciation skills is reported on in this chapter. Two groups of advanced EFL speakers of English received instruction in pronunciation. Part of this training involved acquiring the skill of transcribing longer stretches of speech and, as a result, being able to pronounce them accordingly. One group was carefully and repeatedly instructed in the form and use of the strong and weak forms in class. The other group received no such training – save the general introduction to the matter – but was advised to use the dictionary specified above. Over the period of two and a half months the two groups then performed similar tasks focused on producing connected speech. The results achieved by students indicate that a good mobile dictionary may be an asset when trying to develop one's oral skills holistically and satisfactorily. Users' self-reports also suggest that such an asset must not be blindly followed; the guidance and supervision of a human pedagogue is still required.

Computer assisted language learning (CALL) has raised substantial hopes among educators as to the assistance it can offer in the area of both effective and attractive foreign language instruction. Sound technological tools are particularly suited here as they provide accessible, individualized instruction, also through auditory discrimination and repetition tasks, automatic visual support which allows learners to try to approximate closely the set standard, even though lacking in giving students adequate, accurate and meaningful feedback (Lewis 2007). Even more to the point, mobile-assisted education via various portable devices and apps makes developing various language skills more facilitated, relying on continuity of learning across different physical settings and contexts (Kukulska-Hulme 2013). Mobile devices, which by definition are personal tools that in addition to their primary functions can also support self-directed forms of language learning, can stimulate relatively little enthusiasm for learning the language to grow. Among the skills that are reported to be successfully developed and improved via mobile-assisted language learning (MALL) practices are speaking and pronunciation.

While technologically-enhanced pronunciation instruction undoubtedly exhibits flexibility and incorporates valuable varied instructional modes, it is also true that it comprises certainly more or less evident difficulties in terms of pedagogical measures, technological limitations and teacher-preparedness. Of these three, the first one is the particular concern of this study, yet, the remaining two are believed to be significant in contributing to the quality and effectiveness of instruction.

The major concern as to the pedagogical goals is that the fascination with the potential of new technological applications may lead to ignoring sound pedagogical principles of language (and pronunciation) instruction, in effect driving the technological advances to the detriment of pedagogical criteria otherwise beneficial to the learner (Busá 2007: 165). Accordingly, this study aims to explore the degree to which the recommended use of specific online dictionary can assist in developing comfortable fluency in decoding and producing sound reductions characteristic of connected speech utterances. It also asks about the opinions of online dictionary users pertaining to the perceived facilitative or hindering effects of such (self) instructional resources.

2. Review of literature

2.1 Why focus on connected speech?

Since this chapter's focus is the use of online dictionaries as assistance in developing fluent oral skills, it makes sense to outline the arguments in favour of practicing continuous speech rather than individual sounds or words.

Even in the early days of principled foreign language teaching, the focus on the discrimination and articulation of sounds was considered to be a vital way of improving the perception and production of L2 sounds (Reszkiewicz 1984; Bowen & Marks 1992). In later, more communication-oriented approaches to language teaching, the key role of pronunciation in improving learners' oral skills was widely recognized, also in relation to its contribution to ensuring the success of oral communication. If comfortable intelligibility in a foreign language is the goal of an average learner, they must become aware of which components of the foreign language play a role in the intelligibility of spoken language. Quite apart from what is commonly believed, discriminating and producing foreign sounds is crucial. Busá (2007: 167) reports here on the significance of such elements as differences in speech rate, pitch prominence, pitch range, length and location of pauses in the perception of L2 fluency and speech. Strategies for appropriate vowel and syllable production need therefore to be acquired as well. Levis (2006: 245) expresses these aspects in the following manner: "L2 speakers can be both very advanced in most elements of speaking ability and still be unintelligible due to pronunciation errors". Poor pronunciation, then, is identified with low intelligibility, or, at least, understood as the major factor contributing to communication inadequacy or failure.

Prosodic features affect the perception and production of L2 speech also because of their fundamental role in speech communication. Cross (1995) therefore postulates making classroom speech more like normal speech and thus equipping students to understand spoken English more easily. He believes the various prosodies must be made a focus of language use, practice and correction from the very beginning, especially so because these features of connected speech are still listed as those that need to be rated during oral production tests.[4] One of the features that makes speech in English sound "normal" is the rhythm. To produce rhythmic speech learners must be able to control the feature of vowel reduction. In English, the key words, those that carry message content and so receive emphasis, will characteristically contain one syllable that is stressed and where the vowel retains its full quality. The vowels elsewhere in the word or utterance are usually weakened or reduced. In this sense the existence of the so called weak forms should come as no surprise, and their production should present no special difficulty. This is especially so in the light of the fact that most grammatical (function) words are almost always weakened, typically pronounced with a weak schwa sound (or other short 'weak' vowel like the [ɪ]), unless they are stressed for some special reason.[5] Weak forms are actually the more frequent realisations of function words in English. Characteristically, then:

> [a]s compared with the accented realizations of [function] words (the [strong] forms), the unaccented [weak] forms of these words show reductions of the length of sounds, obscuration of vowels towards /ə, ɪ, ʊ/ and the elision of vowels and consonants.
>
> (Cruttenden 2008: 266)

As regards L2 speakers' realisations of this pronunciation feature, Barańska and Zając (2014) report on studies of nonnative speakers' abilities to reduce function words which suggest that while proficient learners are able to pronounce function words with shorter length than content words, they rarely use reduced vowels in them.

4 "The speaking portion of the Cambridge Certificate of Proficiency in English (CPE) and related tests still use pronunciation as a rated category, with specific mention made of stress, rhythm, intonation and individual sounds" (Levis 2006: 246).

5 Exceptionally, to communicate more meaning or more contrast than in actual words, speakers will choose to emphasize the function word, in such cases, naturally, there is no vowel weakening.

We need to emphasize, then, that we talk here of a system rather than details of realization, and listeners can tune in to such variability without much difficulty, first at the level of conscious recognition and then production. Rhythm of sentences, especially the placement, regularity, and length of intervals between stresses, may be one of the most important indicators of an L2 learner's accent (Rogerson-Revell 2011; Szpyra-Kozłowska 2015). Therefore, they need to be able to learn to hear and ultimately produce the prosodic patterns objectively, as if defying the already-internalized L1 categories. That will lead to operating factors such as L2 pitch range and levels of stress and prominence in their oral productions of L2 syllables and utterances. In the words of Busá (2007: 167): "prosody is what glues sounds in words and words in utterances. It is through prosody that speakers prioritize information, signal emphasis, disambiguate sentences, make meaning in context". Therefore, elements such as segmental duration or rhythmic patterns must be practiced and eventually acquired if they are to contribute to successful communication.

2.2 The pedagogy of pronunciation instruction: some remarks

It has been observed in recent years that the new approaches to teaching of pronunciation are more balanced in focus, with actually more emphasis placed on pitch, stress, rhythm, co-articulation and intonation, and how these are combined to communicate the intended meaning. The general goal now is to achieve comprehensible speech for better overall L2 speech performance. The comparatively new impulse for teaching those aspects has come from various instantiations of technology.

Keeping up with innovations is one of the important challenges that teachers at all levels face in the constantly changing educational scene. Needless to say, teachers must play a part in the result as active agents in the process of change and implementation of new ideas and new practices. Teachers' beliefs and attitudes may support or adversely affect the success of any educational or curricular endeavours, including the use of innovative technology programs. In ideal circumstances, the instructor will act as a guide leading their learners to autonomous extensive out-of-class practice of pronunciation, executed with the help of new technologies and digital tools. It is too common a fact that many teachers are unable to "make effective use of applications because of both lack of training in pronunciation and in the use of technology" (Levis 2007: 185).

Even if the trainer competence is there, what seems more elusive are the actual goals to be achieved as well as the instructional practices to be implemented. Technology – in this case available online lexical resources – acts as a tool, and this tool needs to be appropriate for the specific job, in our case the clearly specified pedagogical requirements. Out of the several principles with which technological materials and applications should be designed that were defined by Pennington (Levis 2007: 187), two appear particularly relevant to the present discussion:

- link pronunciation to other aspects of communication,
- raise users' awareness of how their L1 phonological systems differ from the system of the target language.

Extensive practice in various aspects of connected speech takes care of the first objective: L2 learners find out about the ways in which various reductions and contact phenomena impact comprehensibility and intelligibility among interlocutors. They become aware that there is more to conveying meaning than the words and the structures used, also in contradistinction to what their native language prompts them to apply. They learn to perceive and later to emulate the finer details of utterances which supplement the message conveyed at the lexical plane. Because of technology assistance, they can do it in private, relatively stress-free conditions.

In addition, the design of the present study was such as to fulfill another of Pennington's goals: setting measurable goals and performance targets. The end product of the course of actions taken was to facilitate the acquisition of natural speech features of advanced learners of English. The naturalness aimed at involved working on features such as vowel reductions and other simplifications in the unstressed portions of utterances so that the normal and natural sentence rhythm should emerge. The goal and the target were clear, and the achievement was measurable in a series of tasks.

All this calls for a good degree of pedagogical explicitness, which excludes the idea that we have an application, a technological element which, for one, simply uses a new medium to do the same sort of exercise, and two, does it as if on its own, without pedagogical grounding. One such sound pedagogical requirement to be met is that the instruction proceeds according to the demand (= pull) – technology (= push) chain, and not vice versa. Another one is that not all errors can be treated equally in their impact on listeners – some impact understanding more than others. Prioritizing some elements will contribute to the users' ability to understand at the micro level of word identification and at the communicative level of meaning processing.

The threads and issues explored up to this point, when brought together, lead to formulating the following major and minor aims of the study:

1. To verify the actual usefulness and efficiency of using a designated online lexical resource for developing the users' specific fluency of speech sub-skill as evident in the extensive and consistent production of weak forms in connected speech.

2. To examine the attitudes and preferences among dictionary users via survey tools.
3. To examine the awareness raising potential of the specific tool via survey tool and users' self-report.
4. To establish whether an easily accessible online utility tool can effectively replace the presence of a pedagogue in regards to the target area of pronunciation.

3. The study: Usefulness and effectiveness of mobile dictionaries for developing English pronunciation skills

The fundamental idea underpinning this study is that dictionaries are utility tools which can meet special types of needs. The need defined here is possessing a reliable reference source for verifying the pronunciation of words and longer stretches of speech. The efficiency and satisfaction of dictionary users is measured here via an inspection of their developing and increasing skills in transcribing longer portions of continuous speech phonetically and through tasks checking their oral performance, which involve the production of randomly pre-selected sentences. Additionally, both areas were probed via a survey which examined users' attitudes and opinions.

We follow here the assumption of Barańska and Zając (2014: 282) that, given that the L1 (Polish) sound system has a considerable influence on a learner's L2 productions, it seems safe to assume that realising English function words as unstressed and reduced may prove problematic for Polish learners. Therefore, the focus of the research was on the students' understanding and producing of the reduced variants of function words, known as weak forms as evidenced in their (increasing) transcription skills as well as in oral production tasks of reading a selection of sentences containing the targeted reduced forms. The expected outcome of the procedures is the achievement of greater fluency and effectiveness of communication in English, combined with a more conscious and reflective use of online dictionaries or related mobile apps.

3.1 The subjects and the design

The present study represents a stage in a more comprehensive investigation into the online/mobile dictionary usage patterns for developing text-to-speech skills of learners. Part 1 of the study was completed in October 2015 and the findings were reported on in Buczek-Zawiła (2016).[6] It pertained to establishing the tendencies

6 This part concerned the use of online dictionaries as such; it did not investigate their specific impact on improving (or otherwise) users' pronunciation.

for choosing a particular online dictionary among advanced EFL speakers based on the observations and users' reports. With the growing competence in English they begin to appreciate the ideas that underline the meaningfulness of attention paid equally to the meaning as well as to the form. The opinions forwarded in anonymous questionnaires indicate that a good online dictionary may be an asset in developing lexical knowledge as well as better pronunciation, thus making EFL learners more aware dictionary users.

This time the focus was on verifying the usefulness and effectiveness of one such dictionary, OALD, and more specifically its pronunciation component, for developing fluent and comfortable connected speech as evidenced in the production of reduced variants of certain grammatical words, known as weak forms. This is to be achieved through a small-scale and cross-sectional non-longitudinal class research, to be followed by a short supplementary survey, probing into the participants attitudes and opinions.

Fifty-three subjects participated in the study, but only 31 eventually filled in the survey (part 2) and sent it back. The 32 participants who did the survey following the study were the ones who actually used the designated online tool in their learning experience, as directed by the tutor. It could not be established for certain that the other students know and use the tool; they were consequently excluded from the survey. All participants were freshmen students in the English Studies Department in Kraków, among them 32 were day students, 21 weekend ones. The reasons behind choosing this particular group are connected with aspects such as their age (19–21 – save for a few cases among the weekend group), command of English (above the FCE[7] level), and being (at a minimum) tech-comfy to tech-savvy. Including both day and weekend students as participants stems from a different study pattern that they follow: different amounts of contact hours, greater needs in terms of reliable and instantly available resource, etc. It has to be stated at the outset, though, that the differences in their performance were negligible, and, accordingly, this factor is not taken into account as a separate variable. It is, therefore, assumed that all of them fall into the group of keen online dictionary users, unafraid of new technological applications and constantly at work on developing their English language skills.

Additionally, in the curriculum for year 1 students in the English Department, there is a Practical Phonetics course, comprising, correspondingly, 90/54 hours of instruction for both day and weekend students. One of the components of the course is the IPA transcription module, which requires students to become skilled

7 FCE – stands for the Cambridge First Certificate in English.

in reading and producing phonetic transcriptions of individual words as well as longer utterances and dialogues.

Part of their regular practice is to produce transcribed versions of dialogues or practice sentences for homework. This was accompanied by consistently monitoring the students' homework, frequently pointing out obvious and/or recurring mistakes, and unfailingly supporting their efforts to improve.

The transcribing sort of activity is then reinforced by oral practice of sentences organized into back-chained drills, available in IPA-transcription, and recorded, as per the resources publisher.[8] Sometime towards the end of the semester, minimally after 40 hours of instruction, the students' achievement and progress are evaluated in a series of oral tasks, where they have to produce sets of words and later sets of sentences as accurately and as naturally as they are able. Besides assuring a wealth of material for analysis, the oral practice of sentences as well as the evaluation of the students' progress did not disturb the regular educational process.

For the purposes of the research, the students were divided into two research groups, each consisting of both day and extramural students, in approximately the same proportions. These are their regular college groups to which they had been arbitrarily assigned at the beginning of the academic year. Group 1, consisting of 22 members (14 day and 8 weekend students respectively), were introduced to the subject using printed material[9] only. The material was meticulously discussed by the teacher together with relevant examples. In their case no online resource was specifically recommended or encouraged. The second group of 31 members (18 day and 13 weekend) received a short introduction to the matter while the printed material was recommended for self-study as reference. Instead, the tutor insisted on the students' use of the OALD for all transcription homework with checks on *every* word, including the grammatical ones. The most significant variable in this part of the study was then the different instructional design into weak forms production, coupled with the introduction of OALD as the didactic help.

3.2 Material collected

During the period of approximately two and a half months, the tutor collected written samples from seven homework tasks that the participants in both groups

8 As they appear in one of the handbooks used for the course; cf. Mańkowska et al. (2009).

9 The printed material referred to here is the relevant chapter from Reszkiewicz (1984: 138–148), on occasion supplemented by explanations and examples from Bałutowa (1999: 118ff). The latter is written in Polish, it may occasionally be more accessible to certain students.

did as part of regular class. An example, relating specifically to weak forms practice, is shown in Figure 1 for illustration. This sample comes from one of the better students in the group.

Figure 1: A homework sample from a high-scoring student.

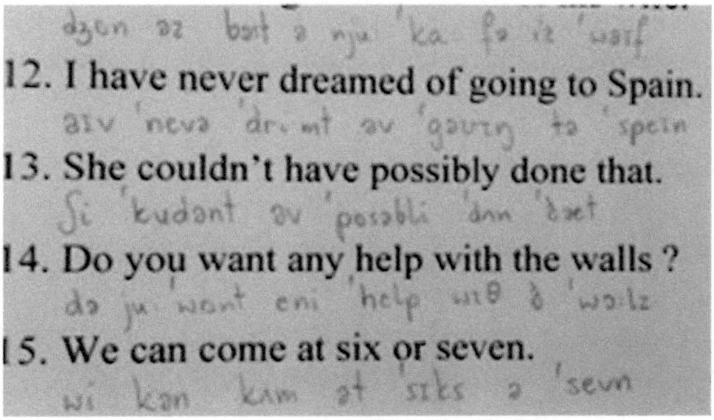

A random but representative selection of students' contributions were analyzed and the mistakes counted. The representation was achieved through ensuring that the same number of samples for each homework task was collected in each of the groups, and that the samples came from high, average and low-scorers. Randomization on the other hand was achieved by collecting samples of different tasks from different participants; that is, it is never the case that one person's complete set of contributions was subjected to the analysis. Both followed largely intuitive and impromptu selection decisions. The results summary is presented in Table 1.

Table 1: Homework tasks results

HOMEWORK TASK	Weak forms TYPES	Weak forms TOKENS	AVERAGE SCORE (%)		
			Total	Group 1	Group 2
[æ] dialogue	14	37	45%	47%	43%
[ɪ] dialogue	11	28	48%	45%	51%
[i:] dialogue	15	36	58%	50%	66%
[ɔ:] dialogue	19	37	78%	64%	92%
-es ending sentences	13	50	70%	63%	77%
-ed ending sentences	16	52	74%	64%	84%
Strong & Weak forms sentences	22	45	80%	74%	86%

The homework tasks are listed in the order they were actually completed by the participants during the course. It is also evident in the progressively higher scores achieved.

When the course was approaching its end, the subjects had to take an oral production task. The task was comprised of 10–12 sentences to be read at a natural pace with *no new* (emphasis mine) lexical items in them - a task listed already as one of the assessment requirements. Figure 2 shows a sample of the oral task sentence reading.

Figure 2: A sample of rater's notes on the oral task.

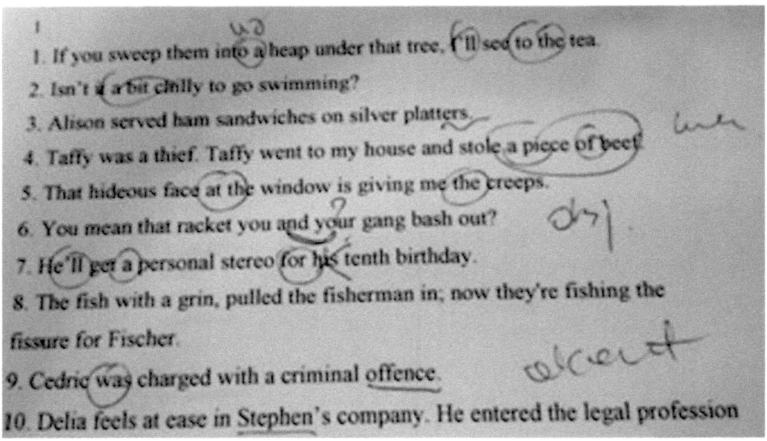
1. If you sweep them into a heap under that tree, I'll see to the tea.
2. Isn't it a bit chilly to go swimming?
3. Alison served ham sandwiches on silver platters.
4. Taffy was a thief. Taffy went to my house and stole a piece of beef.
5. That hideous face at the window is giving me the creeps.
6. You mean that racket you and your gang bash out?
7. He'll get a personal stereo for his tenth birthday.
8. The fish with a grin, pulled the fisherman in; now they're fishing the fissure for Fischer.
9. Cedric was charged with a criminal offence.
10. Delia feels at ease in Stephen's company. He entered the legal profession

Increased attention to language form, as insisted upon by the instructors and the raters, seems to have caused the participants to realise a good deal of function words as unstressed, though not necessarily completely reduced. The summary of the results from the oral task, together with non-parametric statistical validation with the T-test and chi-square test are tabulated for easier reference in Table 2.

Table 2: Oral tasks results

ORAL TASK PERFORMANCE	WF TOKENS (AVERAGE)	AVERAGE SCORE OF CORRECT PRODUCTION	SD	CHI SQUARE: *5.185* T-TEST: *-5.2758* P-VALUE: *0.022*
Group 1	35	25,72	4.11	
Group 2	36	31.03	2.72	

The average maximum score for a sentence reading task was 35 in group 1 and 36 in group 2. The scoring was performed on a scale 0 to 1, where 0 stands for no weak form reduction where expected or the form incorrectly realised. 1 was allocated in instances of weak form token realisation. Tokens were taken into account rather than types, since it is the consistency of use that was the instructional aim.

The table demonstrates a slightly higher rate of weak form realisations for the participants in group 2, those that were specifically instructed in the use of online/mobile OALD dictionary. The scale applied here is semi-nominal, that is it is the ratio of good to bad performances that is of interest here. That is why, rather than conducting a complex multivariate analysis, a simple test of good to bad answers was performed with specific numerical values entered into the contingency table for the chi-square validation. The relatively high chi-square result (coupled with low p-value) testify to the relatedness between the specific instructional procedure used and the result obtained. Namely, it appears that the way in which those reduced forms are taught (with or without the use of OALD) and the scores on the tests are not independent of each other. There is then a significant difference in terms of our sample students' achievement.

3.3 Users' reports

For examining the attitudes and preferences among dictionary users, survey tools are commonly applied, as they help to find out what the users actually think and do with dictionaries, even if the findings remain indirect by recording what users believe happen as opposed to what actually takes place (Tono 2001: 67). Consequently, following the success of the first part of the survey (Buczek-Zawiła 2016), a questionnaire consisting of three major questions was used with participants to meet the demand for reliable empirical information on how online dictionaries are actually being used for developing text to speech skills of participants. First, the participants from both groups were reminded of one of the questions from Part 1: "You are always encouraged by your tutors to use the dictionaries to the fullest extent. In what way did they help you in developing your pronunciation?" A selection of responses offered by them was presented in a tabulated form so that they could reflect on the ideas they had earlier. Their opinions were grouped into three subcategories: those related to audio material available in numerous online dictionaries and related mobile applications, the aspects related to the IPA transcription included there, and finally attention and awareness raising motives.

The participants reported that, on the whole, they stand by their earlier opinions, even if the ones shown in the table were not their own. It should be borne in mind, though, that these answers related to their use of *any* online dictionary, not the specific one (the OALD) which acted as the variable in the research. The questions for Part 2 of the survey, for obvious reasons, could only be addressed to the participants that actually used the OALD for their homework exercises and for class practice. After the interviews with the 31 respondents from group 2, the researcher believes that by that stage in the course the respondents had become more conscious and more mature users of online lexical resources.

Question 1 of the survey was the following: "How did OALD assist you in grasping the idea of weak forms and their use?" The question directed the respondents to the focus area of the study: the weak forms and to the variable, the specific online tool. The comments volunteered by the respondents can easily be grouped into those stressing the positive influence and functionality of the tool and into those regarding the problems encountered. A selection of responses is quoted in Table 3.

Table 3: Respondents' comments to the potential functionality of OALD for weak forms acquisition

POSITIVE INFLUENCE	PROBLEM AREAS
I didn't realize it has entries for small words such as prepositions, pronouns or modals	It doesn't say that the reduced variant is found in unstressed syllables
The most striking feature: the reduced variant listed first, both for BrE and AmE	Without the constant reminder from the tutor I wouldn't always go for the form listed first
Audio files reflect the schwa in the weak form, so I can see it and hear it	It takes some of the responsibility from me, I copy what is there without much thinking
It makes me think that perhaps the reduced form is actually more frequent than the full one	I always need to combine the IPA with the audio – it is a nuisance
It helps to fight the misconceptions that I have, e.g. that words are always pronounced the same	I am not exactly sure when it is that the "edge of an utterance" plays a role. The dictionary doesn't help here
I don't need to refer to other sources, all I need for content and for grammatical words is there	

If one of the major benefits of replacing traditional print materials with online resources is the functionality and usability of the latter (Levy & Steel 2015), then it appears that the study participants are well aware of these benefits. The students' comments provide evidence that for them, the online dictionary (or the related mobile app), while instantly and easily accessible, not only provided sufficient input, but it actually enhanced their competence in the area of weak forms. The negative comments show that at the same time they have become more efficient and more aware consumers of online resources, conscious of the limitations of such resources. They also testify to the necessary presence of the pedagogue to explain the more intricate cases. What transpires from these responses is that in comparison to traditional sources, the online/mobile ones are perceived as more flexible, easier or more comprehensive (cf. the findings of Levy & Steel 2015).

Question 2 required the respondents to rate nine aspects related to pronunciation work with the help of OALD on a 6-point[10] Likert scale, where 0 would mean not useful at all, while 5 meant very useful. As a follow up, in question 3 they were asked to create a personal ranking of the same aspects regarding the use of an online version of OALD in pronunciation practice according to usefulness and importance. The most important criterion was placed highest and the least important in the lowest position. The features to be rated and ranked are listed below:

a. IPA transcription as homework help
b. Audio pronunciation file as homework help
c. IPA transcription as pronunciation guide
d. Audio pronunciation file as pronunciation guide
e. Weak form awareness raiser
f. Weak form practice guide
g. Audio files as input to home repetition based practice
h. Help in deciphering connected speech transcriptions used for class practice
i. Facilitator of class practice through exposure to reduced variants of function words.

The relative usefulness of aspects of OALD-enhanced work regarding improving pronunciation is depicted in Figure 3.

10 The selection of the scale from 0 to 5 rather than 1 to 5 was dictated by the need to try and convert other results, defined in percentage, to a comparable scale.

Figure 3: Mean rating of the usefulness of selected OALD-enhanced aspects of pronunciation work.

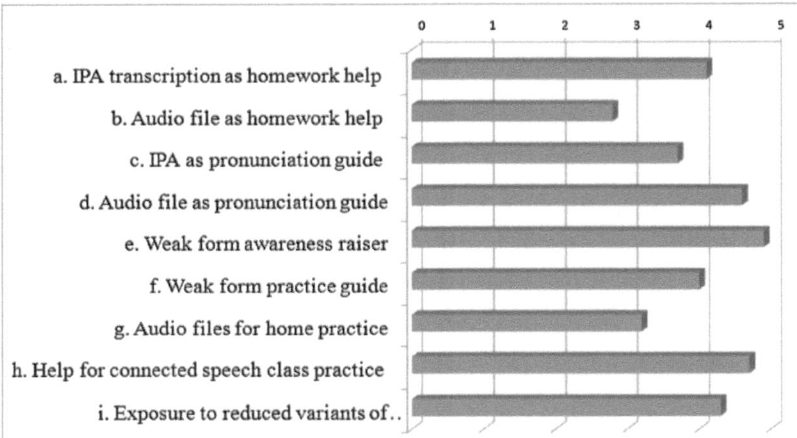

Figure 4 on the other hand illustrates the personal ranking of the same pronunciation-related elements as reported by the participants (group 2). It demonstrates that although there were individual differences regarding particular elements, all of them were ranked very high, with the mean trend line between 70 and 80%. The sole exceptions seem to be item b): audio files as homework help and g): audio files for home practice. It appears the subjects are not prepared at this stage of their language learning to rely substantially on the audio material. This can conceivably be attributed to somewhat under-developed phonemic hearing abilities, a prerequisite to correct sound discrimination and ultimately production (Komorowska 2002).

Figure 4: Personal ranking of usefulness of selected elements of OALD-enhanced pronunciation work.

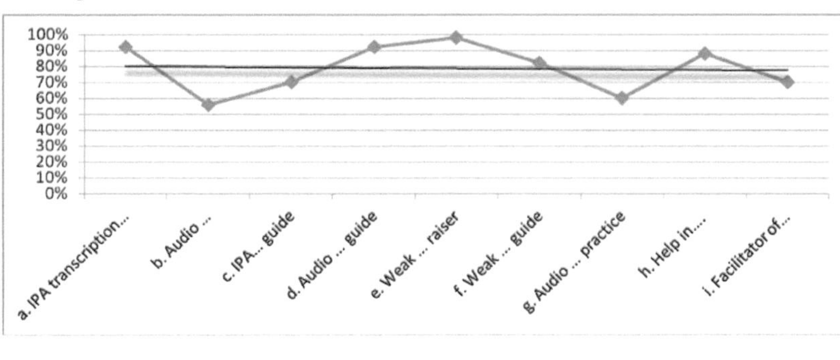

The ranking of the same selected aspects is believed to show significant similarities to the rating, so that a clear correlation between the usefulness and the ranking is observed. Figure 5 combines the outcomes of the two questions in a graphical form. In order to be able to place them on the same scale for clearer comparison, the results shown in Figure 3 have been converted to match the scale range of a Likert scale. The information in Figure 4 is expressed in percentages, which, when converted to numerical values give us the scale range value from 0 to 1. To match them to the 0 to 5 Likert scale range, each result was multiplied by 5 according to a simple proportion. This allows us to place the two result lines on the same graph with the same scale for the point of comparison. Both the subjective perception of OALD usefulness measured in the Likert Scale as well as the ranking of the same aspects produced a similar outcome, as the trace lines help to discern (cf. Figure 5 below). Descriptively expressed, the analysis of ratings reveals that the aspect that stands out as the most important/useful is that the pronunciation portion included in an online version of OALD acts as an awareness raiser when it comes to weak forms.

Figure 5: Correlation between the ranking and the usefulness rating of OALD as used for weak form practice.

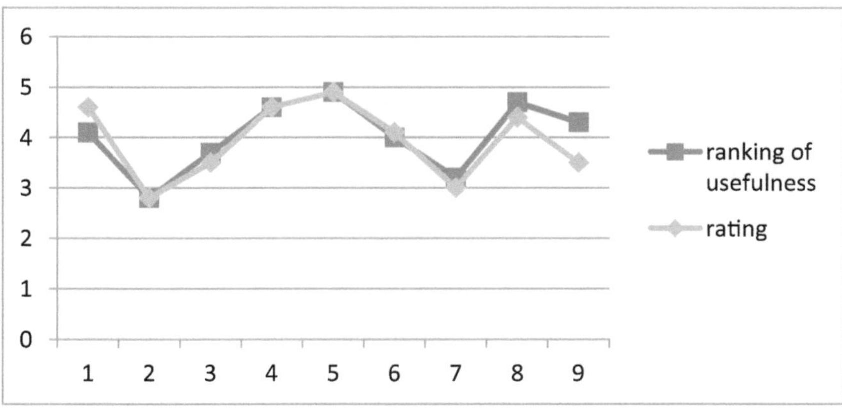

The emerging themes and actual statements from the respondents give ground for claiming that the group 2 participants, on the whole, adopted positive attitudes towards the specific merit of online dictionary use, namely the multimedia/IPA pronunciation information.

3.4 Discussion

Overall, the results of the study suggest that the mobile/online dictionary is now a tool of high usability and functionality, very popular among language learners. For the participants, OALD appears to be tailored to their specific needs and skills. The evidence available from the study invites some optimism with respect to the effectiveness and usefulness of online dictionary use for developing fluent oral skills in its users.

Taken together, the combined results of the homework activities and oral production tasks suggest that the amount of attention paid to speech form may have a considerable bearing on the learners' phonetic performance. As Barańska and Zając (2014: 281) warn, language learners may succeed in producing a given target language form in a controlled context but be less accurate or fail to do so in real life communication when the focus is on meaning transmission. The results accorded with what was assumed initially, namely that for the development of oral and aural accuracy and fluency, the online resource (OALD) would prove useful in both the users' and the tutors' opinions.

The participants' opinions accord with previous findings related to online/electronic/mobile dictionary use (Niewiadomski 2010; Dashtestani 2013; Levy & Steel 2015). They indicate a general positive attitude towards the presence of mobile tools for learning EFL in EFL contexts. Users also generally appreciate highly the pronunciation portion as included in OALD; the transcriptions and the multimedia as well as the possibility of immediately confronting the two. That is believed to help contextualize their learning (Niewiadomski 2010: 282). Users stress the usability and the functionality of the tool, especially when used on wideband-internet-access smartphones, which allow availability at the convenience of the users whenever a specific need arises.

The tutors' perspective takes a mildly less enthusiastic turn; they stress that actually the performance of the participants in the two groups showed no dramatic difference. This absence of unequivocal advantage in the group that used OALD for weak forms practice may stem from several factors.

First of all, it cannot be determined for certain that the participants in the other group did not make use of the same tool. No ban on its use was issued. In light of the comparative novelty of specific pronunciation training taking place in the Practical Phonetics course, pertaining also to IPA transcription, it would be very surprising if the participants relied on the teacher's instructions, printed materials, and their own perception intuitions only. Dictionary consultation must have been the order of the day – though it was perhaps not as intense as in the case of the OALD-users group.

Another factor could be that the task formality itself may have been responsible for the increased accuracy and subjects using more target like forms.[11] In that sense the advantageous effect of OALD – or other materials – could be obscured. This controlled formal context supported the attention to form in the students' performance. They were fully aware that the evaluation constituted a part of the requirements they needed to fulfill to pass the course and thus were prompted to use more target language forms.

Finally, for all participants, the specific task format may have had a bearing. Many of the participants at times exhibited more "strong" realisations in the sentence *reading* tasks and that could be accounted for by the effect of orthography.

It is therefore impossible to decisively qualify the use of online version of OALD as a strong advantage or a mildly beneficial influence. A better grounded designation may only be possible when analysing the long-term effect of the training the participants have received. Such an analysis would provide insights into the retention of the oral skills acquired. While this is true, it is also too much to ask of one study. The small sample size and therefore the limited statistical power, combined with not measuring effect size, can be cited as limitations of the results. These could also be useful in calculating an ideal sample size.

However, returning to the earlier table, it looks like there was improvement in both groups over time. This could speak to the above statement regarding the relative uncertainty as to the usefulness and effectiveness of a particular online/ mobile dictionary use for that particular context. Another factor could be that the task formality itself may have been responsible for the increased accuracy and subjects using more targetlike forms in a test-like situation.

It is entirely possible that the participants will continue consulting OALD in their learning. The users' self-reports indicate strongly that the much appreciated versatility and accessibility of online dictionaries make them especially attractive to the target population of users. The OALD and other such sources will, however, remain a technological tool available everywhere but still relatively useless without proper didactic measures.

4. Concluding remarks

Many technological tools are being developed to assist learners in achieving good communicative competence in an L2. The diverse pedagogic possibilities for

11 Though there are studies in which increased accuracy was not significantly correlated with increased task formality – see the review and the findings in Barańska and Zając (2014).

language learning offered by MALL have been identified before (Traxler 2013). This chapter has reviewed the ways in which online dictionary-assisted instruction can be used to enhance L2 pronunciation teaching and learning. The results of this pilot study demonstrate that using the pronunciation portion of mobile dictionaries to develop and ultimately improve students' oral skills makes sense. Their learning environment is enriched with a novel element, and as a result their learning experiences became richer as well. Yet, caution must be exercised here, as without the active participation of teachers, no computer technology can have a significant effect on students' achievements. Teachers are and must be the main agents in implementing any computer/mobile technology.

Studies show that looking up several different types of information in a dictionary supports vocabulary retention (Töpel 2014). Dictionary user behaviour involves more than that. This chapter ventured to verify the usefulness of online dictionaries for developing more accurate and more fluent speech. It is the belief of the author that such text plus technology transfer to speech is made possible precisely through the use of online lexicographic tools.[12]

References

Baldry, A., Pavesi, M., Taylor Torsello, C., & Taylor, C. (Eds.). (2007). *From DIDACTAS to eCoLingua: An Ongoing Research Project on Translation and Corpus Linguistics.* Trieste: Edizioni Universitá.

Bałutowa, B. (1999). *Wymowa angielska.* Warszawa: Philip Wilson.

Barańska, A., & Zając, M. (2014). The influence of attention to language form on the production of weak forms by Polish learners of English. *Research in Language, 12*(3), 279–290.

Bowen, T., & Marks, J. (1992). *The Pronunciation Book. Student-centred Activities for Pronunciation Work.* London: Longman.

Buczek-Zawiła, A. (2016). Why online dictionaries (plural) make you more open when developing English pronunciation skills – users' self-reports. In M. Marczak & J. Krajka (Eds.), *CALL for Openness* (pp. 123–144). Frankfurt am Main: Peter Lang.

Busá, M. G. (2007). New Perspectives in Teaching Pronunciation. In: A. Baldry, M. Pavesi, C. Taylor Torsello, & C. Taylor (Eds.), *From DIDACTAS to eCoLingua:*

12 No references are made to the use and effects thereof of PED (personal electronic dictionaries) or similar apps. It appears, though, that similar behaviours and tendencies should occur.

an ongoing research project on translation and corpus linguistics (pp. 171–188). Trieste: Edizioni Universitá.

Cross, D. (1995). *A Practical Handbook of Language Teaching*. Hemel Hempstead: Phoenix ELT.

Cruttenden, A. (2008). *Gimson's Pronunciation of English*. London: Hodder Education.

Dashtestani, R. (2013). EFL teachers' and students' perspectives on the use of electronic dictionaries for learning English. *Computer-Assisted Language Learning – Electronic Journal, 14*(2), 51–65.

Hughes, R. (Ed.). (2006). *Spoken English, applied linguistics and TESOL: Challenges for theory and practice*. New York: Palgrave Macmillan.

Komorowska, H. (2002). *Sprawdzanie umiejętności w nauce języka obcego*. Warszawa: Fraszka Edukacyjna.

Kukulska-Hulme, A. (2013). Re-skilling Language Learners for a Mobile World. Monterey. CA: The International Research Foundation for English Language Education. Available at: http://www.tirfonline.org/english-in-the-workforce/mobile-assisted-language-learning/ (date of access: 29 August 2017).

Levis, J. (2006). Pronunciation and the assessment of spoken language. In R. Hughes (Ed.), *Spoken English, Applied Linguistics and TESOL: Challenges for Theory and Practice* (pp. 245–270). New York: Palgrave Macmillan.

Levis, J. (2007). Computer technology in teaching and researching pronunciation. *Annual Review of Applied Linguistics, 27*, 184–202.

Levy, M., & Steel, C. (2015). Language learner perspectives on the functionality and use of electronic language dictionaries. *ReCALL, 27*(2), 177–196.

Mańkowska, A., Nowacka, M., & Kłoczowska, M. (2009). *How much wood could a woodchuck chuck? English pronunciation practice book*. Kraków, Rzeszów, Zamość: Wydawnictwo Konsorcjum Akademickie.

Marczak, M., & Krajka, J. (Eds.). (2016). *CALL for Openness*. Frankfurt am Main: Peter Lang.

Mueller, C. M., & Jacobsen, N. D. (2016). A comparison of the effectiveness of EFL students' use of dictionaries and an online corpus for the enhancement of revision skills. *ReCALL, 28*(1), 3–21.

Müller-Spitzer, C. (Ed.). (2014). *Using online dictionaries*. Berlin, Boston: De Gruyter.

Niewiadomski, K. (2010). Zastosowanie nowoczesnych telefonów komórkowych jako pomocy dydaktycznej w nauce fonetyki języka angielskiego. In M. Pawlak & E. Waniek-Klimczak (Eds.), *Mówienie w języku obcym – sukcesy i porażki uczenia się i nauczania* (pp. 277–285). Poznań, Kalisz, Konin: Wydawnictwo UAM.

Pawlak, M., & Waniek-Klimczak, E. (Eds.). (2010). *Mówienie w języku obcym – sukcesy i porażki uczenia się i nauczania.* Poznań, Kalisz, Konin: Wydawnictwo UAM.

Reszkiewicz, A. (1984). *Correct your English Pronunciation.* Warszawa: Państwowe Wydawnictwo Naukowe.

Rogerson-Revell, P. (2011). *English Phonology and Pronunciation Teaching.* London: Routledge.

Szpyra-Kozłowska, J. (2015). *Pronunciation in EFL Instruction. A Research-Based Approach.* Bristol: Multilingual Maters.

Tono, Y. (2001). *Research on Dictionary Use in the Context of Foreign Language Learning.* Tübingen: Max Niemeyer Verlag.

Töpel, A. (2014). Review of research into the use of electronic dictionaries. In C. Müller-Spitzer (Ed.), *Using online dictionaries* (pp. 13–54). Berlin, Boston: De Gruyter.

Traxler, J. (2013). Mobile learning for languages: Can the past speak to the future? Monterey, CA: The International Research Foundation for English Language Education. Available at: https://www.tirfonline.org/english-in-the-workforce/mobile-assisted-language-learning/ (date of access: 29 August 2017).

Marek Molenda, Michał Adamczyk and Paulina Rybińska
University of Łódź, Łódź, Poland

Beyond the CAPT – Automatic Speech Recognition in pronunciation training

Abstract: This chapter examines the applicability of automatic speech recognition (ASR) software to EFL pronunciation training. Unlike previous authors, such as Hincks (2003) or Liakin et al. (2013), we decided to describe the solutions which do not belong to the computer-assisted pronunciation training (CAPT) category. Instead, the study focused on the ASR systems which transcribe natural speech. As a result of the primary selection, Google Cloud Speech API proved to be the most accessible, mobile-friendly solution. Given the fact that mobility can be viewed as one of the driving forces of the modern world, it was essential to find the solution that puts the ease of access across multiple devices and operating systems first. By providing both the desktop version and mobile application, which can be run on portable devices, including the most commonly used smartphones and tablets, Google API appears to be a reasonable choice.

In the study, EFL students used the software to complete pronunciation tasks designed to maximize the pedagogical value of the system-generated feedback. All the sessions were recorded with a screen capture tool and transcribed. The recordings were analysed and the results were compared with students' answers to questionnaires on their perception of the software. Finally, the data collected was used to create a list of good practices. These guidelines were designed to help language teachers use the non-CAPT ASR systems in pronunciation training.

Keywords: CALL, EFL, computer-assisted pronunciation training, automated speech recognition, M-learning, Google API

1. Introduction

In recent years, pronunciation training, much as any other aspect of English as a foreign language (EFL), has benefited from the constantly improving access to information technologies. In addition to basic tools, such as any form of native speakers' recordings, whose main purpose was to provide English students with a reliable pronunciation model, a number of solutions have been developed in order to facilitate feedback-based learning. One has to stress that non-commercial access to this software remains severely restricted, which might be a serious impediment for students looking for easy-to-use and – preferably – free programs. Thus, in this chapter we took the more egalitarian approach by assessing the usefulness of a free tool based on automatic speech recognition (ASR) technology. We opted for a cross-platform solution which can be easily accessed via portable devices running the most popular mobile operating systems while ensuring the consistency of learning experience, regardless of the type of hardware.

2. Literature review

All the digital solutions which are capable of providing students with automated and meaningful feedback on their pronunciation are based on ASR technology. There is an agreement amongst the researchers that even if programs of this kind do not transcribe the words uttered, which is the case with "typical" ASR software (Liakin et al. 2013: 86), they still belong to the ASR category. Classification based on this premise can be found in Hincks (2002), Liakin et al. (2013), Zechner et al. (2014), and many others.

According to Kim (2006), the technology behind ASR is largely based on the Hidden Markov Model (Ehsani & Knodt 1998). A speech recognizer using this algorithm "computes how close the phonemes of a spoken input are to a corresponding model, based on probability theory" (Kim 2006: 323). In the case of software developed for language pedagogy the result of such an interaction is not limited to text output. On the contrary, there are a number of other ways of providing feedback to EFL students: from more scientifically-minded, such as contrasting the spectograms of the learners' vs native speaker's pronunciation of a given phrase in FluSpeak (Kim 2006: 323), to a gamification-oriented bowling alley used in ISTRA (Indiana Speech Training Aid), where the better the pronunciation, the more pins are knocked down at each attempt (Dalby & Kewley-Port 1999: 427). For an extensive list of offline tools, see Kim (2006).

Two basic functions of ASR software, i.e. teaching and assessing pronunciation, were described by Mak et al. (2003: 23). The former function is often referred to as computer-assisted pronunciation teaching/training, abbreviated as CAPT (Thomson 2011), while the latter was dubbed web-based automated speech evaluation or WASE (Wang & Chen 2009).[1] Since the digital solutions used in both cases are based upon the same concept of human-machine interaction, there is a certain overlap between the studies conducted in both fields, especially in terms of assessing the ASR accuracy (compare Dalby & Kewley-Port 1999 and Zechner et al. 2014).

1 For instance, "training" was used in Thomson (2011), while Liakin et al. (2013) seem to prefer "teaching".

In their review of the CAPT-oriented solutions, Liakin et al. (2013) quote a number of studies which show that the technology meets the requirements described by Chapelle and Jamieson (2008), namely:

- Learner fit
- Explicit teaching
- Opportunities for interactions with the computer
- Comprehensible feedback
- The development of strategies to learn new features on their own.

Conversely, some researchers have stressed the shortcomings of CAPT focusing primarily on software-related problems and certain pedagogical premises. For instance, Hincks reported a high drop-out rate in her subjects who were exposed to CAPT caused by the counter-intuitive graphical user interface (GUI) of the *FreshTalk* program (Hincks 2002: 733). Wang and Chen (2009: 218) cite a number of studies which question the usefulness of spectrogram-based feedback. Some concerns were also raised in relation to the choice of the target pronunciation model. Thomson (2011) stressed that certain programs measure how native-like the accent is, but they do not provide information on its overall quality. Wang et al. (2009) criticized the focus on segmental.[2] Finally, Hincks (2003: 3) discovered that CAPT training was of "limited value" for the students whose pronunciation was more advanced.

3. Study

In this study, we decided to investigate the usefulness of the non-CAPT ASR systems in the context of a self-corrective training session. The choice was largely motivated by the fact that apart from commercially-available software, there seemed to have been relatively little research into freely available, non-pedagogical solutions; the ones that are instantly accessible to any student or teacher who has access to the Internet via a desktop browser or a mobile device. Since many researchers stressed the importance of an intuitive GUI and comprehensible feedback, a decision was made to prioritize these two features.

In accordance with these assumptions, two research questions were formulated:

Q1: Are the non-CAPT, ASR-based systems capable of providing meaningful pronunciation feedback to EFL students?

Q2: Are students able to successfully use such systems, both in terms of technical skills and feedback awareness?

2 More on the ineffectiveness of such an approach can be found in Dziubalska-Kołaczyk (2002).

Since this topic is still largely unexplored, it was decided that research should be conducted in the form of a feasibility study whose major aim is to test the effectiveness of the aforementioned ASR systems and provide a point of reference for teachers and researchers willing to explore particular aspects of non-CAPT digital pronunciation teaching in more depth.

3.1 Software used

In order to ensure the user-friendliness of the programs used, a set of criteria that had to be met by each piece of software was developed:

- No CAPT-based solutions were considered.
- The ASR service had to be available via browser on a PC and Mac. No installation (other than installing the browser itself) should be required.
- The mobile version was expected to work with at least one major OS available in Poland: Android, iOS and/or Windows Phone (see the report on mobile OSs in Poland http://estan.pl/udzial-mobilnych-systemow-operacyjnych-polsce-2015/).
- The software should provide feedback in the form of transcribed text only.
- The "listening time" could not be limited: adding contents with one's voice should keep the system active.
- Users had to be able to choose their target native accent.
- The service should be available free of charge.

Upon the revision of the solutions available, we decided to use Google sound recognition systems. Those services are available via a Chrome browser on a PC/Mac/Chromebook and in the form of a pre-installed application in the case of Android devices. A dedicated, fully-functional mobile application can be also downloaded to iOS.

In order to ensure adequate recording time, the choice fell on the Google Docs suite (https://www.google.com/docs), which makes it possible to dictate longer texts to a browser-based word processor. Google voice recognition is a built-in feature of Android devices, available via system keyboard. In order to replicate our research conditions, Google voice recognition can paired with Android Google Drive mobile applications. iOS users can access the resource by means of Google search app which includes the voice search option.[3]

3 https://itunes.apple.com/us/app/google-search-made-just-for-mobile/id284815942?mt=8

In this study, a plug-in called *Speech Recognition* was used;[4] however, the dictation tool was added as a core functionality to Google Docs on 2/Sept/2015 and has since been available with each official version of the service.[5] It should be noted that both the plugin and the built-in tool make it possible to choose the target accent and that they use the same speech recognition algorithm, i.e. Google Cloud API.[6]

In order for the study to reflect on the structure of the human-machine interaction, we decided that the process of text input and receiving feedback should be recorded. This task might be accomplished with a screen capture tool which makes it possible to compile a real-time recording of the screen with the sound produced by the learner. With hardware requirements being analyzed, a Windows-compatible version of Open Broadcaster was selected as a basic tool for recording students' activity. In order to prevent accidental shutdown of the program, which might be inadvertently done by clicking on the taskbar, we used the full-screen version of Google Chrome, thus making it impossible for the subjects to click away from the browser window.

3.2 Subjects

All the subjects were first-year Polish students of English at the University of Łódź. Their proficiency level was B2/C1, according to the *Common European Framework of Reference for Languages* (CEFR; Council of Europe 2001) guidelines implemented at the University. By the time the research was conducted, they had successfully completed a one-semester course in English pronunciation. According to the syllabus, the students who complete the course should understand the basics of the sound-letter correspondence in English. Moreover, they are supposed to be able to define the characteristics of their target accent (usually Received Pronunciation or General American). These skills were deemed necessary for the successful completion of the task: the understanding of the sound-letter correspondence made it possible for the subjects to analyze the machine-generated output, while accent awareness was essential in order to calibrate the system to listen for specific sounds or clusters.

Nine students, three males and six females, volunteered to take part in the research. All of them attended the same phonetic course. Their average age was

---

4 https://chrome.google.com/webstore/detail/speech-recognition/idmniglhlcjfkhncgbiiecmianekpheh?utm_source=permalink

5 https://googleblog.blogspot.com/2015/09/google-docs-classroom-school.html

6 https://cloud.google.com/speech

19.3, with SD = 1.32. All the subjects chose the RP accent as their target variety of English. The number of subjects situates our research as a small-scale study; however, in the case of screen capture, each participant can generate large amounts of data, depending on the number of actions that they decide to take in order to complete a given task. Based on predictions of how much data would be generated, we decided to limit the number of participants in order to match the envisaged working time proposed by the raters.

3.3 Research procedure

The aim of the first stage of the study was to ensure that no computer-based feedback would be pedagogically harmful to the students. The starting point was the list of segmental and suprasegmental pronunciation problems likely to occur in Polish speakers of English, as described in Sobkowiak (2004) and Baker (2006). On the basis of this data, a set of various items was devised, both single words and longer segments, which students were supposed to input using their voice only (see Appendix). The items were then tested against the Google system in order to make sure that the learners receive meaningful feedback. Each item underwent the process of double blind revision before it was labelled as "useful" or "problematic". As a result, a decision was made to eliminate certain words or phrases which were found to be likely to cause confusion among the subjects. Two examples of analyzed items are presented in Table 1, with target sounds being underlined:

Table 1: Examples of analyzed items

Item	Problems
They found three potato peels in her wardrobe.	**Comment:** When the phrase is pronounced correctly, the system displays "potato peels" only to auto-correct it to "potato pills" (sic!) after a couple of seconds. The phrase "potato peels" produced in isolation yields correct results. Most likely, the context-sensitive algorithms perform keyword analysis and choose the more likely variant regardless of the pronunciation. **Decision:** Since the problem did not occur on a regular basis, the item was included in the list.
computer [stress placement]	**Comment:** There is no negative feedback in the case of incorrect stress placement. Given the lack of counterpart to form a minimal pair, the incorrectly placed stress is not a valid reason for the ASR algorithm to refer to other items. **Decision:** The problem persisted; consequently, the item was eliminated.

Interaction between students and the aforementioned ASR system consisted of a single session divided into introduction, interaction proper, and the follow-up survey. Before a subject was given a list, he or she received individual instruction in using the system. This procedure entailed training sessions during which every participant was allowed to test the equipment by recording a trial sample. Special attention was paid to the "freeze-recovery" procedures which consisted of rebooting the plugin without shutting down the browser. The researcher then ensured that subjects understood that they could only use their voice to input the text. Typing was not allowed, except for *backspace* and/or *delete* keys, as long as they were used to erase incorrectly transcribed words. Finally, students were asked to confirm that they understood the procedures.

Upon receiving the list, students were informed that they were not obliged to input the sentences in the order of appearance. Neither were they expected to succeed in dictating all the items as long as they made at least one attempt to pronounce each segment on the list. The subject was then allowed to work alone in the recording room. The completion of the task was the beginning of the last phase which consisted in filling out the online questionnaire aimed at measuring user satisfaction.

All the recordings of students' work were analyzed in a two-step procedure. Firstly, the screen captures were broken down into segments. Each segment was a single utterance produced by a subject and separated from other segments by silent pauses of at least 1.5 sec. The segments were then listed in a spreadsheet and enriched with the meta-data indicated below.

During the second phase, the following attributes were added to each segment:

- Failure (binary) – the absence of the failure tag meant that the student succeeded in inputting a given segment. It should be noted that the failure is not a negative phenomenon in the context of this study; if not induced by a software glitch, it is expected to be a starting point for the learning process, in which the learner receives negative feedback on their pronunciation. Multiple failures which lead to producing the correct form reflect students' analysis of feedback and attempts to take corrective actions. (whether correctly or not?)
- Correction (binary) – this tag was used whenever the subject tried to self-correct the previously-produced segment immediately upon receiving negative feedback
- False negative (binary) – if the algorithm seemed to fail to identify the incorrect pronunciation, the segment was marked as *false negative*; for the sake of clarity, it should be noted that the corresponding value of *true positive* was defined as the algorithm identifying the problem correctly, i.e. *failure=TRUE*

- Software problem (binary) – whenever the software failed to capture what was registered as a correctly-pronounced item, or when the system did not respond to voice input at all (freezing), this attribute was assigned to the segment
- Cheating (binary) – this attribute was assigned to all instances of students' using the keyboard to input target words
- Mispronunciation code (multiple values) – since a type-token approach to mispronunciations was adopted, each type received a unique code. The codes were added to relevant segments, thus forming tokens.

Having received training in transcription conventions, two pronunciation teachers from the University of Łódź processed the data. Blind tests were conducted to control the inter-rater reliability. The rates were found to be totally consistent as regards the number of problems which were identified (100%) and very highly consistent in terms of segmentation, i.e. the identification of boundaries between the items (96%).

3.4 Data presentation

3.4.1 Binary tags

The subjects produced 311 segments in total, with the average of 34.56 segments per student and SD=10.05. The number of tags assigned to the segments is presented in Figure 1:

Figure 1: The frequency of occurrence of tags in the database. All the values expressed as a percentage were calculated in relation to the total number of recorded segments, labelled as "All segments".

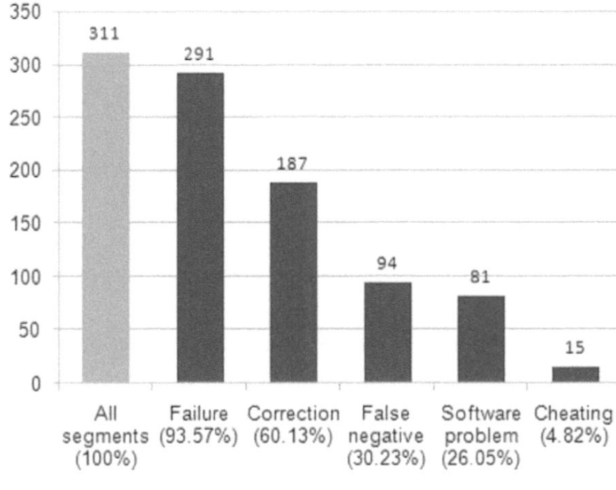

The high number of "failure" tags indicates that there were relatively few instances when students succeeded in inputting the target segment. These problems might be attributed to a number of variables generated either by software or by users. In order to determine the impact of the software on the total number of failures, the ratio of frequency of occurrence of the "software problem" tag to the "failure" tag was calculated. The result is 27.84%, which means that slightly more than a quarter of all failures to input the target item was due to the software. This ratio is presented in Figure 2.

Figure 2: The ratio of software problems to user-induced failures.

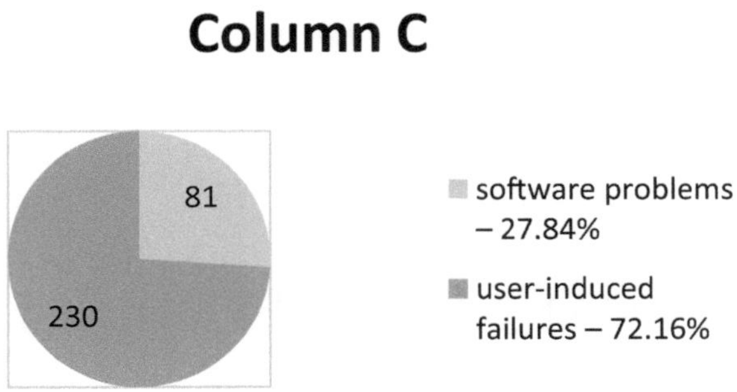

The occurrences of self-corrections were analyzed to establish subjects' success rate expressed as a percentage of successful attempts. It was found that in approximately one fifth of the cases (19.25%) the succession of failures acted as corrective feedback and led to the final successful inputting of a given item. This value reflects the effectiveness of the system in terms of directing students towards target pronunciation. However, the fact that some students did not manage to produce the correct form does not mean that they did not receive valuable feedback; in spite of being unable to pronounce the item correctly, they might have realized that they make pronunciation errors.

Despite the preliminary evaluation of the materials, almost a hundred utterances were classified as "false negatives". While the human factor makes it the least reliable of all binary descriptors of system performance, this value is still highly indicative of the ASR algorithms being more "liberal" than human raters.

The fact that the "cheating" tag could be found in fewer than 5% of all segments means that the data can be considered as reliable. On the contrary, the presence of such problems might indicate user impatience and dissatisfaction with the system.

3.4.2 *Mispronunciation codes*

In the process of transcribing the data, 25 types of mispronunciations were identified; these were realized as 131 tokens. The type-token ratio is 0.19, which can be expressed as 5.24 tokens per each type. However, the SD=5.73 indicates that the distribution of the tokens is not even, as this is presented in Figure 3.

Figure 3: The distribution of tokens representing mispronunciations.

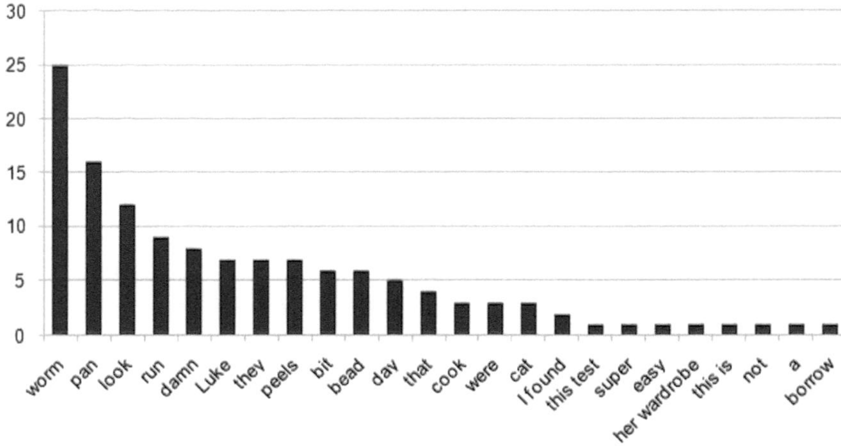

Most of the items listed in Figure 3 are target words, containing sounds whose pronunciation was expected to be most problematic for the students. The remaining suprasegmental problems, related to stress placement, were relatively rare given the total of five tokens.

Vowels seemed to constitute the majority of problems encountered by the learners. The mispronounced word "worm" was correctly transcribed by the software as "warm", "pan" as "pen" and "look" as "Luke", which gave the students the opportunity to see how a given word might be understood by a native speaker when it is free from defining context. Conversely, the rendering of the mispronounced "damn" as "them" might have been confusing for the user. In this case, it was clear that the system prioritized the vowel over the correctly produced/d/sound.

3.4.3 *User satisfaction*

Over three quarters of respondents (83%) consider the tool in question to be "useful" or "very useful" for learning English pronunciation. The values of this parameter, referred to as "user (dis)satisfaction", were not found to be statistically correlated with respondents' success rate. Also, no significant relationship was found in the case of self-assessment of one's pronunciation skills and the number of recorded mispronunciations.

User feedback was decomposed into single propositions which were divided into positive and negative comments. Positive feedback was collected on:

- Software accuracy
- Task design
- Intuitive interface (recording and changing target accent were mentioned in this context)
- Reliability of Google API as a diagnostic tool

Below, are examples of feedback we received, split between four major categories. Students' comments on the piece of software were translated from Polish to English. In some cases, a small portion of text was added to increase clarity of the comment; it is enclosed in square brackets.

- Software accuracy:
    - o "The program catches even tiny little differences between words".
- Task design:
    - o "I liked it that at any time I could delete the wrong word and try to say it again, this time – correctly".
- Intuitive interface:
    - o "I didn't notice any technical issues while running the software: it was easy to handle".
    - o "[I liked] it that instead of using a keyboard we can do the same thing using our voice, and at the same time, practice our pronunciation".
    - o "There was no need to type the words in, what usually takes a lot of time".
- Reliability of Google API as a diagnostic tool:
    - o "[The software] shows pronunciation errors (incorrect pronunciation, a different word)".
    - o "[The program allows me to] check the correct pronunciation".
    - o "I liked it that I could pick the accent and see if I pronounce words correctly".

While positive comments were made on software accuracy, it was also found that almost all the negative feedback was connected with this aspect. As for software accuracy, the participants found it important that the program was capable of identifying even small differences in pronunciation. Students comments were analysed and matched with specific sections of the recordings in order to identify the source of the problem. The results of this analysis are presented in Table 2.

Table 2: Analysis of negative feedback. Comments were translated from Polish

Comments	**Description**
Target words were divided into smaller units by the program, though it might as well be my fault.	This phenomenon was observed in the case of problems with intonation and/or unclear pronunciation.
Despite correct pronunciation, one word was inaccurately transcribed.	In this case, "worm" was mispronounced (and transcribed) as "warm". Upon receiving corrective feedback, the student unsuccessfully tried to change the pronunciation and length of the vowel.
The program tends to freeze.	Unfortunately, we observed some instances of this problem. Before recording their voice, students received training in "freeze recovery" procedures.
Sometimes strange words would appear, e.g. "they were" → "weather".	The words "they were" were mis-transcribed as "day weather". One of the reasons might be the fact that the subject pronounced "day" instead of "they" which could trigger context-sensitive algorithms to transcribe the proceeding word as "weather".
The program fails to transcribe separate words.	Separate words were harder to pronounce, as the context-sensitive algorithms were not able to offset the effects of mispronunciations. For instance, in the case of the word "damn", the system is far more liberal if it is used in a phrase "damn it!" In isolation, the/æ/sound requires more effort.
I didn't like deleting the mispronounced words.	This aspect might have been irritating since lags were observed in the browser-based Google Docs as opposed to traditional word processors. It might be hypothesized that improving the speed of the Internet connection would remedy this problem.

Negative feedback given by the students can be further divided into two categories. The first one are complaints which are undeniably valid and require re-adjusting the parameters of the digital workspace in order to create a user-friendly learning environment. In the context of this study, the materials should be further improved to meet software requirements, and hardware upgrades should be considered.

The other category are the students who blamed their mispronunciations on software failures, oftentimes in spite of corrective feedback. Such learners might benefit from access to external tools or extended pre-session training. One should bear in mind, however, that having high confidence in their pronunciation might prevent students from making any attempts to approach the problem from the analytic perspective as it was observed in the case of "worm".

3.5 Discussion

The data obtained in the study offer a number of ways of assessing the usefulness of Google ASR in the language classroom. For the sake of clarity, the impact of the technological factor on the overall assessment is reflected on first, and then it is followed by human factor analysis.

While the majority of *failure* tags are ascribed to the human factor, the frequency of occurrence of machine-generated phenomena, i.e. *software problems* and *false negatives*, may be worrying. The former ones are hardly controllable by the teacher as the freezing of the system should be addressed by the software developer. It is not unrealistic to expect it to happen in the foreseeable future as this shortcoming might simply discourage the customers from using the system. Conversely, the *false negatives* can and should be filtered out by the teacher. While an attempt to do this before the beginning of the study was not overly successful, the data obtained in the course of the research might be used to detect and remove problematic items from the list.

The task of preparing teaching materials is made difficult by one more feature of the ASR, namely, the algorithms which predicts words based on the probability of occurrence of a given item in specific contexts. Such an approach makes it almost impossible for the teacher to use nonsense examples as those might be simply transformed into more conventional phrases, even if pronounced correctly. One of the ways of tackling this problem is creating and testing minimal pairs of sentences, where both phrases are comparably likely to occur in the language (corpus analysis would be useful in this case). Alternatively, one might resort to minimal pairs of words, where no context is provided.

Despite the workload which might be imposed on the teacher by the discussed shortcomings of the system, the solutions based on Google API were found to be user-friendly. Although the training sessions were relatively short, each subject knew how the system works and what they were supposed to do. This opinion was reinforced by the results of the questionnaire: no student complained about the GUI, and some openly praised it.

Another important feature of the system is its availability, both in terms of money and ease of access. Since this free-of-charge solution is fully integrated with a popular browser, it helps to cover most of the computer market. Furthermore, the same system can be accessed via majority of mobile devices, which makes it especially attractive for teachers interested in *BYOD* policy and the *flipped classroom* model.

The latter of the two aspects of the use of ASR, namely the human factor, proved to be more significant than initially expected. One of the most problematic discoveries was the one of students' "cheating". While it might be a manifestation of the dissatisfaction with the system, as it was hypothesized in the previous section, it also shows a product-oriented attitude of some learners. Such an attitude makes it harder for students to understand that the purpose of the activity is to practice rather than to produce a sheet of perfectly-transcribed phrases.

While "cheating" is an issue which stems from students' attitude, problems on the analytic level were also discovered; most notably in the case of interpreting feedback. Initially, it was assumed that students would naturally find it easier to understand that by making a pronunciation mistake they actually pronounce another word. However, there is evidence in the data that the learners were unable to interpret such feedback, and some blamed it on the software. Two ways of tackling this problem were suggested; the first one is improving the perceived reliability of the ASR by revising the worksheet, and the second one is more training in analytical approaches to system output. Additionally, one might consider providing students with access to sources which offer phonetic transcription of the target words. In this case, it seems important to make sure that the learners do not receive such feedback prior to the analysis phase.

In sum, the answers to both research questions, despite the reservations, are positive. Meaningful feedback might be generated if the teachers carefully select the contents of the task and the software developers work on the system reliability. The aforementioned inclusion of the voice dictation function as a native element of the Google Docs seems promising in the context of providing a trouble-free user experience.

The problems connected to feedback awareness reveal the weaknesses of the task-based approach where the ASR is likely to be considered a tool rather than a source of meaningful feedback. This approach seems to fail to guarantee that students pay enough attention to computer-generated feedback as a source of information. Therefore, we postulate that even though the simplicity and the intuitiveness of the feedback seems to be increased in comparison to the CAPT solutions, training sessions still seem necessary in order to make the feedback more meaningful to the students.

As was demonstrated, there are certain shortcomings in the system which need to be tackled in order to make it a fully-functional learning tool. However, one may believe that such a situation is possible, provided that enough effort is invested in preliminary evaluation of materials and student training.

4. Pedagogical implications

The use of the Google speech recognition system has potential benefits, but while it is relatively easy for learners to use, it requires careful preparation on the part of the teacher. We suggest taking a two-pronged process, with emphasis respectively on the technological and human factors.

The technological aspect consists of adjusting the materials and hardware to software requirements. Thus, the following suggestions for the teachers:

- Make sure that your hardware and Internet connection are capable of running the program/application without lags and freezing.
- Prepare recovery procedure for your students in case of freezing.
- Prepare and organize a training session. While normally very little time is necessary to provide students with effective training, this step seems to be crucial when one wants to avoid most of the software-related problems.
- Compile a list of items according to your regional requirements, and then test it carefully using the software.
- Avoid homophones and nonsense phrases.
- Use minimal pairs of words or sentences. In the latter case it is recommended to verify their likelihood of occurrence in a reference corpus.
- Organize a pilot test session in order to eliminate the items from the list which might still be problematic.
- Supervise the actual session in order to provide assistance.
- Collect feedback on the system and respond to your students' needs.

Although the actions listed above are relatively time-consuming, it should be noted that some of them need to be performed just once. For instance, a pre-tested worksheet might be used with a number of groups and on multiple occasions; unless unexpected problems arise, there is little need to modify it.

The latter group of suggestions are aimed at reducing the negative impact of the human factor on the effectiveness of pronunciation training. Upon the analysis of the data, the following list was devised:

- Make sure that students who are to participate in the activity have enough training to be able to understand the basic rules of sound-letter correspondence in the English language.

- Confirm that your students are familiar with the pedagogical rationale behind the exercise. It is important to stress that this is a process-oriented activity.
- Verify your students' ability to analyze ASR feedback: a preliminary training session is strongly recommended.
- Consider providing students with access to reference materials.

We hope that our suggestions help the teachers who would like to use the non-CAPT ASR for pronunciation training choose the tools and create effective teaching procedures. It is also highly-recommended to monitor the progress of the speech-recognition technology as the appearance of new or significantly-improved solutions seems relatively probable. When it happens, we hope that our framework and research methods remain applicable and that they facilitate the process of software evaluation.

Finally, we would like to stress that the pronunciation training based on the Google API is likely to have one more potentially positive effect, namely enhanced integration with the voice recognition systems. By avoiding typical mistakes that can occur in this context, the students will be more likely to successfully use mobile devices, wearable technologies, GPS, and many other voice-operated systems.

References

Baker, A. (2006). *Ship or Sheep?: An Intermediate Pronunciation Course.* Cambridge: Cambridge University Press.

Chapelle, C., & Jamieson, J. (2008). *Tips for Teachers: Computer-assisted Language Learning.* New York: Pearson Longman.

Council of Europe. (2001). *Common European Framework of Reference for Languages: Learning, Teaching, Assessment.* Modern Languages Division, Strasbourg: Cambridge University Press.

Dalby, J., & Kewley-Port, D. (1999). Explicit pronunciation training using automatic speech recognition. *Journal of the Computer Assisted Language Learning Consortium, 16*(5), 425–445.

Dziubalska-Kołaczyk, K. (2002). Conscious competence of performance as a key to teaching English. In E. Waniek-Klimczak & P. J. Melia (Eds.), *Accents and Speech in English* (pp. 97–106). Frankfurt am Main: Peter Lang.

Ehsani, F., & Knodt, E. (1998). Speech technology in computer-aided language learning: Strengths and limitations of a new CALL paradigm. *Language Learning & Technology, 2*(1), 45–60.

Hincks, R. (2002). Speech recognition for language teaching and evaluating: A study of existing commercial products. In J. H. L. Hansen & B. Pellom (Eds.), *Proceedings of ICSLP 2002* (pp. 733–736). Denver, CO: Carnegie Mellon University.

Hincks, R. (2003). Speech technologies for pronunciation feedback and evaluation. *ReCALL, 15*(1), 3–20.

Kim, I. S. (2006). Automatic speech recognition: Reliability and pedagogical implications for teaching pronunciation. *Educational Technology and Society, 9*(1), 322–344.

Liakin, D., Cardoso, W., & Liakina, N. (2013). Mobile speech recognition software: A tool for teaching second language pronunciation. *Cahiers de l'ILOB, 5,* 85–99.

Mak, B., Siu, M., Ng, M., Tam, Y. C., Chan, Y. C., Chan, K. W., Leung, K. Y., Ho, S., Chong, F. H., Wong, J., & Lo, J. (2003). Pronunciation learning via automatic speech recognition. In J. Burstein & C. Leacock (Eds.), *Proceedings of the HLT-NAACL 03 workshop on Building Educational Application Using Natural Language Processing* (pp. 23–29). Stroudsburg, PA: Association for Computational Linguistics.

Sobkowiak, W. (2004). *English Phonetics for Poles.* Poznań, Poland: Wydawnictwo Poznańskie.

Thomson, R. I. (2011). Computer assisted pronunciation training: Targeting second language vowel perception improves pronunciation. *CALICO Journal, 28*(3), 744–765.

Wang, M. J., & Chen, H. C. (2009). Pedagogical practice and students' perceived effectiveness of web-based automated speech evaluation. *Journal of Asia TEFL, 6*(4), 217–243.

Waniek-Klimczak, E., & Melia, P. J. (Eds.). (2002). *Accents and Speech in English.* Frankfurt am Main: Peter Lang.

Zechner, K., Evanini, K., Yoon, S. Y., Davis, L., Wang, X., Chen, L., Lee, C. M., & Leong, C. W. (2014). Automated scoring of speaking items in an assessment for teachers of English as a foreign language. In J. Tetreault, J. Burstein, & C. Leacock (Eds.), *Proceedings of the Ninth Workshop on Innovative Use of NLP for Building Educational Applications* (pp. 134–142). Baltimore, MD: Association for Computational Linguistics.

Appendix

The list of items given to students

This test is going to be super easy.

What a lovely cat!

I found potato peels in her wardrobe.

Can I borrow a pan?

Look, it's Luke!

This is not a worm.

I'm thinking…

That day they were surprised.

ran

cook

bit

Damn!

bead

Agnieszka Bryła-Cruz
Maria Curie-Skłodowska University, Lublin, Poland

Authentic podcasts as a linguistic and cognitive resource for advanced learners of English

Abstract: This chapter argues that thanks to the vast potential of computer-assisted language learning (CALL) and mobile learning in particular, English can be taught more holistically. The undeniable ubiquity of portable devices in everyday life has inspired language educators to integrate podcasts into the curriculum, which seems an excellent idea considering their versatility, accessibility and, above all, portability. Even though using podcasts in technology-enhanced education is not a new idea and there exist plenty of web pages with podcasts elaborated for pedagogical purposes, the approach presented in this chapter is innovative in that it deals with authentic podcasts, i.e. podcasts designed for English native listeners. Moreover, the benefits of implementing these podcasts go beyond linguistic growth only. In this chapter it is shown how the audio material is employed so that students enhance listening and speaking skills, focus on vocabulary as well as critically approach the content, and interact with the ideas. In the process, learners refine their linguistic skills and become more knowledgeable citizens of the world. Last but not least, they are stimulated to embrace the countless benefits of podcasts and realize that learning can happen anytime and anywhere as long as they are willing to exploit their handheld (and held dear) devices for educational purposes.

Keywords: podcast, CALL, mobile learning, content-based instruction, integrated teaching, listening skills, foreign language teaching, translator education

1. Introduction

This chapter argues that thanks to the vast potential of technology-enhanced education and mobile learning in particular, English can be taught more holistically to advanced learners. Authentic podcasts, which can be reproduced on a variety of portable devices, constitute a useful resource to implement a truly integrated approach to foreign language teaching, i.e. the one where linguistic knowledge and skills are not separated from other types of knowledge and skills. This is in line with content-based instruction (CBI), where the target language is not viewed as the only object of study, but rather a vehicle through which the learner can expand their horizons on relevant and up-to-date topics (Brinton, Snow & Wesche 1989). Moreover, the omnipresence of mobile appliances and the fact that we live (and learn) in an increasingly digitalized era mean that podcasts can be aligned with a common lifestyle in an unobtrusive and cost-free way.

On the one hand, CBI programs render the language learning process more attractive and motivating for the students because their focus is shifted from the language itself onto ideas, opinions, and issues. The task of communication becomes more natural and the language acquisition is more effective because students learn language most effectively when there is an emphasis on relevant and meaningful content rather than on the language itself (Dueñas 2004). On the other hand, given the fact that most coursebooks do not provide enough "food for thought", the teacher needs to look for appropriate content elsewhere. It places more workload on language instructors and the process of preparing classes is more time-consuming. Relying on podcasts for attractive and pedagogically rich supplementary resources seems a very good choice, as will be argued in the subsequent sections.

In what follows I share my experience of using authentic podcasts in the classroom with the subsequent discussion of the countless benefits which stem from it. I begin with a brief explanation of the term podcast. I then proceed to present various ways in which authentic podcasts (not specifically designed for learning purposes) can be adapted for use with advanced learners of English to practise listening and speaking skills, and expand vocabulary but also develop a variety of thinking skills (paraphrasing, summarising, information gathering, organizing, analyzing) as well as provide students with topics of intellectual substance. In this way, students learn the language, enhance their learning strategies, and absorb cognitively relevant content.

The last goal is considered particularly relevant for translation-oriented fields of study, which I observed when for 7 years I taught practical English to the students of Applied Linguistics. As potential translators they need to develop their language skills and also constantly expand their general knowledge about the world in order to be able to comprehend and translate various types of texts. Translation didactics underline the importance of "cognitive complements" and insist that broad general knowledge is essential to understand contexts and utterance circumstances. Translators need to be able to retrieve from their minds extralinguistic knowledge in order to produce logical, accurate and valuable translations (Delisle 2003). For this reason, making use of authentic podcasts, which enable the integration of particular content with language teaching aims, seems an ideal choice when teaching English to translator apprentices. Since podcasting provides access to authentic materials, students can have an insight into issues such as history, politics, culture, science and current events.

2. Podcasts and language learning

In a nutshell, podcasts are audio files, typically in mp3 format, that can be freely downloaded from the Internet. The term "podcast" emerged in 2004 as a combination of "iPod" and "broadcast" meaning a pre-recorded audio file downloadable from the Internet on a computer or any portable device. The acronym "pod" means "portable on demand," as podcast can be listened to at the listeners' convenience, i.e. when, where and the number of times they wish. The conspicuous feature of podcasts is that they work in the form of pull technology (the listeners select the content they want to engage with) as opposed to push technology characteristic of radio and TV (the providers predetermine what the listeners are exposed to). Typically, podcasts come in a regularly updated series and the listener can subscribe to them by simply clicking a button. As a result, he or she is automatically notified of each new episode which has been uploaded or even receives a downloaded copy directly onto their computer or portable device. Putting ubiquitous mobile technology (smartphones, iPods, Mp3 players, PDAs, wireless laptops) at the service of language learning is an excellent way to take advantage of students' favourite devices in order to foster their involvement with diverse linguistic content and draw them to the target culture. Podcasts have a huge educational potential because of their versatility, accessibility and, above all, portability (King & Gura 2009). They are a great example of mobile learning because listening to them can be personal, informal, spontaneous, and pervasive, i.e. "so integrated with daily life that is hardly noticed" (Kukulska-Hulme 2006: 2). Importantly, it can take place when the learner is not "at a fixed predetermined location" (Kukulska-Hulme 2006: 1).

Podcasts can be divided into two broad categories depending on their authors, i.e. those made by bigger entities and those created by individuals. The former group encompasses podcasts through which corporations, professional groups, libraries, and universities make updates about their organizations. Other podcasts belonging to this category include those posted by radio stations (e.g. the BBC, the Voice of America, The National Public Radio), science journals (e.g. Scientific American) and news organizations, who regularly make their content available online. In contrast to the above mentioned, individuals who upload podcasts do it not for commercial but entertainment reasons. They focus on themes of personal or social interest and usually adopt a talk radio format mixed with songs or enriched with background music. Such independent podcasts tend to be interactive and respond to the questions or comments left by the listeners on different kinds of social media online.

As regards the source of podcasts, they can be located and accessed in several ways: by visiting the providers' own websites or blogs, via podcast directories (databases), or by performing a google search. The convenience of using podcast directories is the fact that the audio files are arranged thematically. In the BBC podcast directory, the content is organized by radio stations and genre (news, music, religion & ethics, sport, comedy, etc.). Additionally, specific searches can be done by typing the key words.

Even though podcasting was originally meant for spreading information and entertainment, its potential for teaching and learning languages was recognized very quickly by educators and learners alike. There exists a plethora of websites dedicated to learning the English language with the use of podcasts.[1] Because of the abundance of ELT podcasts available on the Internet, there are directories which host only podcasts designed for learning purposes, e.g. a sub-page of the Internet TESL Journal: http://iteslj.org/links/ESL/Listening/Podcasts/. Many of these podcasts are accompanied by transcripts and printable worksheets for further grammar or lexical practice. Some of them (e.g. http://www.breakingnewsenglish.com) provide whole lesson plans based on podcasts.

In addition to this, teachers and learners can create their own podcasts to supplement the language course. As noted by Stanley (2006), podcasting projects, in which students work individually, in pairs, groups or with an instructor have multiple language advantages and are highly motivating. Apart from stimulating the students, such joint undertakings have been found to reduce learners' anxiety and create a sense of belonging to a learning community.

Yet, in what follows the focus is neither on podcasts created for language practice, nor on those recorded by the learners themselves. I will take a closer look at authentic podcasts, in other words those originally designed not for pedagogical purposes but for English native speakers. The podcasts come from the BBC directory (Channel 4), and the webpages of "TED Talks", "Science Update" and "The Naked Scientist". The choice of the podcasts has been dictated by my personal preferences: these are the podcasts I regularly listen to and enjoy. These two facts may at first seem irrelevant, but in fact there is a rationale beyond them. Firstly, it is advocated that for teachers to avoid being overburdened with finding appropriate podcasts, they should rely on those they naturally listen or subscribe to. It happens quite frequently that while listening to an audio file the teacher encounters instances of grammar problems, vocabulary or topics he or she is about to cover in class. Finding appropriate podcasts does not amount to extra work if the teacher is accustomed to listening to them anyway (as mentioned above, thanks to the

1 For example, http://www.podcastinenglish.com/, http://www.bbc.co.uk/podcasts/genre/learning/, http://learnenglish.britishcouncil.org/en/listen-and-watch/)

portability of podcasts they can be reproduced at the listeners' convenience, e.g. while walking or driving). Secondly, it is important that the teacher chooses the podcasts they are fond of and whose content they feel at ease with rather than force themselves upon themes they are not comfortable with. This is particularly important in the case of CBI, when apart from language skills there is an intention to discuss and comment on certain ideas and issues present in the podcast.

While the selection of podcasts does not need to be particularly time-consuming and can happen naturally or even accidentally, adapting podcasts to the classroom use is a deliberate process which involves time and planning. Authentic podcasts may be too long to be listened to in full during the lesson. Even though advanced learners of English are able to process longer stretches of speech than beginners, a listening activity which lasts a consecutive 20 or 40 minutes would not be a good idea. Firstly, little time would be left for the practice of productive skills and other areas of language use. Secondly, it would be difficult for the teacher to know how much the learners actually understand. Thirdly, instead of being an attractive element of classes, extensively long podcasts would be associated with a forced and boring task. For these reasons the manipulation of audio files with special programs is unavoidable. Nowadays, however, it can be overcome very easily thanks to free downloadable software. Mp3 Cutter is a simple tool which enables the user to slice longer audio files. In a few clicks one can select a relevant part and save it as a separate mp3 file. Thanks to such programs, the teacher controls how much of a given podcast the students hear in class. The successive parts of the listening tasks are interwoven with comprehension or vocabulary exercises and oral activities. Needless to say, the teacher can (and should) encourage students to listen to the whole podcast on their own.

3. Authentic podcasts and language pedagogy

Numerous studies on the broad use of podcasts for educational purposes highlight flexibility as a key feature of students' engagement with podcasts (e.g. Rosell-Aguilar 2007; Ashton-Hay & Brookes 2011; Salmon & Nie 2008; Onsrud 2009). Collis and Moonen (2010: 218) define flexibility as "a movement away from a situation in which key decisions about learning are made in advance by the instructor or learning institution, towards a situation where the learner has a range of options from which to choose". In other words, flexibility is understood in a few dimensions, such as time, space, pacing and also learner's choice and control. These elements are inextricably connected with the fact that podcasts can be reproduced on omnipresent portable devices and thus enable mobile learning which assigns the central position to the learner and real life communication.

"The time-shifting capability of podcasting allows students to listen over and over again at any time and at any place" (Huan & Thong 2006: 8). In addition to determining the time and location of studying, the learner also controls the pace and sequence (repeatability) of reproducing the material, which, in its turn, is also chosen independently by the listener (Salmon & Nie 2008; Viswanathan 2009).

An important benefit of introducing podcasts in the classroom is to present students with samples of authentic language. As Little (1997: 226) points out: "We cannot expect learners to cope with target language communication in the world outside the classroom if we do not prepare them by bringing examples of that communication into the classroom". L2 classes should constitute the first space where students interact with authentic language and this contact is monitored and assisted by the teacher in a well-planned lesson (McBride 2009). King and Gura (2009: 182) observe that "[b]ringing authentic materials into the learning experience has long been a favored practice of teachers and podcasting is one way that technology makes this previously difficult practice infinitely easier". Podcasts are excellent and easy to access samples of real language used for meaningful communication (Warschauer & Healey 1998; Thorne & Payne 2005). Moreover, as recommended by Stevick (1989: 147), a good approach to language learning should involve "lots of listening before speaking" and "tie the language to some coherent reality". These requirements are met satisfactorily by podcasts and thus they comply with a socio-cognitive view of language learning.

Another advantage of using podcasts is to show students a very useful tool for broadly understood development as well as make them more autonomous. This approach is consistent with a constructivist view of the learning process which advocates an active way of constructing knowledge through exploration, observation and interpretation (Cooper 1993; Rosell-Aguilar 2007). Rather than treating podcasts as something merely additional but not necessary, I am convinced that "those of us in higher education owe it to our students to bring podcasting and other rich media into our courses so that they can lift their learning to a whole new level" (Campbell 2005: 44). Initially, learners will listen to podcasts for a defined stretch of time and perform the tasks and activities designed by the teacher. Gradually, they will gain the necessary skills and strategies to approach authentic audio input. As a result, they will develop confidence and a positive attitude towards listening to authentic podcasts and will search for texts suiting their interests on their own.

The ultimate goal of working with authentic podcasts in the classroom is to create in learners a habit of regular extensive listening not only for conscious target language practice but also for pleasure. As noticed by Clark and Walsh (2004), hearing has multiple advantages as a medium for learning. Thanks to podcasts and their salient feature of portability listening is socially acceptable (and can be done in a variety of settings while walking, commuting, shopping, etc.) and is deeply embedded in the modern lifestyle.

Needless to say, the correlation between the development of listening skills and becoming a proficient foreign language user has been recognized widely (Feyten 1991; Brown 2001; Rost 2011). Listening is considered the fundamental skill in foreign language learning because it is crucial for understanding and because reception precedes production. According to Gruba et al. (2009: 402), "in the context of foreign language learning, podcasts are most often used to teach listening skills". However, the linguistic benefits of employing podcasts as teaching resources go beyond the development of receptive skills. Pronunciation and broadly understood oral competence are perhaps the most immediate beneficiaries of extensive listening (Ducate & Lomicka 2009; Knight 2010), but podcasts can accelerate and facilitate the learning of vocabulary and grammar as well (Kaplan-Reiserson 2005; O'Bryan & Hegelheimer 2007; Borgia 2010). The findings of Hawke's (2010) research on teaching English for Special Purposes suggest that podcasts used as supplementary materials encourage students to focus on the content (in this case it encompassed scientific lexis) and contribute to the expansion of discipline- related vocabulary and knowledge.

This section presents my own suggestions as to how chosen authentic podcasts can be used in the classroom with advanced learners of English as a linguistic and cognitive resource. The presentation is organized thematically as the main criterion beyond the podcast selection was to match the thematic domains (defined in the syllabus of the course) with a particular broadcast. It should be noted that I do not present scenarios of the whole lessons here, but rather possible ways of incorporating authentic podcasts in a didactic unit, which can be further altered and suited to the teacher's needs. The design of the listening activities complies with an integrated approach which views listening as a complex and multi-dimensional process (Flowerdew & Miller 2005). Listeners actively reconstruct and interact with the input by either filling in the gaps, capturing the key idea or summarizing and paraphrasing the content. Both bottom-up and top-down processing strategies are employed, which is in line with an interactive model that synthesizes the two processes (Rumelhart 1975). Moreover, students practise the mirco-skills indispensable for dealing with more complex ideas in academic writing or reading (Richards 1983).

It should be pointed out that while I have implemented the learning activities presented below with a few groups of students, I have not conducted any form of explicit evaluation of the use of podcasts, such as students' questionnaires or pre- and post-teaching tests. All the conclusions regarding the educational benefits of podcast use are drawn on the basis of regular final tests, my observations, and continuous assessment performed in the classroom as well as students' voluntary comments provided during or after the course (spontaneous conversations or e-mails from ex-students).

3.1 Emigration

This lesson employs a podcast which comes from a series of thought-provoking talks entitled "Four Thought" downloaded from the BBC, Channel 4. It is recorded live and has an average duration of 20 minutes. During the lesson the students are exposed to two extracts lasting 8 minutes and 1 minute, respectively.

As a warm-up at the pre-listening stage the students are assigned a pair work activity. Their task is as follows: "Make a list of possible reasons why people choose to emigrate. After you have finished, think whether you can divide these causes into any categories". The students themselves usually notice that emigration can be voluntary or involuntary and enumerate the following factors: personal, economic, political, etc. After this brainstorm, the teacher introduces two sociological terms: push and pull factors and the students again look at their lists and try to divide the items into these two broad categories. The speaking activity is followed by a lexical exercise. Its aim is to activate the vocabulary students are already familiar with as well as explain the meaning of some terms which will appear in the listening. The task is to match the words with their definitions.

Having done that, students are given a speaking task concerned with discussing controversial statements on the topic of emigration (e.g. People should stay and live in the country where they are born). After the speaking activity, which gives students an opportunity to express and exchange their own views comes the listening task. In the post-listening activity students think of the Polish reality from the perspective of immigrants and foreigners. They are also encouraged to reflect on their own experience of living/studying abroad.

At the very outset the students are informed about the source of the extracts (the BBC) and the background data of the speaker: Heaven Crawley, Professor of International Migration at Swansea University. This has a motivating effect on the learners as they treat the listening task as a more life-like activity, i.e. listening to a real person talking about relevant and up-to-date problem at a reliable radio station. They listen not only in order to answer a set of questions, but to learn something new from the person who is respectable and knowledgeable on the topic. Figure 1 below includes the tasks in Listening Comprehension 1.

Figure 1: Tasks for Listening Comprehension 1 (Emigration).

LISTENING COMPREHENSION 1

Pre-listening

→ Make a list of possible reasons why people choose to emigrate. After you have finished, think whether you can divide these causes into any categories.

→ Match the following words and phrases with their definitions.

asylum seeker
pandemic
remittance
refugee
brain drain
diaspora
mobility

a) emigration of trained and talented individuals from the country of origin to another country resulting in a depletion of skills resources in the former
b) a person who seeks safety from persecution or serious harm in a country other than his or her own and awaits a decision on the application for refugee status
c) money earned or acquired by non-nationals that are transferred back to their country of origin
d) a large group of people with a similar heritage or homeland who have since moved out to places all over the world
e) all types of movement from one location to another
f) disease that occurs over a wide geographic area and affects a very high proportion of the population
g) a person who is forced to migrate from their home country and cannot return for fear of persecution

→ In pairs discuss the following statements. Which of them would you disagree with?

- Everybody should be able to live where they choose. Freedom of movement is a civil right.
- In an ideal world nobody would need to emigrate.
- People should stay and live in the country where they are born.

While-listening (8 min.)

Heaven Crawley, Professor of International Migration at Swansea University shares her experience of working with refugees and asylum seekers. Listen to a part of her talk and answer the following questions.

→ What are the reasons for negative social attitudes towards refugees and asylum seekers?
→ What advice does the speaker give to help us overcome those negative attitudes?
→ On what occasions does she mention the following emotional states?

anger
curiosity
resilience
compassion

Post-listening

Do you think there should be more help available to immigrants (or foreigners in general) to adapt to their new country. Think of Poland as an example. Do you have any experience of living/studying abroad?

It must be noted that the duration of the recording is longer than those typically found in coursebooks. Students should be informed in advance about this fact as, sadly but realistically, they may not be used to listening in English for longer stretches of time. They should be instructed that one of the reasons beyond exposing them to audio materials like this is to accustom them to longer listening sessions, enhance their concentration and, last but not least, encourage them to listen extensively beyond the classroom. It is crucial that students know exactly what information they need to find in the extract so that they do not get frustrated when unable to follow everything they hear. Also, the students should be reminded that they will need to use the skills of synthesis as the information they are supposed to gather is scattered across the recording. After they have listened to the audio material, the students report on their answers, compare them with the rest of the group and are allowed to provide any comments they wish.

Having completed Listening Comprehension 1, students are informed that the speaker, apart from being an expert at migration, is also a balloon pilot. They are presented with a picture of a balloon in their handout and are asked to work in groups of three and think of possible analogies between ballooning and refugee experience. This task allows students to use their imagination, and usually they manage to generate interesting ideas, e.g. being unable to predict exactly the landing point, being uncertain of the destination, seeing the world from a different perspective than the rest of people, feeling detached from ordinary things, etc. After they have completed the speaking task, students listen to what the speaker herself thinks about these two apparently remote spheres of her life (working with refuges and piloting a balloon). At this point they are curious and motivated to compare their own views with the ones of the speaker, so they complete attentively the Listening Comprehension 2 (see Figure 2). As a post-listening activity, students are asked to come up with their own associations with the word "refugee" using the letters of the word as the initials, e.g. R (random) E (escape) F (fear) U (unpredictable) G (giving up) E (exile) E (entrance).

Figure 2: Tasks for Listening Comprehension 2 (Emigration).

LISTENING COMPREHENSION 2

Pre-listening
Think of possible links/similarities between ballooning and refugee experience.

While-listening (1:12 min.)
Apart from being an expert on migration, the speaker is also a balloon pilot. What analogy does she find between and ballooning and refugee experience? (1 min.)
ballooning ---? --- refugee experience

Post-listening
Think of a word (phrase) which begins with the following letters and which you associate with refugees.
R
E
F
U
G
E
E

The benefits stemming from the class are of dual type: linguistic and extralinguistic. The podcast-based lesson gives the students a chance to develop their speaking and listening skills as well as expand their vocabulary associated with the topic of emigration. The fact that students listen for global understanding as well specific information requires them to practise extremely useful skills, i.e. the paraphrase and summary of spoken text. Being able to express the meaning in alternative ways is a useful tool for any creative language user, translators in particular. Apart from linguistic gains students develop cognitively and broaden their general knowledge, which makes them more aware of and sensitive to the problems present in the modern world. Their motivation is boosted because they engage with meaningful and authentic input many of them can personally relate to and talk about in their L1. Using podcasts is thus a chance to encourage learners to pay attention to the content and approach it from both bottom-up and top-down perspectives (Flowerdew & Miller 2005). Similar dual (i.e. linguistic and cognitive) benefits of the application of podcasts in the classroom were reported in Isanto's (2011) empirical study. In addition to refining listening skills and grammatical competence, learners gained cultural knowledge about the target community. In Hawke's (2010) study podcasts contributed to the expansion of vocabulary and knowledge related to science.

3.2 The theory of evolution

This lesson is based on podcasts drawn from two sources. The first one is the podcast "Talkback" from the BBC (Radio Ulster) in which the host discusses with his guests the most recent events and controversial topics and invites the listeners to participate in the debates. The average duration of episodes is 35 minutes During the lesson students are exposed to two selected extracts lasting 3:29 minutes and 1:52 minutes, respectively. The second audio material is extracted from "TED". It is a nonprofit devoted to spreading ideas in the form of short (approx. 18-minute-long) powerful talks. "TED" talks are recorded live; they welcome the speakers from all over the world and cover nearly all possible topics. During the lesson students listen to just a portion of the text lasting 3:24 minutes.

Before students hear the first extract, they are asked to discuss in pairs the questions 1. and 2. from their handout: "What is the theory of evolution in a nutshell?", "How many people in the UK (%) still don't believe in evolution? What might it be due to?" It gives students a chance to refer to their background knowledge and also realize how much they actually remember about the Darwinian theory of evolution. This pre-listening exercise also activates some key terms, e.g. natural selection, survival of the fittest, fossils, species. Having exchanged their views in pairs, students are informed that they are going to listen to a part of an authentic radio programme from the BBC, which hosts Richard Dawkins, a prominent British evolutionary biologist, ethologist and popular science writer. They listen to confirm their predictions. Again, providing some brief biographical data about the speaker is considered motivational as students realize they are going to deal with solid information delivered by one of the most renowned contemporary scientists.

In the second part of the listening students are asked to find answers to the following questions: "Were our ancestors monkeys?", "Where did Darwin take the idea of evolution and natural selection from?" Before they listen, they are encouraged to share their views on these issues. After listening and discussing the answers, the teacher can write on the blackboard some terminology and facts which students might not have been able to pick up from the recording or might have doubts about. These may include the name of Thomas Malthus (a late 18th century social economist who inspired Darwin to formulate the theory of natural selection), geographical distribution, food supply, overpopulation, breeding, competition. Figure 3 contains the tasks for Listening Comprehension 1.

Figure 3: Tasks for Listening Comprehension 1 (Evolution).

LISTENING COMPREHENSION 1

Part 1.

Pre-listening
Discuss in pairs the questions below.
1. What is the theory of evolution in a nutshell?
2. How many people in the UK (in %) still don't believe in evolution? What might it be due to?

While-listening (3:29 min.)
Listen to find the answers to the questions in the recording.

Part 2.

Pre-listening
Discuss in pairs the questions below.
1. Were our ancestors monkeys?
3. Where did Darwin take the idea of evolution and natural selection from?

While-listening (1: 52 min.)
Listen to find the answers to the questions in the recording.

Post-listening (to Part 2 and Part 3)
Try to guess how many people in Poland still find it difficult to accept the theory of evolution. What might be the possible reasons?

In the next task (Listening Comprehension 2, Figure 4) students discuss in pairs a controversial statement "Religion is corrosive to science and science is corrosive to religion". After they have exchanged their opinions on the statement, they are asked to share their views about the correlation between intelligence and religion with the rest of the group. Having done that, they learn that the author of the statement is Richard Dawkins, introduced in the previous recording. They are told that the scientist is also an atheist (a "militant atheist" as he self-labels). Students listen again to the same extract and their task is now to focus on the speakers' arguments and also to note down any instances of irony and humour employed as persuasive devices. Students are also asked to evaluate critically the arguments, i.e. they reflect on how convincing the speaker is.

Figure 4: Tasks for Listening Comprehension 2 (Evolution).

LISTENING COMPREHENSION 2

Pre-listening
Discuss in pairs to what extent you agree with the following statement:
"Religion is corrosive to science and science is corrosive to religion."

While-listening (3:24 min.)
Task 1. Listen to find out what arguments are given to corroborate this statement.
Task 2. Listen again and note down any instances of irony and humour employed by the speaker as persuasive devices.

Post-listening
Evaluate critically the arguments given by the speaker. How convincing is he?

The benefits of the lesson are both linguistic and extralinguistic. Students enhance their speaking and listening skills as well as revise, reinforce and enrich vocabulary and knowledge related to the topic of evolution. The listening material provides an opportunity to focus on discourse organization and elements like persuasion and argumentation.[2] Pragmatic comprehension, which involves making inferences about the speaker's intentions and going beyond literal meaning (Rose & Kasper 2001), is also practised. When spotting instances of irony and humour, students are stimulated to discover the speaker's attitude and arrive at the contextualized meaning intended by the speaker. In this way the cognitive strategy of elaboration is applied (Vandergrift 2003). Additionally, students expand their knowledge about one of the most powerful and controversial theories of all times. They are engaged in meaningful content and practise formulating their own ideas as well as responding critically to the ones they hear.

3.3 Senses

This lesson employs podcasts from "Science Update" and "The Naked Scientist". Both are devoted to the latest discoveries in science, technology and medicine. The episodes of "Science Update" last only 60 seconds, which is a very convenient feature, for the files do not require any further modifications for the classroom use and can be reproduced at full length. During the lesson students hear two one-minute podcasts. In addition to that, there is a listening task based on

2 Since I conducted this lesson in the same group of students I had taught academic English (writing class) to two years prior, we revised some topics from that course, among others critical thinking and logical fallacies.

"The Naked Scientist". It has an average duration of 30 minutes; for the sake of this lesson students hear an extract which lasts 4:33 minutes.

As a pre-listening activity, students are asked the following questions: "If you had to give up one of your senses, which one would it be? Why? Which sense can't you imagine your life without? Why?" They discuss the questions in pairs first and then with the rest of the group. This warm-up is meant to activate schemata, recall the names of the five senses (sight/vision, smell/olfaction, touch/tactition, taste/gustation, hearing/audition) and arouse interest in the topic. When answering the aforementioned questions, many students tend to sacrifice the sense of touch deeming it relatively unimportant. Some of them justify their choice by saying that being deprived of the sense of touch can actually be beneficial because one does not experience unpleasant sensations like pain, excessive cold or heat. They are not aware of the dangerous consequences related to not having the sense of touch.

Therefore, students are asked to read an extract about the condition in which tactition is impaired (hereditary sensory and autonomic neuropathy type 2, hence HSAN2). First they skim the text to capture the gist and then their task is to fill in the gaps doing word formation. The text comes from the following website and has been adapted by the author: http://ghr.nlm.nih.gov/condition/hereditary-sensory-and-autonomic-neuropathy-type-ii. A brief extract of the text is included in Figure 5.

Figure 5: A sample paragraph from a reading comprehension and word formation task used as a lead-in to the lesson (Senses).

These sensations are impaired in people with HSAN2. In some affected people, the condition may also cause mild **1……………………. (NORMAL)** of the autonomic nervous system, which controls **2……………………… (VOLUNTEER)** body functions such as heart rate, digestion, and breathing.

Apart from practising word formation, students learn about this rare, yet interesting, condition. This is also the aim of the listening comprehension tasks, i.e. to reveal certain facts regarding the human senses students most probably are not familiar with.

The first recording deals with the sense of smell (olfaction). It contains the description of a sniff test which is employed to trace down problems with smelling, which tends to be the first casualty in debilitating brain diseases (like Alzheimer's). The decreased ability to identify odours may be, thus, a signal of serious brain disease. The students' task is to learn how the sniff test is performed. They listen for global understanding and practise the skills of paraphrase and summary.

The questions which the students need to answer is in Figure 6 below.

Figure 6: Tasks for Listening Comprehension 1 (Senses).

LISTENING COMPREHENSION 1

Pre-listening
In pairs discuss the following questions: If you had to give up one of your senses, which one would it be? Why? Which sense can't you imagine your life without? Why?

While-listening (1 min.)
Did you know that a simple sniff test may help doctors pick up the scent of debilitating brain diseases? Listen to learn in what way.

Post-listening
Would you consider undergoing a test like this? Those of you who have decided to give up the sense of smell, does this recording make you change your mind?

The second recording focuses on the sense of sight (vision) and colour blindness (see Figure 7). First, students are asked to brainstorm what they know about colour blindness and the areas of human activity which can possibly be affected by this condition. This time they listen for detail and need to capture the exact phrase from the recording, namely: "sensitivity to a different colour dimension". The post-listening stage consists in revising some idioms with the word "red" (to see red, red tape, red herring, red-handed). Students are asked to think of the possible link between seeing red colour (in stop signs, Mc Donald's, the teacher's pen) and human emotions (anxiety, alertness, restlessness, being in a rush).

Figure 7: Tasks for Listening Comprehension 2 (Senses).

LISTENING COMPREHENSION 2

Pre-listening
What is colour blindness? What spheres of life can be affected by this condition?

While-listening (1 min.)
You may be surprised to learn how colour blind people see. Listen and fill in the missing information.
The scientists conclude that some colour blindness is not blindness at all but rather ....

Post-listening
It has been proved in yet another study that seeing red colour around exerts a big influence on people's emotions and even behaviours. Can you think of this possible link? What does the idiom "to see red" mean? Do you know any other expressions with the word "red"?

The third recording provides interesting facts about the sense of olfaction (Figure 8). Since this sense has already been talked about during the lesson and there is no special need to activate the schemata, the pre-listening stage is relatively brief and requires the students to answer a straightforward question: "What is the most relaxing smell for you?" While listening to the extract, the students' task is to decide whether five statements they are presented with are true or false. They listen both for global understanding and for detail. The skills of paraphrase and summary are necessary to perform the task as the information is sometimes scattered throughout the extract and they need to be able to synthesize it. The post-listening stage is focused on grammar. Students revise the fact that verbs related to senses can function as both dynamic and stative verbs, but this implies the change in meaning and grammatical behaviour.

Figure 8: Tasks for Listening Comprehension 3 (Senses).

LISTENING COMPREHENSION 3

Pre-listening
What is the most relaxing smell for you?

While-listening (4:33 min.)
You will hear a part of a talk about the sense of smell. Decide whether the statements below are true or false according to what is said in the recording. Circle T or F, respectively

1. The pattern in which the receptors are activated enables the brain to identify a given smell. **T F**
2. The mechanism of smelling things around you and inside your mouth is basically the same. **T F**
3. Accidents and allergy tend to cause a permanent loss of the sense of smell. **T F**
4. The sense of sight is predominant in humans. **T F**
5. Humans have approximately 350 types of smell receptors, some of them inactive. **T F**

Post-listening
The verb "to smell" and other verbs related to senses (feel, taste, see, hear) can be used both in dynamic and stative sense. Provide your own sentences to illustrate this usage, e.g. Your perfumes smell wonderful. vs. She's smelling the soup.

The three recordings briefly described here contribute to the development of listening skills, reinforce vocabulary and idiomatic language related to human senses and give students a chance to practise the paraphrase and summary of texts. Apart from linguistic benefits, students expand their knowledge on the topic of senses and learn some new facts about an immensely important aspect of their life, which can be useful in daily activity. All of these render the listening tasks more purposeful and motivating. As reported by various empirical studies and surveys conducted among students, podcasts have the potential of enhancing learners' intrinsic and extrinsic motivation (O'Bryan & Hegelheimer 2007; Kavaliauskienė & Anusienė 2009). I have not examined explicitly my students' response towards podcast-based classes but through their active involvement in discussions and genuine interest in the source of podcasts, I inferred they had a positive attitude both towards the medium as well as the content and were willing to continue listening to podcasts of their own accord.

4. Conclusions

This chapter has meant to argue that authentic podcasts are an ideal way to implement a broadly understood integrated approach to foreign language teaching, i.e. to enhance language skills, engage students in cognitively demanding content, and foster a positive attitude towards extensive listening, thereby making learners more autonomous. Thanks to their portability, variety and accessibility, podcasts are a resource which is more and more widely used and attractive to learners and teachers alike. It has been presented how authentic podcasts (primarily from the BBC but also from "TED", "Scientific Update" and "The Naked Scientist"), can be incorporated in the syllabus as both a linguistic and cognitive resource for advanced learners of English.

Having implemented the activities discussed in the present chapter and relying on my observations as well as formal assessment (final tests), I can make a claim that authentic podcasts contribute to the enhancement of listening skills (listening for global understanding and listening for a particular piece of information) and also stimulate students to speak and acquire contextualized vocabulary and phrases. Extensive listening has a positive effect on students' pronunciation since they receive authentic input which is a perfect sample of native speech. The skills of paraphrase and summary, indispensable for creative language users and translators in particular, are also practised. The listening material provides an opportunity to focus on discourse organization, i.e. finding the thesis statement, evaluating arguments and tracing down instances of logical fallacies. Students become sensitive to elements like irony, humour and the attitude of the speaker.

The benefits of podcast-based lessons go beyond linguistic growth. The fact that the focus is shifted from the language itself onto the ideas students are dealing with at the moment makes it more motivating and enables them to expand their knowledge. Constant cognitive development is particularly relevant for (future) translators, whose training should focus on specialized techniques and knowledge without neglecting the general knowledge necessary for understanding contexts and utterances. The podcasts discussed here cover the topics of emigration, evolution, and senses, introducing students to interesting facts delivered by expert speakers. I received feedback from a student of mine a few years after she graduated that she was going to undertake social studies as her second major and she mentioned my classes and particularly the topic of emigration as one of the factors which had raised her interest in the area.

Furthermore, authentic podcasts can motivate students to listen extensively outside the classroom and thus promote mobile learning. Scaffolding provided during the lesson guides students how to approach authentic audio materials and fosters positive attitude towards them. Consequently, language learners are stimulated to embrace the countless benefits of podcasts and realize that learning can happen anytime and anywhere as long as they are willing to exploit their handheld (and held dear) devices for educational purposes. If this is achieved, the benefits of authentic podcasts for foreign language learning and cognitive development, which is then embedded in everyday life, become constant and limitless.

References

Abraham, L.B., & Williams, L. (Eds.). (2009). *Electronic Discourse in Language-Learning and Language Teaching*. Amsterdam: John Benjamins Publishing Company.

Ashton-Hay, S., & Brookes, D. (2011). Here's a story: Using student podcasts to raise awareness of language learning strategies. *EA Journal*, *26*(2), 15–27.

Bobrow, D.G., & Collins, A. (1975). *Representation and Understanding: Studies in Cognitive Science*. New York: Academic Press.

Borgia, L. (2010). Enhanced vocabulary podcasts implementation in Fifth Grade Classrooms. *Reading Improvement, 46*(4), 263–272.

Brinton, D., Snow, M., & Wesche, M. (1989). *Content-Based Second Language Instruction*. Boston, MA: Heinle & Heinle Publishers.

Brown, C. L. (2004). Content based ESL curriculum and academic language proficiency. *The Internet TESL Journal, 10*(2). Available at: http://72.14.253.104/search?q=cache:fmJzxFxDlBwJ:iteslj.org/Techniques/BrownCBEC.html+criticisms+of+content+based+instruction&hl=ko&ct=clnk&cd=4 (date of access 6 July 2016).

Brown, H. D. (2001). *Teaching by Principles: An Interactive Approach to Language Pedagogy*. White Plains, NY: Longman.

Campbell, G. (2005). There's something in the air: Podcasting in education. *Educause Review, 40*(6), 32–46.

Chan, A., & Lee, M. (2005). An MP3 a day keeps the worries away: Exploring the use of podcasting to address preconceptions and alleviate pre-class anxiety amongst undergraduate information technology students. In D. Spennemann & L. Burr (Eds.), *Good Practice in Practice: Proceedings of the Student Experience Conference 5–7th September '05* (pp. 58–70). Wagga Wagga, NSW: Charles Sturt University.

Clark, D., & Walsh, S. (2004). *iPod-learning*. Brighton, UK: Epic Group Plc.

Collis, B., & Moonen, J. (2010). Flexibility in higher education: Revisiting expectations. Revista Comunicar, *19*(37), 15–25.

Cooper, P. (1993). Paradigm shifts in designing instruction: From behaviourism to cognitivism. *Educational Technology, 33*(5), 12–19.

Crandall, J., & Tucker, R. (1990). Content-based instruction in second and foreign languages. In A. Padilla, H.H. Fairchild, & C.M. Valadez (Eds.), *Foreign Language Education: Issues and Strategies* (pp. 187–200). Newbury Park, CA: Sage.

Delisle, J. (2003). *La traduction raisonnée.* Ottawa: Les Presses de l'Université d'Ottawa.

Ducate, L., & Lomicka, L. (2009). Podcasting: An effective tool for honing language students' pronunciation? *Language Learning and Technology, 13*(3), 66–86.

Dueñas, M. (2004). The whats, whys, hows and whos of content-based instruction in second foreign language education. *International Journal of Language Studies, 4*(1), 73–96.

Feyten, C. M. (1991). The power of listening ability: An overlooked dimension in language acquisition. *The Modern Language Journal, 75*(2), 173–180.

Flowerdew, J., & Miller, L. (2005). *Second Language Listening: Theory and Practice.* Cambridge: Cambridge University Press.

Gruba, P., Clark, C., Ng, K., & Wells, M. (2009). *Blending technologies in ESL courses: A reflexive inquiry*. Available at: https://pdfs.semanticscholar.org/e3b9/7bcbc1e8a731148ba166fac61a42b71a9752.pdf (date of access: 22 February 2017).

Gura, M. (2006). Moving instructional podcasting beyond coursecasting. *Perspectives: New York Journal of Adult Learning, 4*(2), 31–33.

Hardman, M. C. (2009). *Developing a Teachers' handbook for Content-Based Instruction at Brigham Young University's English Language Center*. Available at: http://scholarsarchive.byu.edu/cgi/viewcontent.cgi?article=2710&context=etd (date of access: 7 September 2015).

Hawke, P. (2010). Using internet- sourced podcasts in independent listening courses: Legal and pedagogical implications. *Jalt CALL Journal*, *6*(3), 219–234.

Huan, T. Y. & Thong, M. K. (2006). Audioblogging and Podcasting in Education. Available at: http://citeseerx.ist.psu.edu/viewdoc/download?doi=10.1.1.459.9418&rep=rep1&type=pdf (date of access: 22 February 2017).

Istanto, J. W. (2011). Pelangi Bahasa Indonesia podcast: What, why and how? *Electronic Journal of Foreign Language Teaching, 8*(1), 371–384.

Kaplan-Leiserson, E. (2005). *Trend: Podcasting in academic and corporate learning.* Available at: http://www.learningcircuits.org/2005/jun2005/0506_trends (date of access: 31 October 2016).

Kavaliauskienė, G., & Anusienė, L. (2009). English for specific purposes: Podcasts for listening skills. *Coactivity: Philology, Educology, 17*(2), 28–37.

King, K., & Gura, M. (2009). *Podcasting for Teachers: Using a New Technology to Revolutionize Teaching and Learning.* New York: Information Age.

Knight, R. A. (2010). Sounds for study: Speech and language therapy students: Use and perception of exercise podcasts for phonetics. *International Society for Exploring Teaching and Learning, 22*(3), 269–276.

Kukulska-Hulme, A. (2006). Mobile language learning now and in the future. In P. Svensson (Ed.), *Fran vision till praktik: Sprakutbildning och Informationsteknik (From vision to practice: language learning and IT)* (pp. 295–310). Sweden: Swedish Net University.

Little, D. (1997). Responding authentically to authentic texts. A problem for self-access language learning? In P. Benson & P. Voller (Eds.), *Autonomy and independence in language learning* (pp. 225–236), New York, NY: Longman.

McBride, K. (2009). Podcasts and second language learning: Promoting listening comprehension and intercultural competence. In L. B. Abraham & L. Williams (Eds.), *Electronic Discourse in Language Learning and Language Teaching* (pp. 153–167). Amsterdam: John Benjamins Publishing Company.

O'Bryan, A., & Hegelheimer, V. (2007). Integrating CALL into the classroom: The role of podcasting in an ESL listening strategies course. *ReCALL, 19*(2), 162–180.

Onsrud, E. M. (2009). *Podcasting in the foreign language classroom: Improving communication* (Unpublished master's thesis). University of Wisconsin-Stout, Wisconsin.

Padilla, A. M., Fairchild, F. F., & Valadez, C. M. (Eds.). (1990). *Foreign Language Education: Issues and Strategies.* Newbury Park, CA: Sage.

Richards, J. C. (1983). Listening comprehension: Approach, design, procedure. *TESOL Quarterly, 17*(2), 219–238.

Rose, K. R., & Kasper, G. (Eds.). (2001). *Pragmatics in Language Teaching.* Cambridge: Cambridge University Press.

Rosell-Aguilar, F. (2007). Top of the pods: In search of a podcasting "podagogy" for language learning. *Computer Assisted Language Learning, 20*(5), 471–492.

Rost, M. (2011). *Teaching and Researching Listening.* Edinburgh Gate: Pearson Education Limited.

Rumelhart, D. E. (1975). Notes on a schema for stories. In D. G. Bobrow & A. Collins (Eds.), *Representation and Understanding: Studies in Cognitive Science.* (pp. 211–236) New York: Academic Press.

Salmon, G., & Edirisingha, P. (Eds.). (2008). *Podcasting for Learning in Universities.* Berkshire: Open University Press.

Salmon, G., & Nie, M. (2008). Doubling the life of iPods. In G. Salmon & P. Edirisingha (Eds.), *Podcasting for Learning in Universities* (pp. 1–11). Berkshire: Open University Press.

Schmidt, J. (2008). Podcasting as a learning tool: German language and culture every day. *Die Unterrichtspraxis/Teaching German, 41*(2), 186–194.

Spennemann, D., & Burr, L. (Eds.). (2005). *Good Practice in Practice: Proceedings of the Student Experience Conference 5–7th September '05.* Wagga Wagga, NSW: Charles Sturt University.

Stanley, G. (2006). Podcasting: Audio on the Internet comes of age. *TESL-EJ, 9*(4), 1–7.

Stevick, E. W. (1989). *Success with Foreign Languages. Seven Who Achieved I and What Worked for Them.* New York, London, Toronto, Sydney, Tokyo, Singapore: Prentice Hall.

Svensson, P. (Ed.). (2006). *Fran vision till praktik: Sprakutbildning och Informationsteknik (From vision to practice: language learning and IT).* Sweden: Swedish Net University.

Thorne, S., & Payne, J. S. (2005). Evolutionary trajectories, Internet-mediated expression, and language education. *CALICO Journal, 22*(3), 371–397.

Vandergrift, L. (2003). From prediction through reflection: Guiding students through the process of L2 listening. *The Canadian Modern Language Review, 59*(3), 425–440.

Viswanathan, R. (2009). Using mobile technology and podcasts to teach soft skills. Available at: http://www.irma-international.org/viewtitle/21946/ (date of access: 22 February 2017).

Warschauer, M., & Healey, D. (1998). Computers and language leaning: An overview. *Language Teaching, 31,* 57–71.

Links to the podcasts:

Emigration:
http://www.bbc.co.uk/programmes/b03sztyl

The theory of evolution:
https://www.youtube.com/watch?v=2t2UhVA-lDk

https://www.youtube.com/watch?v=VxGMqKCcN6A

Studies in Computer Assisted Language Learning

Edited by Anna Turula

Vol. 1 Anna Turula/Maria Chojnacka (eds.): CALL for Bridges between School and Academia. 2015.

Vol. 2 Mariusz Marczak/Jarosław Krajka (eds.): CALL for Openness. 2016.

Vol. 3 Joanna Pitura / Shannon Sauro (eds.): CALL for Mobility. 2018.

www.peterlang.com

www.ingramcontent.com/pod-product-compliance
Ingram Content Group UK Ltd.
Pitfield, Milton Keynes, MK11 3LW, UK
UKHW041828100926
8556IPUK00002B/79

9 783631 744550